## Racial Americana

SPECIAL ISSUE EDITOR: JOHN L. JACKSON JR.

A Little Black Magic   393
JOHN L. JACKSON JR.

The Last Word on Racism: New Directions for a
Critical Race Theory   403
SHARON P. HOLLAND

Hip-Hop Women Shredding the Veil: Race and
Class in Popular Feminist Identity   425
MARCYLIENA MORGAN

"Mary Lou Williams Plays Like a Man!"
Gender, Genius, and Difference in Black Music
Discourse   445
NICHOLE T. RUSTIN

The Negro Digs Up Her Past: "Amistad"   463
ELIZABETH ALEXANDER

Getting Out of the Hole   481
BRACKETTE F. WILLIAMS

Our Flesh of Flames   501
AMIRI BARAKA AND THEODORE A. HARRIS

Hunted Everywhere: Collaging the Capitol,
a Manifesto   509
THEODORE A. HARRIS

The
South
Atlantic
Quarterly
Summer 2005
Volume 104
Number 3

"Making a Collection": James Weldon Johnson
and the Mission of African American Literature
521
TESS CHAKKALAKAL

Culture against Race: Reworking the Basis for
Racial Analysis   543
JOHN HARTIGAN JR.

Cosmopolitanism and Planetary Humanism:
The Strategic Universalism of Paul Gilroy   561
DON ROBOTHAM

How the Hindus Became Jews:
American Racism after 9/11   583
VIJAY PRASHAD

Notes on Contributors   607

The
South
Atlantic
Quarterly
Summer 2005
Volume 104
Number 3

Visit Duke University Press Journals at www.dukeupress
.edu/journals.

*Subscriptions.* Direct all orders to Duke University Press,
Journals Fulfillment, 905 W. Main St., Suite 18B, Durham,
NC 27701. Annual subscription rates: institutions, $140;
e-only institutions, $126; individuals, $35; students, $21.
Add $12 postage and 7% GST for Canada. Add $16 postage
outside the U.S. and Canada. Back volumes (institutions):
$140. Single issues: institutions, $35; individuals, $14. For
more information, contact Duke University Press Journals at 888-651-0122 (toll-free in the U.S. and Canada) or
919-687-3602; subscriptions@dukeupress.edu.

*Permissions.* Photocopies for course or research use that
are supplied to the end user at no cost may be made
without explicit permission or fee. Photocopies that are
provided to the end user for a fee may not be made without payment of permission fees to Duke University Press.
Address requests for permission to republish copyrighted
material to Permissions Coordinator, Duke University
Press, 905 W. Main St., Suite 18B, Durham, NC 27701;
permissions@dukeupress.edu.

*Advertisements.* Direct inquiries about advertising to
Journals Advertising Specialist, Duke University Press,
905 W. Main St., Suite 18B, Durham, NC 27701;
journals_advertising@dukeupress.edu.

*Distribution.* The journal is distributed by Ubiquity
Distributors, 607 DeGraw St., Brooklyn, NY 11217; phone:
718-875-5491; fax: 718-875-8047.

The *South Atlantic Quarterly* is indexed in *Abstracts of
English Studies, Academic Abstracts, Academic Index, America:
History and Life, American Bibliography of Slavic and East
European Studies, American Humanities Index, Arts and
Humanities Citation Index, Book Review Index, CERDIC,
Children's Book Review Index (1965– ), Current Contents, His-
torical Abstracts, Humanities Index, Index to Book Reviews in
the Humanities, LCR, Middle East: Abstract and Index, MLA
Bibliography, PAIS,* and *Social Science Source.*

The *South Atlantic Quarterly* is published, at $140 for insti-
tutions and $35 for individuals, by Duke University Press,
905 W. Main St., Suite 18B, Durham, NC 27701. Periodicals
postage paid at Durham, NC, and additional mailing offices.
Postmaster: Send address changes to *South Atlantic Quarterly*, Box 90660, Duke University Press, Durham, NC
27708-0660.

ISSN 0038-2876

John L. Jackson Jr.

A Little Black Magic

Social constructionism continues to rack up rhetorical victories vis-à-vis contemporary identity politics and the encompassing culture wars. Its heuristic power is undeniable, its foundational presuppositions ubiquitous. This anti-essentialist position serves as dogma, *doxa*, and even hardwired habitus, despite the fact that its social hegemony is not more than a couple generations old. No matter, hoist the flag and cue the marching band, public displays of identificatory deconstructionism—specifically racial deconstructions—are the order of the day. So much so, in fact, that some recently retooled versions of sociobiology avoid explicitly invoking race at all, even and especially when arguing for genetic explanations of group differences.

There was little overt reference to race in, say, 1994's controversial *The Bell Curve*, which only made it all the more useful to unabashedly hereditarian raciologists of the Arthur Jensen and William Shockley persuasion. *The Bell Curve* exemplified a culturalization of race, an ethnicization of race thinking, that clearly still trucked in—more powerful for its Trojan-horsed sublimations—genetic notions of race in decidedly nonracial idioms. An explicit invocation of race

The *South Atlantic Quarterly* 104:3, Summer 2005.

would have been far too predictable, too retro, too easily dismissed as racism proper.

Even when *The Bell Curve*'s arguments get revamped and more explicitly reracialized for the twenty-first century, these redemptively biological formulations just defang themselves with perfunctory claims about racial genetics' ultimate irrelevance for public policy.[1] Race is real, they argue, but that really doesn't matter. In an age of social constructionism, it seems, even neo-eugenics must bow to its analytical status as lone hermeneutical superpower. However, at the same time that genetics-based start-up companies unequivocally champion the view that "race is a social construction" on their Web sites and in their glossy brochures, they simultaneously sell genetic answers to laypeople's questions about African origins and ancestors—a racialized version of the proverbial cake, had and summarily eaten, too.

Clearly, there is something about the connection between race and affect that social constructionist challenges may not necessarily short-circuit— or even address. The rhetorical avoidance of race does not automatically buttress its antiessentialist cause. In fact, taking away race's vocal chords, the acoustic concreteness of its explicit bark, does not mean that one has defused its bite. If anything, race becomes more compelling in silence, when unspoken—as "tactility and distraction" more than explicit thematic, taking advantage of what Michael Taussig calls "a very different apperceptive mode, the type of flitting and barely conscious peripheral vision perception unleashed with great vigour by modern life."[2] When race and racism work best, we don't even think to talk about them; they cannot really be seen. We noddingly eschew any and all public policy implications.

In an attempt to highlight race's conspicuous falsehoods, some full-fledged deconstructionists argue that letting go of race as a salient social and individual category is the precondition for ending racism in practice. Sociocultural constructions have real productive force, they say, a social power that must be defused before racialized minorities can ever accept the glories and privileges of full citizenship. Such *hard* versions of constructionism work for the cultural Left and the cultural Right, for extremists and moderates alike. In our social constructionist world, even the most unapologetic racist can be found arguing that races don't really exist. Here, one can cite the likes of Leo Felton, New England's famous "black white supremacist," a biracial love child of the 1960s who hid his black father's existence from fellow Nazi skinheads while committing antiblack hate crimes with ravenous abandon. Felton refuses to reduce the whiteness he feels inside, the whiteness of his soul, to any narrowly biologized definition of black identity predicated on America's one-drop rule of hypodescent. Race is not biology, he says. It is not about the body at all. To ground his case, Felton uses the esoteric and Nazi-friendly work of Nietzschean Ulick Varange. "We attain now," Varange writes, "to the grand formula for the 20th century out-look on Race: *Race is a horizontal differentiation of men.* The materialism of the 19th century, confusing race with anatomy, regarded Race as a verti-cal differentiation of men."[3] Taking his cue from Varange's 1948 formula-tion, Felton disconnects racial identity from anatomy and uses that space to fold his unbrown body into a debiologized notion of white privilege. Fel-ton's example indicates that divorcing race from genetic determinism does not inevitably inoculate society from bigoted, racist oppression—even the seemingly internalized and self-inflicted kind.

To appreciate just how denigrated and hollow race has truly become, one need only recognize that electoral politicians seem to be the folks most unselfconsciously and consistently invoking it these days, usually giving lip service to its continued value with platitudes about mosaics and melt-ing pots and patchwork quilts where every single color is vitally important, particularly come election time. They have no patience for utopian theo-ries of "planetary humanism."[4] Of course, that is only because politicians are greedily pragmatic about such matters, hitching their rhetorical reins to the most obvious thoroughbreds—even when constructionists might advise them, counterintuitively, that the carts themselves really do all the actual pulling.

Many scholars use the term *postraciality* to mark this antiessentialist and hyperconstructionist moment, a term that privileges identificatory decon-struction over and above any other heuristic project. All roads lead to the dissolved racial subject, and even Gayatri Spivak has recanted her former articulation of strategic forms of essentialist praxis. Racial Americana, I would argue, is something like the flipside to academia's current postracial zeitgeist—its orthogonal off-ramp, carrying us to a place where racial decon-struction is less heuristic finish line than anxious starting block. It parses race as one of the nation-state's fundamental constitutive elements, inex-tricably central to future understandings of how biopolitical, nanopolitical, and necropolitical strategies constrain the hopes and dreams of national citizenries. This is a biopolitics that flags phenotype as final arbiter of hier-archical difference, categorizing and codifying bodies along a continuum of recognizable somatic privilege.[5] It means a nanopolitics mining the human genome for invisible racial solidities and causal absolutes, for submolecular answers to visual social inequalities.[6] Likewise, the necropolitical impulse to control and determine life's ultimate death, thereby consolidating claims on social control and sovereignty, might help us to better explain death row's dark-hued tint.[7] In each of these instances, race becomes a powerful and necessary frame for thinking "the body in pain,"[8] both individual bodies and the collective body politic.

Racial Americana, therefore, is skeptical of postraciality, cynical even, and in this sense is explicitly in dialogue with the notion of a Pax Americana, a phrase ambivalently marking/countermarking the country's period of ostensible peace after World War II—a peace belied by overt wars in Korea and Vietnam, by covert military actions in Latin America, by structural violences against the struggling poor, and by ever impending nuclear annihilation. Racial Americana, likewise, underscores academia's current phase of racial détente, an identificatory peace born of collective agreements among scholars about the need to transcend racial essentialisms at all costs, a high-ground response to Afrocentric excesses, white supremacist machinations, and the subtly quotidian nuances of "inferential racism."[9] However, each one of these specific configurations (Afrocentrism, white supremacy, and everyday, inadvertent raciology) mandates distinct analytical scaffolding for comprehension and transformation. By conflating these very different instantiations of racial ideology, an essentializing ethos can remain safely ensconced within adamantly antiessentialist projects—political projects most likely to falter at the nexus where an abstract antiessentialism meets the particularities of local difference.

*Americana* itself is usually glossed as a way to invoke, even celebrate, the folksy specificities of this country's historical, geographical, and material provincialisms: the Americanness of apple pie and small-town baseball, of what Ishmael Reed lampoons as "those jockey-dressed amulets on the Southern Lawn of America's consciousness."[10] This last example begins to hint at race's centrality to such quaint particularities, to the idiosyncrasies of a most "peculiar institution" and its aftermath. *Racial Americana* seeks to examine those aspects of Americanity that, like Reed's amulets, constitute American exceptionalism through the historical prism of racial animus, affect, and privilege. It is the Americana of everything from Ray Charles's soulful blues-strummed authenticities to Michael Jordan's tongue-extended slam-dunks (MJ, that bald-headed icon of postracial American desire), from segregated housing markets to ethnic grocery stores, from handmade Kwanzaa gift-giving to photographed black bodies limply hung from southern trees. Racial Americana emphasizes the inextricable linkages between race and nationhood, even and especially in a globalizing context wherein many theorists are sounding the death knell for both these kinds of "imagined communities." It focuses on the symbiotic relationship between race and gender, a relationship specifically carved from the history of sexually vulnerable and exploited black bodies, the hazy and chattel-slaved distance between "mama's baby and papa's maybe."[11]

As much as we might try, every single day it gets more difficult to escape the truths of racial Americana, to escape its sordid history. The more we squirm, the harder we fight, the tighter our chains seem to become. They are always with us, returning from repression at the very instant of their supposed dissolution. An attempt to theorize race in the beginnings of a new century might start with one of academia's quintessential examples of racial Americana: the habitual invocation of William Edward Burghardt Du Bois, black son of the New England Berkshires and fiery racial conscience for subsequent generations of Americans of all colors and classifications.

Du Bois is racial Americana personified, and we usually beckon Du Bois by rote, without even a second thought—some kind of race-based Rorschach response. Like a scholastic reflex, the invocation is purely psychomuscular: a tapping on the racial knee leads to an almost involuntary extension of the Du Boisian leg. It has all become second nature. This is not meant to disparage Du Bois—or those scholars who study his foundational work on race and racism. Du Bois is just a handy, evocative, and overdetermined example of the commonsensicalities that define racial Americana today: its taken-for-grantedness, its prefabbed architectonic footprints. And this is precisely the subject these special-issue contributors engage—an attempt to extend Du Boisian analysis into the strictures of late capitalism's newest millennium, into its own inevitably exhausted collapse.

If Du Bois proved all too easily prophetic about the twentieth century and its colored lines, the beginnings of this newest century have spawned divergent pronouncements about the potential tomorrows of race relations and racial discourse in American society. Clearly, the Jim Crowed categories of black victims and white victimizers hardly seem up to the task of wringing complete social sense out of a nation-state where the highest-ranking African American judge is consistently hostile to any and all discussions of racial community; where the influx of workers from South America, Central America, and the Caribbean can be said to "brown" every single member of the national citizenry; where the second conservative real-life Bush presidency boasts a much more racially diverse staff than a hyperliberal progressive Bartlett presidency depicted on network television's *The West Wing*; where Chinatowns fear the threat of gentrification just as adamantly as Harlems do; and where (thanks to a vocal multiracial movement) census taxonomies change faster than the tampered-with stock prices of Fortune 500 companies. But what kind of racial theorizing helps us to understand the differences within similarity that cloud our analytical engagements with the everyday realities and surrealities of racial reasoning? More than ever, we need to create new ways of understanding the social facts that underpin race (as belief system, as common sense, as pseudopatriotism, as interpersonal shortcut, as biological mythmaking) and what those underpinnings forewarn about the possible futures of social difference in the United States.

In this volume, contributors have been challenged to push beyond Du Bois, not because we have exhausted useful readings of his powerful prose, which we surely have not, but rather because he haunts us still, has never gone away: the perpetually chanted incantation that always already grounds authoritative claims about race making, claims that provide itineraries for portions of the social journey yet to come. But what does that future entail? Where do we go from here? And how much do we need the conjuring of Du Bois's ghost to get us there?

What might be most telling about this Du Bois–inflected charge, however, is that most of the contributors took the mandate so seriously that they moved beyond Du Bois altogether, moved beyond his very invocation. For many of the authors in this volume—Tess Chakkalakal on African American anthologies, Nichole Rustin on Mary Lou Williams's musical masculinities, Donald Robotham on cosmopolitan utopianism—there is nary a mention of this canonical figure. Certainly not in the fiction of Brackette Williams or the poetic manifesto of Elizabeth Alexander. Most of the scholars offer no direct invocation of Du Bois at all, which is less dismissal than measured nonfetishization. For there are far more fetishes to be summoned in this land of racial Americana, much more than simple Du Boisian rearticulation, and these scholars are determined to unmask such alternative incarnations: popularized recollections of the transatlantic slave trade; culture's debt to cloaked assumptions about race; Derrida's significance for discussions of Tupac Shakur and everyday racism; September 11's role in revising the character of contemporary cross-racial coalitions. All of these moves— from contributors who define themselves as anthropologists, sociologists, literary theorists, performance studies scholars, linguists, novelists, poets, and visual artists — bespeak an interdisciplinary ethos organized around the prospect of transcending Du Bois so as to dwell in the immanence of racial irreducibility, an irreducibility tethered less to biological determinism than to an adamant refusal of make-believe transcendence, of a priori racial transcendentalism.

Not inconsequentially, the genre differences between and among these entries are another rather significant part of this story. The volume includes ethnographic fiction, memoir, poetry, art, and autobiography, not to mention both academic and popular essays. Indeed, racial Americana doesn't just allow for such generic eclecticisms; it demands them. Anything else would risk losing sight of this mobile and protean category, artificially boxing it up into a singularly impoverished presentational form.

The scholars in this volume highlight several important attributes of racial Americana. For one, they refuse a certain localization of social analysis. Racial Americana is about so much more than American exceptionalism, and it is comprehensible only within a larger global context of deterritorialized identities and transnational flows. With invocations of slave ships and imperialist unilateralisms, of Haitian foremothers and internationally circulating Norton readers, these scholars demand that we understand American race relations within a decidedly international framework. To think racial Americana is to think about racial formations that circulate all over the world — even when their details morph and mutate with every border crossing.[12]

Moreover, this is no zero-sum game, where race's centrality is predicated on concomitant marginalizations of class, sexuality, religion, nationality, and so on. We are not talking about some inflexible notion of racial reasoning that would imagine gender to be static and utterly beside the intellectual point. Racial Americana demands a blackness that is gender-conscious, variously contextualized, and willing to view culture as an utterly political and politicized site, but it also recognizes the dangers of playing with racial fire in the first place — its burns that never vanish, its quick-paced volatilities and spontaneous conflagrations, its cannibalistic propensity to consume everything in its path.

Recognizing the hazards of this discursive landscape, *Racial Americana*'s contributors use everything at their disposal — self-reflexivity, popular culture, feminism, political economy, psychoanalysis, and more — to imagine race as still decidedly alive and well. Not in a lazy and disingenuously genetic sense, but in a way that admits our inability to fully outrun this monstrous creation. In fact, maybe this monster isn't even alive at all, not really, not in the way we might think. Instead, *Racial Americana* imagines the realities of race as much more like the walking dead, active but hollowed out, human and thinglike at one and the same time. How else do we comprehend a schizophrenic race that simultaneously disavows biology and searches for nanopolitical anchorings? One that eschews racial language to argue an even more absolutist and essentialist case?

No, race is not alive, not anymore. We've killed it, deconstructed it to death, social-constructionized it out of fully animate existence. But it is hardly that easy. Instead, our beast has risen from the dead and haunts our every waking hour. It is the bogeyman in our collective social closet, make-believe but all the more frightening for its irreality, its ghostly intangibility. We can't kill racial reasoning with human genomes or social constructionism because, in some very fundamental ways, we killed race long ago,[13] and its death is part of what plagues us today, keeps us all up at night. We can't find the corpse, and there still seem to be sightings everywhere — of both its waking life and its strangely uncanny demise.

What we have now, what *Racial Americana* highlights, is a zombified notion of race, one that we constantly put to work, much like Zora Neale Hurston describes the matter in her performative ethnography of Haitian voodoo.[14] Zombies are occupational slaves, she says, and they do all the labor we ourselves would never want to undertake. These walking dead are not just commodity fetishes (in the Marxian sense) but a commodified form of death itself, slaving away for the masters who fear their very own Frankensteinian fiends, masters who would feebly wish their creations off into illusory oblivion — that is, had they not already grown overly dependent on them for some much-needed surplus value.

The task, then, is not to find out why and how race's telltale heart continues to beat. That may already be conceding far too much. Instead, racial Americana might trade in deconstruction for exorcism, for an analytic of the séance, a starting point that imagines the dead to have agency — even if only as the sacred sacrifices we make to the gods of collective social reproduction. There is an interiority to the thingness of the corpse, an animation still, and wrestling with the realities of race in a self-consciously post–Du Boisian and post-postracial moment entails taking that internality seriously. It means talking with the dead, channeling them, and not sorely underestimating their social effectivity. These dead walk, talk, struggle, and strain. In so doing, they also chain us to the scene of our past crimes. If we've killed race, yet it still moves, real analysis might take more than social deconstruction—the analytical equivalent of feebly petitioning the dead corpse that chokes us with an incredulous last-breath protest: "But you're dead. You're supposed to be dead. You're not real. This can't be re—*ugh*."

To escape the clutches of our own cultural creations, we need new incantations, new charms and southern amulets, new spells for countering the powerful magics of pseudoscience and social constructionism. *Racial Americana* is a small attempt to create this alternative magic, and the pieces in this volume represent various paths along that variegated and mystical roadway, alternative tactics for breaking death's ironclad choke hold. This counterspell will demand all the writerly weapons at our disposal—poetry, fiction, collage, memoir, essay, research report, philosophical treatise, and even the deeply felt anecdote—to cobble together a rendering of place, power, and history that can take race seriously without accepting it at face value.

Fine, race is not real, but that only makes it more powerful, more difficult to deny. Therefore, our critical goal is not simply to expose race's enabling fictions; we must also find ways to rewrite them—with new plot twists and heroes and dramatic narrative cliffhangers. It is not enough to cry "fiction" in a crowded classroom, not if the fiction in question still resonates for students as profoundly true-to-life. Our task is a bit more performative than that. It entails teasing out fiction's productive force, finding where its power lies, and determining what keeps bringing our dead things back to palpable life. *Racial Americana* offers a group of social critics and scholars trying to rethink race while unthinking it in the selfsame instant. That is a special kind of magic indeed—contradictory, paradoxical, self-deconstructed. Only in America! But this is a racial America that's all around the world, an imperialist zombie that might just be circulating the kernels of its own global undoing with every new escape from its coffin.

## Notes

Three groups at Duke University provided financial support for the four-color printing in this issue: the Department of Cultural Anthropology, the Program in African and African American Studies, and the John Hope Franklin Center for Interdisciplinary and International Studies. We gratefully acknowledge their generosity.

1    I am thinking of Vincent Sarich and Frank Miele, *Race: The Reality of Human Differences* (Boulder, CO: Westview, 2004).

2    Michael Taussig, *The Nervous System* (New York: Routledge, 1992), 145.

3    Ulick Varange, *Imperium: The Philosophy of History and Politics* (Sausalito, CA: Noontide, 1948), 300.

4    Paul Gilroy, *Against Race: Imagining Political Culture beyond the Color Line* (Cambridge, MA: Harvard University Press, 2000), 327.

5    For a discussion of Foucauldian biopolitics and its links to questions of sovereignty and the nation-state, see Giorgio Agamben, *Homo Sacer: Sovereign Power and Bare Life* (Stanford, CA: Stanford University Press, 1998). Also, for a specific look at the nanopolitics of race, see Gilroy, *Against Race*. For an argument specifically organized around biopolitics' ties to state racisms, see Michel Foucault, *"Society Must Be Defended": Lectures at the Collège de France, 1975–1976*, trans. David Macey (New York: Picador, 2003).

6    For a discussion of biopolitics that marks time with the nanopolitical, see Adriana Petryna, *Life Exposed: Biological Citizens after Chernobyl* (Princeton, NJ: Princeton University Press, 2002).

7    See Achille Mbembe, "Necropolitics," *Public Culture* 15.1 (2003).

8    See Elaine Scarry, *The Body in Pain: The Making and Unmaking of the World* (New York: Oxford University Press, 1985).

9    See Stuart Hall, "The Whites of Their Eyes: Racist Ideologies and the Media," in *The Media Reader*, ed. M. Alvarado and J. Thompson (London: British Film Institute, 1990), 532.

10   Ishmael Reed, *Mumbo Jumbo* (Garden City, NY: Doubleday, 1972), 216.

11   See Hortense Spillers, "Mama's Baby, Papa's Maybe: An American Grammar Book," *Diacritics* 17.2 (1987): 64–81.

12   See Kamari Clarke and Deborah A. Thomas, *Globalization and Race: Transformations in the Cultural Production of Blackness* (Durham, NC: Duke University Press, forthcoming).

13   Here, I am thinking of the long line of antiessentialist race work, from the older efforts of people like Frederick Douglass and Franz Boas to the recent research by Stephen Jay Gould and Richard Lewontin—as well as more recent scientific findings by Ning Yu and Alan Templeton.

14   Zora Neale Hurston, *Mules and Men* (New York: Perennial Library, 1990).

Sharon P. Holland

The Last Word on Racism:
New Directions for a Critical Race Theory

Dismayingly, institutionalized racism and prejudice
endure too, long after the abolition of slavery, or the
desegregation of public institutions, or the protest
marches or the shattering acts of violence. Racism, it
turns out, can take the heat.
—Joy Gregory, on her adaptation of Studs Terkel's
"Race: How Blacks and Whites Think and Feel about
the American Obsession" in *Playbill*

## A Shopping Plaza, A Primal Scene

A few days after Tupac Shakur's death, I pulled
into a grocery store parking lot in Palo Alto, California, with my friend's fifteen-year-old daughter. We were listening to one of Shakur's songs
on the radio—because he was a hometown boy,
the stations were playing his music around the
clock: a kind of electromagnetic vigil, if you will.
An older (but not elderly) white woman with
a grocery cart came to the driver's side of my
car and asked me to move my vehicle out of
its spot beside hers so that she could unload
her groceries. The tone of her voice conveyed
the fruition of expectation—it was not only a
request, but also a demand that would surely
be met. The southerner in me would have been

The *South Atlantic Quarterly* 104:3, Summer 2005.
Copyright © 2005 by Duke University Press.

happy to help; the critic in me didn't understand why she couldn't simply put her groceries in on the other side, where there were no other cars or potential impediments. I told the woman that I would gladly wait in my car until she unloaded her groceries—that way, there would be plenty of room for her to maneuver.

While she did this, I continued to listen to Shakur's music and talk with my friend's fifteen-year-old daughter, Danielle. We were bonding, and I was glad that she was talking to me about how Shakur's death was affecting her and her classmates. When I noticed that the woman had completed her unloading, I got out and we walked behind her car toward the Safeway. What happened next has stayed with me as one of the defining moments of my life in Northern California. As we passed the right rear bumper of her car, she said with mustered indignation, "And to think I marched for you." I was stunned at first—when something like this happens to you, you see the whole event in slow motion. I recovered and noted that I had two options: to walk away without a word, or to confront the accusation—to model for Danielle how to handle with intelligence and grace what would surely be part of the fabric of her life as a black woman in the United States. I turned to the woman and I said, "You didn't march for me, you marched for yourself—and if you don't know that, I can't help you."

When average people participate in racist acts, they demonstrate a profound misreading of the subjects they encounter. The scene above dramatizes a host of racialized relations: the expectation that black women will cease connection with their own "families" in order to respond to the needs of white persons; the comprehension of a refusal to do so as a criminal act; the need to subject black bodies to the rule of race; and the absolute denial of the connection between seemingly disparate peoples that the words *civil rights march* connote. For that woman in the parking lot, the civil rights struggle was not about freedom for us all, it was about acquiring a kind of purchase on black bodies. I would be given the right to participate in "democratic process," but the ability to *exercise* such a right would be looked upon with disdain, and at times outrage. This scene from a mall stays with me as if that woman and I were locked in a past that has tremendous purchase on my present. In my mind, we hover there touching one another with the lie of difference and nonrelation balancing precariously between us—like the characters Rosa Coldfield and Clytie (Sutpen) at war on the dilapidated staircase in Faulkner's *Absalom, Absalom!* The psychic violation of my moment in the parking lot haunts me still; but it is the intimacy of that moment that arrests me. The woman *expected* something from me—though one usually does not expect anything from strangers. Moreover, our connection as women, tenuous though it might have been, was completely obscured, if not obliterated, by this racist act. It was then that I began to think about the word *race* under the auspices of racism, the thing that, according to the epigraph for this essay, "endures."

Racism defends us against the project of universal belonging, against the findings, if you will, of the human genome project. Racism, after all, "can take the heat." We cannot think about race without thinking about the racism that defines race, interprets it, and decrees what the personal and institutional work of race will be. Racism requires one to participate in a *project of belonging* if the work of producing racial difference(s) is to reach fruition. I have used the phrase "project of belonging" to signify two sets of relations. One is a "real" biological connection, a belonging that occurs at the level of family (blood relation). A crude understanding of race is that it is always already the thing that happens in the blood: think "one-drop rule," think "blood quantum," think "blueblood," and think "sangre pura." The second set of relations is the result of the work of identifying with others, a belonging usually imposed by a community *or* by one's own choice. Given the slipperiness of identity, identifying with others can be a fictitious and fantastic undertaking. Fantasy, of course, can oscillate between delusion and creative hope.

Where racism imposes racial purity however, *law and practice* will code the identification across differences as impossible, even if it happens, even if it is real. Even though every human visage and quotidian encounter bear witness to this reality and the twin practices of Indian removal and transatlantic slavery attest to it, miscegenation remains an impossibility. In order to mine this contradiction between human practice and jurisprudence, I use the phrase "blood strangers" to understand this process. While the word *race* creates the possibility for blood strangers, it also employs its primary ally and enforcer, racism, to police the imaginary boundary between blood (us) and strangers (them). Racism transforms an already porous periphery into an absolute. Racism makes it necessary to *deny* all kinds of crossing. Racism can also be described as the emotional lifeblood of race. Racism is the "feeling" that articulates and keeps the flawed logic of race in its place. Ultimately, we have race, but it lacks emotion, so we often speak of race through various theories of its fictional and transitive nature. But sit-ing/citing *everyday* racism is almost like stating a belief in the paranormal. We focus on race, but not on the everyday system of terror and pleasure that in varying proportions makes race so worthwhile a category of difference to many.

This essay is an experimental exploration of the intimacy that everyday racism relies upon. The work here is not focused upon egregious or spec-tacular acts of racist violence, but instead investigates the more quotidian acts of racism—the kind that separate (and simultaneously conjoin) black and white in family genealogies, the sort created by a simple touch or a word uttered between blood strangers. This essay functions as reconnoi-ter, deploying and then interrogating a series of scenarios, passages, and scenes (from engagements with the likes of Jacques Derrida, Toni Mor-rison, William Faulkner, and Thomas Jefferson, among others) in order to understand the workings of race. Throughout this piece, touch appears as an appropriate metanarrative for racism because it articulates similar dangers—touch both engenders outrage and identifies connection in past, present, and future. The touch, I suggest, manifests itself as the psychic life of difference, transforming two categories of being (human and nonhuman) into a charged space of pleasure *and* of possibility.

## The Last Word

Critical musing about the end of race or about the inadequacies of the cate-gory altogether have assumed that race pilots itself through national narra-tives, fictional enterprises, or family albums. This is not the case. Even as we pronounce the death of race, we cannot overlook the fact that our attempts to articulate it into oblivion, to pronounce the last word on race, simply have not worked. In keeping with the speculative nature of this essay, I want to shift here to a metaphoric rendering of the last word, in order to meditate upon our *simultaneous* search for the end of race and our strivings for an adequate articulation of it. An apt example of this arduous quest is Toni Morrison's selection of the final word of *Beloved*. In her essay "Home," she discusses its ending and writes: "Someone saw the last sentence of *Beloved* as it was originally written. In fact, it was the penultimate sentence if one thinks of the last word in the book . . . as the very last sentence. In any case the phrase, 'Certainly no clamor for a kiss,' which appears in the printed book, is not the one with which I had originally closed the book."[1] Upon her editor's suggestion, Morrison looked for a word that was not so "dramatic" or "theatrical" as the original, now erased ending. She continues:

> I was eager to find a satisfactory replacement, because the point that gripped me was that even if the word I had chosen was the absolute right one, something was wrong with it if it called attention to itself—awkwardly, inappropriately—and did not complete the meaning of the text, but dislodged it. It wasn't a question of simply substituting one word for another that meant the same thing. . . . I am still unhappy about it because "kiss" works at a level a bit too shallow. It searches for and locates a quality or element of the novel that was not, and is not, its primary feature. The driving force of the narrative is not love, or the fulfillment of physical desire. The action is driven by necessity, something that precedes love, follows love, shapes it, and to which love is subservient. In this case the necessity was for connection, acknowledgment, paying-out of homage still due. "Kiss" clouds that point. (6–7)

Closing her remarks on writing *Beloved*, Morrison adds,

> My efforts were to carve away the accretions of deceit, blindness, ignorance, paralysis, and sheer malevolence embedded in raced language so that other kinds of perception were not only available, but were inevitable. That is the work I thought my original last word accomplished; then I became convinced that it did not, and now am sorry I made the change. The trouble it takes to find just one word and know that it is the note and that no other would do is an extraordinary battle. (7)

The right word can also bring the acknowledgment that puts the erotic life of the text in motion, a place in *Beloved* where categories of difference can also be at play. Morrison has not revealed what that word might be, but I can't help but think that the original last word hovers somewhere between *fuck* and *touch*. Regardless, Morrison documents the quest for the penultimate pronouncement on race—if one can think of the novel as a relentless meditation upon the slavery's racist brutalities—as ultimately unfruitful. Nevertheless, she does capture the inadequacy of the word *kiss* for an articulation of fraught and dangerous relations between white and black subjects under slavery's racist imperative. Morrison's struggle with the word *kiss* and her attempts to work around "raced language" point to the complex nature of racism and our attempts as writers and critics to write a narrative of its permutations. Her reliance upon and repudiation of the erotic life of racism—the "kiss" between (blood) strangers—indicates that we do find racism in the arena where intimates make "connection."

French philosopher Jacques Derrida also attempts to explore "the last word" in his 1985 essay "Racism's Last Word"—more aptly translated from the French as "The Last Word on Racism."[2] Derrida, however, deploys the metaphor in a different fashion. Speaking of the word *apartheid*, he notes that the word remains the same no matter what the natural language in which it is embedded. He observes that "no tongue has ever translated this name—as if all the languages of the world were defending themselves, shutting their mouths against a sinister incorporation of the thing by means of the word, as if all tongues were refusing to give an equivalent, refusing to let themselves be contaminated through the contagious *hospitality* of the word-for-word."[3] Derrida uncannily uses a turn of the tongue similar to that employed by Zora Neale Hurston in *Their Eyes Were Watching God* (1937). Janie, the primary protagonist, pronounces: "Mah tongue is in mah friend's mouth." Feminist and African Americanist critics have consumed reams of white paper devising intricate and seductive theories about this statement. Surely one is that the phrase "mah tongue is in mah friend's mouth" is both a figure of speech and an erotic declaration; its mimetic qualities abound. If we take the tongue, must we also accept the word—"the contagious hospitality of the word-for-word"—or can we have our pleasure and leave its disconcerting language behind? This is where Hurston might trouble Derrida.

Like Hurston, Derrida envisions tongues exchanging. His concept of "contagious hospitality" underscores the problem of treating the tongue as a contaminant, insisting that the inevitable exchange (commingling) is dangerous, that the act of transference/translation itself is corrupt.[4] The hospitality he refers to here is often interpreted as from outside, and the implication is that apartheid therefore comes from some "foreign" place—that its word is not given to us by our "friends." Thus "hospitality" is a contagion, making the wor(l)d a dangerous place. Perhaps the most pernicious aspect of any sustained conflict between peoples is that phrases like "separate but equal," "the final solution," and "apartheid" are not the creations of institutions, of governing bodies, or of our enemies. They are the inventions of our intimates, our friends, our neighbors, and our blood relations. Remember the transatlantic slave trade, Indian removal, and the Holocaust; witness Algeria in the 1950s, Bosnia in the 1990s—the list is endless. Friendship is often the first "gift" of war.

Many of Derrida's critics often take exception with his focus upon the play of language, rather than upon the more concrete nature of material conditions.[5] I would argue that Derrida's language play opens up new possibilities for our understanding of racism and its legacy of action. In addition, his vision of racism points to our inability to own it, to see it as a possibility for past, present, and future. Working with the tongue and the word, or, more precisely, with the simultaneity of repudiation and acceptance that so characterizes racism's contradictory terrain, Derrida highlights the active nature of racism. He continues:

> At every point, like all racisms, it [apartheid] tends to pass segregation off as natural — and as the very law of the origin. Such is the monstrosity of this political idiom. Surely, an idiom should never incline toward racism. It often does, however, and this is not altogether fortuitous: there's no racism without a language. The point is not that acts of racial violence are only words but rather that they have to have a word. Even though it offers the excuse of blood, color, birth — or rather, because it uses this naturalist and sometimes creationist discourse — racism . . . institutes, declares, writes, inscribes, prescribes. A system of marks, it outlines space in order to assign forced residence or to close off borders. It does not discern, it discriminates. (331)

The discrimination that is racist practice marks the contradiction embedded in this "political idiom." Knowing how to use an idiomatic phrase in any language is the beginning of mastery, as it simultaneously demonstrates to others that the master's tools are no longer in the master's house. Words in the mouths of those who are the objects of racist discourse are always already purloined. The trope of the tongue works in two directions: we engage in a word-for-word, tongue-for-tongue reciprocation or we perform a refusal through abstraction — refusing to incorporate the word in our own lexicon (making word and deed an aberration), rejecting it as someone else's experience (racism is for/happens to one group over another), someone else's language (the word does not befit the deed, the act), and ultimately, someone else's problem. And the problem of racism is always someone else's to own — it has a place in that it occurs at the level of the everyday, but it does not have a home — it manifests, but only as a fantastic event — an abhorrence in an otherwise lovely day. Its exceptionality is its beauty. If the word does not have a place (no origin, no nation), a point of passing/passage (two tongues intertwined), it ceases to exist.

Morrison's agonizing over the last word of *Beloved* parallels the play in Derrida's journey through the minefield of racism. In Derrida's cosmos, racism is both actor and acted upon—it is possessed (its last word) and possessor (the last word on racism). The play of words, the exchange, the mark of racism is understood as a both/and phenomenon. Moreover, Derrida's personification of the word also describes the *experience* of racism itself—where someone else's perpetuation of a racist act against a subject often feels like the definitive moment, feels like an endpoint, but at the same instant reveals its second life, as the act of hate speech or physical violence reveals itself as the beginning, where the two lives of actor and acted upon become sutured in the erotic dance of painful recognition, trauma, and shame. Racism choreographs such a dance that subject and object will replay and relive as they move through the material world, together and apart. The violence of racism locks the two in a peculiar and erotic psychic life—a place where they have surely touched one another, where the encounter betrays the prohibition of erotic life and establishes its importance, its necessity. What the touch does engage is the desire of thinking communities to destroy the idea that language belongs to anyone at any given time no matter what their epistemological cosmos might be (for example, in a psychoanalytic register, the "touch" might be called preoedipal language, but that would still require its belonging to someone, to the mother and child). For example, the touch cuts across ("abrogates," to echo Faulkner) the desire to name and form meaning through language. Perhaps this is Derrida's idea all along: that the word (*apartheid?*) staves off intimacy is precisely the effect of racism's last word—it calls attention to the action that engenders its necessity.

### Faulkner's Touching Moment

In his essay "*Le toucher*: Touch/to Touch Him," Jacques Derrida expounds upon the myriad objectives of the touch. He writes:

> For to touch, so one believes, is touching what one touches, to let oneself be touched by the touched, by the touch of the thing, whether objective or not, or by the flesh that one touches and that then becomes touching as well as touched. This is not true for all the other senses: one may, to be sure, let oneself be "touched" as well by what one hears or sees, but not necessarily heard or seen by what one hears and sees, whence the initial privilege of what is called touch.[6]

Both physical and psychic, touch is an act that can embody multiple, con-flicting agendas.[7] It can be both a troubled and troublesome component in the relationship between intimates, as in the case of Derrida;[8] or, alterna-tively, the touch mediates relations between friends and strangers. In fact, the touch can alter the very idea as well as the actuality of relationships, morphing friends into enemies and strangers into intimates. For touch can encompass empathy as well as violation, passivity as well as active aggres-sion. It can be safely dangerous, or dangerously safe. It also carries a mes-sage about the immediate present, the possible future, and the problematic past. Finally, touch crosses boundaries, in fact and imagination.

In brief, the concept of the touch has an antecedent in recent significant thinking about race in the trope of the "intersection," a place where dif-ferences come together. This trope has been generative for such scholars and feminists as Ann du Cille, Cherrie Moraga, Valerie Smith, and Kim-berlé Crenshaw. Often, they have often employed it to describe the tender space that women of color occupy in the nexus of antiracist and feminist struggles.[9] Crenshaw's 1992 essay that introduced the term *intersectionality* was part of a large scholarly movement. It generated publications that were written at the crossroads of race, gender, and sexuality and that prolifer-ated in the decade of the 1990s and later.[10] As intersectionality describes the painful possibility of the simultaneous *effect* of race and gender, so does the touch provide another point of contact where race and gender(s) collide.

Ironically, even though we shrink from our experience of quotidian racism, we are apparently incapable of living without categories of differ-ence, even when those categories are at worst hurtful and at best fictions in and of themselves. My central questions here are: "What makes difference work?" and "How do we accomplish its goals?" I again come back to racism as the action that makes race matter. In a psychoanalytic register, Freud offers an account of our need to differentiate. He surmises: "Even where the original inclination to identification has withstood criticism—that is, when the 'others' are our fellow men—the assumption of a consciousness in them rests upon an inference and cannot share the immediate certainty which we have of our own consciousness."[11] In other words, even when we recognize someone as "human," we destroy the pleasure of recognition and of reci-procity. We do not permit ourselves fully to see the human we encounter as having the same consciousness or even the *potential* for the same as ours. While the purpose of this essay is not to engage Freud's complex delibera-tions about the human psyche, it is noteworthy that the work of difference, as conceived of by Freud and perhaps as experienced by all of us to some extent, is never really complete. Our desire for absolute difference cannot be satiated. It keeps coming back to question the legitimacy of our own claim that we possess a single and unique consciousness. There is no endpoint to our gambits with the other, which breaks in upon our singularity, causing us to react indignantly, "Oh, it's *you* again?" We feel the same burden when touched by another. The touch, crossing boundaries, affirms the inadequacy of this boundary between selves.

The power of the touch as both boundary and trespass is wonderfully illustrated in one of William Faulkner's greatest novels. In an infamous scene in *Absalom, Absalom!* Rosa Coldfield exhibits hysterical rage when Clytie (Thomas Sutpen's "half-black" daughter) arrests her ascent of the staircase at Sutpen's Hundred by placing a hand upon her arm. Behind this gesture and the anger it provokes is a terrible story. For *Absalom* is organized around a family saga that takes place in the old and the new South and extends beyond the Civil War. In 1833, Thomas Sutpen arrives in the town of Jefferson, Mississippi, with a "design" to build a mansion and establish a hundred-acre plantation: "I had a design. To accomplish it I should require money, a house, a plantation, slaves, a family—incidentally, of course, a wife. I set out to acquire these, asking no favor of any man."[12] Shortly afterward, he marries Rosa Coldfield's older sister Ellen. As the novel takes several temporal and narrative shifts, we hear the convoluted tale of Sutpen's early years. Before his arrival in Mississippi, Sutpen's first attempt at fulfilling his design went awry when he discovered that the woman he married in Haiti was not white, but Creole. He put her aside in New Orleans and traveled to Mississippi. But his design is again challenged when the son from this first union, Charles Bon, plans to marry his own half-sister, Judith— Sutpen's daughter and Rosa's niece. Charles Bon is literally the past coming back to haunt Sutpen's design. In order to prevent the marriage, Henry Sutpen (son of Ellen and Thomas) kills Charles and then disappears. Henry's reasons for committing murder are a matter of speculation throughout the text.

In the novel's present tense (January 1910), the narrative is pieced together as Quentin Compson and Shreve Davenport sit in their Harvard dormitory recalling the story as told to Quentin by Rosa and Colonel Compson. Rosa's first-person narrative, contained in chapter 5 of *Absalom*, encompasses both her return to Sutpen's Hundred just after Henry Sutpen kills Charles Bon and the seven-month period when Rosa, Clytie, and Judith wait for Thomas Sutpen to return after the Civil War. When Rosa arrives at the foot of the stairs in 1864, within two years of Ellen's death, Henry Sutpen has killed Charles Bon and vanished; Judith, Bon's intended, stands outside the door she will not open, clutching her wedding dress in one hand and the picture of Charles's New Orleans wife (like father, like son) in the other. Clytie stands between Rosa and the door beyond which the dead body of Bon resides.

In this signal passage, we find Rosa obsessed with Clytie's "black arresting and untimorous hand on my white woman's flesh" (115). Listen to Rosa's rage, which exemplifies my concept of "the touch":

> Then she touched me, and then I did stop dead. Possibly even then my body did not stop, since I seemed to be aware of it thrusting blindly still against the solid yet imponderable weight . . . of that will to bar me from the stairs; possibly the sound of the other voice, the single word spoken from the stair-head above us, had already broken and parted us before it (my body) had even paused. I do not know. I know only that my entire being seemed to run at blind full tilt into something monstrous and immobile, with a shocking impact too soon and too quick to be mere amazement and outrage. . . . Because there is something in the touch of flesh with flesh which abrogates, cuts sharp and straight across the devious intricate channels of decorous ordering, which enemies as well as lovers know because it makes them both. . . . But let flesh touch with flesh, and watch the fall of all the eggshell shibboleth of caste and color too. Yes, I stopped dead—no woman's hand, no negro's hand, but bitted bridle-curb to check and guide the furious and unbending will—I crying not to her, to it; speaking to it through the negro, the woman, only because of the shock which was not yet outrage because it would be terror soon, expecting and receiving no answer because we both knew it was not to her I spoke: "Take your hand off me, nigger!" (115)

What makes Rosa's obsession with Clytie's touch so remarkable is that even in the midst of absolute chaos and trauma, Rosa chooses to focus upon that touch and its possibility. Here, the touch assumes experiential knowledge, while it also calls upon its witnesses and players to testify to it as both connection and repudiation, making it part of that person's experience and daring her to disown it. The parallels to Derrida's conceptualization of nations refusing an intimate exchange—"word-for-word" refusal—

are several and uncanny. When Rosa finally utters the word *nigger* at the end of this rambling scene, it is almost anticlimactic; she has already proven that the touch does transform, or at least it has the possibility to translate, to convey meaning from one to another. The touch is vividly personified, and as an entity in the text it is always already present—it does not happen to Rosa, so much as it *connects* Rosa and Clytie in a past whose imbrication occurs through blood and law. Rosa and Clytie become, literally, *blood strangers*. Like Derrida's conceit about racism's incorporation and repudiation by national bodies, Rosa's narrative refuses the touch at the same time that it proves its inevitability throughout time, rather than in time. In essence, the touch transforms, becomes legible because it moves beyond "the Negro" and becomes "it"; Rosa begins to see the touch as her adversary ("I crying not to her, to it; speaking through the Negro, the woman"), and as she realizes this, she also embraces its unequivocal presence. Simultaneously, the surrogacy performed here—the fact of Rosa's voice speaking through "the Negro"—mimics the problem of generation, its biological and psychic roots.

Faulkner renders the touch between Clytie and Rosa as not solely violent but also erotic. The touch is so compelling here that the prevailing narrative of race is undone and a multitude of possibilities find fruition. The language of the passage is entirely visceral—as Rosa's body moves forward within the action of the novel, her mind is arrested and preoccupied with the inevitability of the touch. The mind/body split that Rosa endures mimics the structure of racism—how everyday people play the game of distancing themselves from racism, by seeing it as not part of their daily routine, but as someone else's devastating failure at communication. She runs headlong into the truth of the past—her blood relationship to Sutpen's black and white family—that renders the language of getting there absolutely inarticulate. Language is literally "broken"—ungendered and unraced. It hovers in chapter 5 of *Absalom* witnessing its own demise, as there is no adequate language for Rosa's experience of Clytie's touch, which is why we have such a convoluted articulation of this moment by Rosa. The touch they share potentially unmakes gender, as it dismantles racial difference because the two women are called upon (through Rosa's voice) to contemplate the meaning of difference, to reside in the space where a gendered connection is made (im)possible by racism's quotidian assault. Rosa's panic is made all the more inviting because of Clytie's relative silence—a silence that Faulkner makes very few attempts to move beyond. But Clytie's action, singular and momentary though it might be, is profound, and it breaks upon the climactic scene, spreading like a virus in Rosa's mind.

In another manifestation of difference, Rosa remarks: "Even as a child, I would not even play with the same objects which she [Clytie] and Judith played with, as though that warped and Spartan solitude which I called my childhood . . . had also taught me not only to instinctively fear her and what she was, but to shun the very objects which she had touched" (116). Faulkner identifies Rosa's personification of objects as they become intermediaries between one body and another. Rosa's objects *are* constitutive of the human. How we become human, then, is always already mediated by an ever-present touch of the material, the object, the not-us, threatening incorporation. Moreover, to put Freud in play, what Rosa reacts to is not the threat of belonging to (sharing the same gene pool with) Judith and Clytie; she later says that she sees them as no different than she. Rosa's reaction to Clytie's touch introduces the threat of belonging. But the anxiety caused by this threat is only perceived—it is only a performance, if you will, because each character in *Absalom* fully understands that the commingling he or she loathes has already taken place. The objects at work in *Absalom* take on the position of the virtual body, representing both terror and pleasure and eliciting a simultaneous response from the reader—titillating fear and absolute disavowal.[13]

To think of the body through the trajectory of the flesh is to also think through the existential paradigms of Maurice Merleau-Ponty, Frantz Fanon, Simone de Beauvoir, and, more recently, Hortense Spillers.[14] In her "classic manifesto of the liberated woman,"[15] de Beauvoir speaks to the presence of the erotic and its connection to the lives of women. She offers that "eroticism implies a claim of the instant against time, of the individual against the group; it affirms separation against communication; it is rebellion against all regulation; it contains a principle hostile to society."[16] Decades later, Audre Lorde would make a similar claim for the revolutionary power of the erotic for women.[17] If the erotic has as its principle a hostility to social norms, a claim *against* time and simultaneously *for* body as well, then the touch that Rosa *describes* and *experiences* resonates with the idea of what it means to be human and female, of what it means to subject oneself to constant regulation. Since the publication of *The Second Sex*, feminist critics and philosophers have been resurrecting and reinterpreting de Beauvoir's take on some of existentialism's major tenets. Rosa's rage is perhaps a product of the erotic's signal meaning—how it speaks the text of all relations, psychic or otherwise. For Beauvoir, the erotic has its place in both the personal and the political. The connection between peoples, refused or accepted, changes and even distorts time, making personal interactions political. In Rosa's case, her rage is of both a political and a personal nature. Clytie exists under a double prohibition—she is forbidden by law to lay a hand upon a white woman, *and* she is encouraged by custom and practice not to touch Miss Rosa.

The intimate moment that Rosa and Clytie share is ordinary. Quotidian intimacy forces us to realize the other as someone we interact with and have an impact upon—our acknowledgment of this connection represents the touch and its fruition. We do not create intimacy; it is there awaiting our recognition.[18] Let me rephrase this: We are bound intimately to others whether or not we realize or acknowledge such connection. The touch is the sign without a language to make it legible to others. Rosa's experience of Clytie's touch creates a psychic presence so powerful that it draws another woman, Judith Sutpen, into its web. In the end, the women—Rosa, Clytie, and Judith, like the three Fates—become "one being" (129). For Faulkner, the touch "abrogates"—it nullifies our stubborn insistence upon separation, between races, sexes, or nations, if you will. After all, in Faulkner's modernism, black and white bodies do not always occupy separate spheres. What is at stake here is not presence at all, but the idea of it; the knowledge, no matter how circumscribed—that "presence" is only (as with Clytie) half the story.[19]

### Jefferson's Grave Disturbance

In the spring of 2001, NPR's Morning Edition ran a report about the Thomas Jefferson Heritage Organization and its attempt to preserve the "character" and "reputation" of our third president. The organization had produced a six-hundred-page report stating that the DNA evidence linking Jefferson to Sally Hemings's children was inconclusive. John Work, an eighth-generation relative of Jefferson and president of the Thomas Jefferson Heritage Society, was "deeply disturbed by the thought that President Jefferson slept with a young slave."[20] What astounds me is that Jefferson's relative champions do not see the fact that he owned slaves in the new republic as any kind of stain on his character or reputation. Jefferson's detractors see the connection to Hemings as evidence of the "complicated" nature of early American society. His advocates see this "evidence" as a complete occlusion of what it means to be a "founding father" in the first place. What is in jeopardy is (white) paternity.

In addition to this report, NPR also ran a story on Alice Randall's novel *The Wind Done Gone*, a parody of Margaret Mitchell's *Gone with the Wind*, told as a series of diary entries by the illegitimate and enslaved half-sister of Scarlett O'Hara. The Mitchell estate successfully sued to stop the initial publication of Randall's parody, citing violation of copyright law by infringing upon the estate's sequel rights. The decision was eventually overturned in appellate court, and *The Wind Done Gone* eventually reached the public. NPR's Cheryl Crowley interviewed several writers and critics, one of whom was Lauren Berlant of the University of Chicago. All of them noted the dominance of the now infamous classic, how its "mythic portrayal of the South" is more widely read and available than histories of "plantation life" and "reconstruction." Berlant, speaking for the academy, argues that the novel has achieved a kind of "normative" status in the imagination, providing a cultural fantasy that endures.[21] Even Jefferson's own words cannot curb our lust for the fantasy of slavery—its human refuse, if *refuse* here denotes both trash and renunciation. In his most direct, but brief, account of slavery in *Notes on the State of Virginia*, Jefferson remarks:

> There must doubtless be an unhappy influence on the manners of our people produced by the existence of slavery among us. The whole commerce between master and slave is a perpetual exercise of the most boisterous passions, the most unremitting despotism on the one part, and degrading submissions on the other. Our children see this, and learn to imitate it; for man is an imitative animal. This quality is the germ of education in him. . . . The parent storms, the child looks on, catches the lineaments of wrath, puts on the same airs in the circle of smaller slaves, gives a loose to his worst of passions, and thus nursed, educated and daily exercised in tyranny, cannot but be stamped by it with odious peculiarities. The man must be a prodigy who can retain his manners and morals undepraved [*sic*] by such circumstances.[22]

We are left to wonder if Jefferson is that prodigy and, therefore, exception to the will to tyranny. If the root of the word *prodigy* vacillates between the marvelous and the monstrous, the potential for human action is so mercurial here as to be of no consequence. Here, the psychic life of language holds open the poles of slavery's behavioral enterprise. The institution of slavery is truly what Coleridge sought in the demonic imagination—

a beautiful but horrific sublime, a state wherein all possibility, imagined or otherwise, is managed and contained. Jefferson is Sula watching her mother burn, not because he or she is spiteful, but because he or she is *interested*. Moreover, this passage is flooded with what I would call negative language about the category of the human. Human exchange gives way to "commerce," and any and all human connection is arrested by a series of relations that make the figures in Jefferson's hypothetical scene part of the machinery of slavery itself. The possibility of attaining or engaging in the kind of status bestowed upon the category "human" is withheld from everyone in Jefferson's short narrative, and what we are left with are the "odious peculiarities" that also manage to thrive without a proper name.

Jefferson's poignant dismantling of the human through the perpetuation of a pervasive and therefore dominant narrative makes American slavery legible *only* as a fiction — and yet one worth preserving by any means necessary. The sexual practice of the nation's third president and the story at the root of *Gone with the Wind* are both haunted by the touch — the image of Jefferson sleeping with (touching) Sally Hemings or the idea of Scarlett O'Hara's (half-)black sister putting her pen to paper (touching) the legacy of Scarlett and Rhett.[23] The prohibition against the touch extends even to the grave, as Jefferson's relatives and those of Sally Hemings continue to quarrel about the burial ground at Monticello. The idea of separate but equal ground annoyed descendants of Hemings, one of whom remarked, "Nothing's changed in two hundred years, has it?" On the other hand, John Work sent a letter to over seven hundred family members "complaining that the lines between the two cemeteries 'would blur' over time and lead to 'a graveyard of Jefferson's descendants, *both real and imagined.*'"[24] Whiteness forms the stuff of the real, and blackness is always already imagined territory. Jefferson's white relatives want to spare his legacy, his image, from the "odious peculiarities" associated with slavery; his black relatives want to put an end to our understanding of such relations as "odious" or "peculiar" at all. When we think of slavery in America, we'd rather have the violent touch of enslaved and free bodies or the love that dare not speak its name — both accounts serve as romanticized fictions of past events. We are constantly hovering between these two inventions and are reminded that any attempt at the truth about slavery is simply unavailable to us. John Work's racism polices the border between black and white, male and female. At this contested border stands the body of a black woman; the fight over generation(s) and our claim upon them always enlists a gendered and raced standard.

If touch can be interpreted as the action that bars one from entry and also connects one to the sensual life of another, then we might go so far as to say that racism has its own erotic life. The particular legacy (if not genius) of the Confederacy is that it was able to convince an entire nation to look toward the future for events that had already taken place in the past, to believe that emancipation would result in rampant miscegenation. Think about the kind of shame and then rage you might provoke when you ask someone to articulate the problem of racism (I am thinking of Du Bois here)—not from some one else's history, but from their own. Even though property is everything in America, you will find difficulty in getting your neighbor to own this small piece of our collective pie.

Let me offer the following series of relationships. Our understanding of slavery as Americans vacillates among the good, the bad, and the ugly. Some see its touch as violent; others, like the purveyors of the legacy of Mitchell's novel, view it as doing more good than harm. Any attempt to revisit this myth called the past is likely to be viewed as just plain ugly. In Faulkner's imaginary the abrogation of the touch is precisely the problem—we are flailing at institutional structures like family, like race, without the proper implement; for Faulkner it is the touch that both sears the flesh and provides the opportunity for its suture.

### Coda: Slavery's Posthumanity?

> But the posthuman does not really mean the end of humanity. It signals instead the end of a certain conception of the human, a conception that may have applied, at best, to that fraction of humanity who had the wealth, power, and leisure to conceptualize themselves as autonomous beings exercising their will through individual agency and choice.
>
> —N. Katherine Hayles, *How We Became Posthuman*

The idea that humans can, do, and will merge with machines reflects a future that has an origin (I am going against one of deconstruction's primal urges here, so bear with me) in a past situated in the labor relations of slavery. Let me offer a series of somewhat radical hypotheses to illustrate my larger point. Rather than move toward a conclusion here, I want to offer a few radical directions for further study.

The practice of slavery caused its population—whether enslaved or free, black, white, or indigenous—to think differently about what it meant to be human. White subjects, as the primary inhabitants of the category of the human, merged with enslaved peoples/chattel/property in order to continue to grease the wheels of a lucrative economy otherwise known as slavery. As the category of the human and the object came together to produce offspring—perhaps half human, half chattel, but nevertheless fraught—the possibility of posthumanity became embedded in the human/object paradigm of the slavocracy. In other words, the posthuman condition is not only present as a historical component of experience, it is an important component of our understanding of what took place between here and there, between freed and enslaved, between the human and the nonhuman. A theory of the posthuman might make its home in the space before technology as we know it, rather than at a critical endpoint. It might have a place in the moment when the human literally was, to remember Sartre, "like a machine."[25]

From the human to the posthuman and toward the dissolution of the human/animal binary, recent investigations in either direction give credence to the psychoanalytic concept of the return of the repressed. That critics, both scientific and philosophical, have endeavored to draw and quarter the category of the human in an effort to free it from several dichotomous arrangements leaves ample room for an investigation of slavery's systemic machinations. Even N. Katherine Hayles admits that her larger project "show[s] what had to be elided, suppressed, and forgotten to make information lose its body," as she envisions her book as "a 'rememory' in the sense of Toni Morrison's *Beloved*: putting back together parts that have lost touch with one another and reaching out toward a complexity too unruly to fit into disembodied ones and zeros" (13). But embedded in Morrison's story of fugitive slave law and human flesh is the following command from Schoolteacher, slave owner–cum–pseudo-scientist: "I told you to put her human characteristics on the left; her animal ones on the right. And don't forget to line them up."[26]

Morrison has always been fascinated by numbers and systems. One example of this preoccupation is her brilliant trope of the three Deweys in *Sula*, where the white, the Indian, and the black are rendered identical (in name only). Hayles's understanding of her project in *How We Became Posthuman* embraces both the possibility of touch and the freedom associated with random assembly of both objects and humans. Between the touch and its signifying freedom lies the possibility for a companion project—a connection, if you will, between the aims of my study and the goals of post-human studies. Since either side can and does speak for the human, its integration or disintegration should no longer be the "it" that we seek to engage. From Jefferson to Faulkner and back again, an ordinary scene is transformed by the narration of small events and quotidian occurrences into evidence of something much more pernicious. That racism is ordinary—a key principle in Critical Race Theory—is no surprise; that its banal quality should collide with and therefore affect the human/animal divide might also come as no small wonder. In any event, everyday racism has a continuum from past to present, and this endurance leads us back to the beginning, giving credence to the sentiment of the epigraph for this essay: "Racism, it turns out, can take the heat."

## Notes

The title of this article is taken from a more accurate translation of the title of Jacques Derrida's essay "Racism's Last Word."

1   Toni Morrison, "Home," in *The House That Race Built: Black Americans, U.S. Terrain*, ed. Wahneema Lubiano (New York: Pantheon, 1997), 6. Subsequent citations are given parenthetically by page number in the text.

2   Derrida was not the last scholar to have at the end of racism. A full decade later, Dinesh D'Souza would publish *The End of Racism: Principles for a Multiracial Society* (New York: Free Press, 1995).

3   Jacques Derrida, "Racism's Last Word," trans. Peggy Kamuf, in *"Race," Writing, and Difference*, ed. Henry Louis Gates Jr. (Chicago: University of Chicago Press, 1986), 331.

4   In his essay "On 'Captive' 'Bodies,' Hidden 'Flesh,' and Colonization" (in *Existence in Black: An Anthology of Black Existential Philosophy*, ed. Lewis R. Gordon [New York: Routledge, 1997]), G. M. James Gonzalez observes that "tongue (language, voice, rhetoric) and thought (ideology) have been among the deadliest instruments of colonialism. . . . Tongue and thought are, therefore, infectious and untrustworthy within the colonizer and the colonized; for the colonized has also been infected" (127).

5   Derrida's essay was published with a lengthy critique by Anne McClintock and Rob Nixon, "No Names Apart: The Separation of Word and History in Derrida's 'Le dernier mot du racisme,'" to which Derrida also responded (all in *Race, Writing, and Difference*, ed. Henry Louis Gates Jr. [Chicago: University of Chicago Press, 1992]). In essence, they remind Derrida, as one must rarely remind Morrison and Hurston, that a word's meaning is not separate from its history, and this relationship gives us a word's politics, forms the epicenter of its nervous system. For Derrida, it is precisely this logic of relation—the idea that history creates meaning rather than confounds it—that causes a word to adhere in one place and experience repudiation in another. I believe that McClintock and Nixon misunderstand Derrida's intent. Derrida doesn't necessarily repudiate racism's checkered history so much as he wants to isolate the word itself and deploy it as a floating signifier, or contaminant. What he finds is that so long as racism is perceived as someone

else's problem by those who live in its midst, history cannot adequately account for it. His view is radical in that it emphasizes a lack of responsibility for racism that is epidemic in global cultures.

6   Jacques Derrida, "*Le toucher*: Touch/to Touch Him," *Paragraph: The Journal of the Modern Critical Theory Group* 16.2 (1993): 136.

7   This essay is indebted to the long history of ruminations on the touch in both philosophical and feminist traditions. For other explorations of "touch," see Carolyn Vasseleu, *Textures of Light: Vision and Touch in Irigaray, Levinas, and Merleau-Ponty* (New York: Routledge, 1998); and Elizabeth Grosz, "Merleau-Ponty and Irigaray in the Flesh," in *Merleau-Ponty, Interiority and Exteriority, Psychic Life and the World*, ed. Dorothea Olkowski and James Morley (Albany: SUNY Press, 1999), 145–66.

8   Derrida wrote "*Le toucher*" as a tribute to the work of his friend and colleague Jean-Luc Nancy.

9   Kimberlé Crenshaw first used the term *intersectionality* in 1992. Ann du Cille used intersection as a trope in her 1994 essay on black women in the academy, "The Occult of True Black Womanhood: Critical Demeanor and Black Feminist Studies," *Signs* 19.3 (1994): 591–629.

10   See Teresa de Lauretis, ed., *Feminist Studies/Critical Studies* (Bloomington: Indiana University Press, 1986); Marianne Hirsch and Evelyn Fox Keller, eds., *Conflicts in Feminism* (New York: Routledge, 1990); Judith Butler and Joan W. Scott, eds., *Feminists Theorize the Political* (New York: Routledge, 1992); Anne C. Herrmann and Abigail J. Stewart, *Theorizing Feminism: Parallel Trends in the Humanities and Social Sciences* (Boulder: Westview, 1994); and Dana Heller, ed., *Cross Purposes: Lesbians, Feminists, and the Limits of Alliance* (Bloomington: Indiana University Press, 1997), to mention only a few.

11   Quoted in Akira Mizuta Lippit, *Electric Animal: Toward a Rhetoric of Wildlife* (Minneapolis: University of Minnesota Press, 2000), 99. Lippit uses this passage from Freud's essay "The Unconscious" to demonstrate Freud's reliance upon the narrative of evolution (borrowed from Darwin) to engage the "estrangement of human beings from subjectivity" (98).

12   William Faulkner, *Absalom, Absalom!* (1936; New York: Vintage International, 1990), 218.

13   Similarly, N. Katherine Hayles explores the role of "virtual bodies" in cyberculture and asks: "What to make of this shift from the human to the posthuman, which both evokes terror and excites pleasure?" (4).

14   See Lewis R. Gordon's introduction to *Existence in Black*; and Hortense Spillers, "Mama's Baby, Papa's Maybe: An American Grammar Book," in *Black, White, and in Color: Essays on American Literature and Culture* (Chicago: University of Chicago Press, 2003).

15   This phrase, from the Vintage Books paperback, is clearly meant to be a marketing tool rather than a substantive critical endorsement.

16   Simone de Beauvoir, *The Second Sex* (New York: Knopf, 1952), 212.

17   See Audre Lorde, "Uses of the Erotic," in *Sister Outsider* (New York: Crossing Press, 1985).

18   See Derrida's "*Le Toucher*." I want to thank Tom Cohen and J. Hillis Miller for bringing this work to my attention.

19   For the protracted discussion of presence/absence, see Derrida, *Of Grammatology*, trans. Gayatri Chakravorty Spivak (1974; first American edition, Baltimore: Johns Hopkins University Press, 1976).

20 Emily Harris, "Study Doubts Jefferson Fathered Hemings' Child," Morning Edition, *National Public Radio*, April 13, 2001.

21 Rey Chow explores a parallel project on orientalism as fantasy in her English Institute piece, "The Dream of a Butterfly" (collected in *Human, All Too Human*, ed. Diana Fuss [New York: Routledge, 1996]).

22 Thomas Jefferson, *Notes on the State of Virginia*, ed. Frank Shuffelton (1785; New York: Penguin, 1999), 168.

23 The romance of Scarlett O'Hara and Rhett Butler is a perfect example of white supremacist heterosexual love and has remained the ideal in that portion of the American imaginary where slavery is remembered, if at all.

24 Associated Press, "Jefferson Heirs Plan Cemetery for Slave's Kin," *New York Times*, April 21, 2002.

25 In a 1945 essay, "What I Learned about the Black Problem" (trans. T. Denean Sharpley-Whiting, in Gordon, *Existence in Black*), Jean-Paul Sartre remarks: "These untouchables . . . their business is with the elevators, suitcases, shoes; they attend their tasks like machines, and you pay no more attention to them as if they were machines."

26 Toni Morrison, *Beloved* (New York: Knopf, 1987), 193. Alexander G. Weheliye has a brilliant reading of this reference in Hayles's work. See "'Feenin': Posthuman Voices in Contemporary Black Popular Music," *Social Text* 71, 20.2 (Summer 2002): 21–47.

Marcyliena Morgan

Hip-Hop Women Shredding the Veil:
Race and Class in Popular Feminist Identity

Until the late 1950s, one of America's worst-kept secrets was its repression of blacks, other nonwhites, the working class, and women. African American communities lived behind a veil that hid their complex and personal struggle to define manhood and womanhood within an ideological system that denied them social, cultural, and moral citizenship.[1] One result of this veiling has been contempt toward African American women in the United States and the world. If W. E. B. Du Bois's notion of double consciousness represents two voices, two worlds, and the "real" black soul,[2] then black women live in a state of schizophrenia where there are multiple voices and messages about what it means to be a woman and what it means to be black in relation to men. Nearly a century ago, Du Bois foresaw this complex state of affairs when he wrote: "So some few women are born free, and some within insult and scarlet letters achieve freedom; but our women in black had freedom thrust contemptuously upon them. With that freedom they are buying an untrammeled independence and dear as the price they pay for it, it in the end will be worth every taunt and groan."[3]

While feminists today find problematic the

The *South Atlantic Quarterly* 104:3, Summer 2005.
Copyright © 2005 by Duke University Press.

sort of society that Du Bois describes—one that requires patriarchal protection—the notion that women should be protected nevertheless provided
some form of safety and propriety. It also was the basis of American cultural views of "the good woman" and the cult of true womanhood.[4] The
good woman needs and gets protection and is provided for. Yet this ideology does not include and was never intended to include black women. Not
only was the black female slave denied protection from assault; she was also
forced to perform physical labor under harsh circumstances while under
constant surveillance.[5] Following slavery, black women had to engage in
paid labor to support themselves and their families. Consequently, since
they did not benefit from a white patriarchy that could or would provide
for and protect them, they experienced limited freedom to control economic aspects of their lives. However, as Mullings warns, "this window
of freedom, narrow and equivocal as it is, poses a problem, a threat to
the dominant society's rationalizations of gender hierarchy."[6] The price
was "special" treatment for surviving their collective ordeal and emerging with a defiant sense of the self that embodies an unspoken critique of
America and what it calls a "good woman." They were labeled with and routinely worked within the limitations of contested notions of mammy, matri-
arch, castrator, manipulator, and whore. Today, the situation for the black
woman remains one where she is routinely derided for her sexuality, social
class, determination, commitment to family, passion, and public displays of
womanhood. She must deal with confrontations similar to the one canoni-
cally described by Du Bois in 1902—confrontations predicated on cloaked
interrogations from white Americans about what it must feel like to be a
racial problem. However, unlike Du Bois, instead of responding with "seldom a word" to the question "How does it feel to be a problem?" young
urban black women respond with actions that suggest their answers come
with an open palm in the interrogator's face and the response: "You're the
one with the problem!" This article will examine the moves that hip-hop
women make to eradicate "the problem" and shred the veil of racism, sexism, and classism within African American communities and America in
general. It focuses on how hip-hop performers use discursive strategies to
transform the notion of "real" American womanhood through public performances that become resources for racial and feminist identity—and for
ongoing political contestation.[7]

## Do Right Woman

In the midst of hip-hop's rise into America's consciousness, concern over both the representation and involvement of women often has been in the form of scandal, moral panic, and cultural and political hysteria. Since the mid-1990s, politicians and public figures such as C. Delores Tucker, as well as respected musicians like Dionne Warwick, have publicly derided hip-hop artists for what they deem to be widespread misogyny and violence in lyrics, videos, and staged performances.[8] In contrast, scholars and many feminists, while highly critical of sexism and violence in hip-hop, argue that it is a product and representation of male-dominated culture and should be criticized within American culture and media representation.[9] While well intentioned, this public debate does not improve the day-to-day life of the young women hip-hop fans and artists. Their reality is fraught with numerous physical threats and stereotypical media images of young urban women who are frequently cast in sexist, racist, paternalistic, contested, and convoluted notions of the strong, angry, promiscuous, childbearing, wild black woman. Moreover, the representations of these notions of young urban women occur within a panoply of discursive practices and symbols of womanhood, motherhood, sexuality, class, authority, race, influence, and desire. It should come as no surprise that hip-hop women are not only aware of representations of their generation but are also invested in understanding the musical, social, political, and cultural history of black women that led to these representations. Female MCs use hip-hop to develop and display their lyrical skills as well as present and challenge what it means to be a young black woman in America and the world. They do not use their musical and verbal genre to destroy the veil of race, gender, and class discrimination. They prefer to render it diaphanous, so that it can be seen and manipulated as symbol, warning, and memory of what it meant to live under its tyranny and the dangers of underestimating dominant society's desire to erect it once again.

African American musical traditions often connect younger generations to mothers, women, workers, singers, activists, and organizers who have struggled to place the lives and values of black working-class women within general American and African American culture. Musical forms have a central role in African American culture as a major source of socialization, social change, political thought, and expression of desire, religious belief, and love.[10] The music, history, and memories of past generations are the seeds of the hip-hop generation, and the women prepare to both run with them and use them to incinerate race and gender stereotypes—if necessary. The history that these musicians deliver to the hip-hop generation includes details of how black women were treated as property under slavery and denied rights to their bodies and any argument of femininity, family, and motherhood. Evidence of a sense of connectedness to their female predecessors often appears as responsibility and entitlement in the practiced lyrics of artists. One strategy is the performance of racially marked and "strong woman/sister" authenticity that challenges pernicious stereotypes and uses figures such as Angela Davis (e.g., the artist Medusa) to represent uncompromising revolutionary commitment and spirit. Others look to Mother Africa (embodied in, say, Queen Latifah), explicitly promote self-respect, and engage in educational dialogue with men and women who lack knowledge of their history and culture. Still others offer a variety of street-smart perspectives (e.g., Eve, Rah Digga, Missy Elliott) and that of the down-to-earth, thoughtful, and conscious woman (e.g., Lauryn Hill, Mystic).

Irrespective of style, hip-hop women share the same value of performance: hard, skillful, provocative, and intelligent rhyming. They are skilled MCs, and they represent the lives of women in hip-hop and the world. Medusa, a prominent underground MC, describes herself as "One Bad Sista" who speaks with her ancestors by her side and contemplates their sacrifices and triumphs through the power ("gangsta") and wisdom of her womb and vagina as she croons, "This pussy gangsta."[11] This explicit reference is simultaneously sexual and nonsexual, defiant and compliant. It is the unambiguous telling of the black woman's story as she carries, produces, and attempts to protect that which she holds dear.

### Ain't No Way

Female MCs devour and set to rhyme black women's history, social life, and dreams of being treated with respect as women in America. Virtually every female rapper has "shouted out" the names of strong, talented women who were symbols of excellence and leadership. These names include Angela Davis, Harriet Tubman, Sojourner Truth, Rosa Parks, Nina Simone, Bessie Smith, Billie Holiday, Aretha Franklin, and more.[12] Though not all female MCs are versed on the details of the treatment of black women in the United States, they are well aware that black women had to struggle to be valued as both women and black people in American history. For many black women, a claim to womanhood has been a matter not only of social practice but also of the courts.

The tragic 1855 case *State of Missouri v. Celia* set the stage for how black women would be treated and viewed by society for decades to come. After attempting to resist repeated rapes by her master that left her pregnant and sick, Celia struck and killed him and then tried to destroy the evidence. During her trial for murder, the defense's argument was that in the state of Missouri, women are protected from rape and therefore Celia should be subject to a lesser sentence. The court ruled that the assault did not constitute rape, since she was a slave rather than a woman, and thus could not be adjudicated under laws that protect women.[13] The precedent had been set. Because she was a slave, Celia was not a woman. Later, because black women worked to support their families, unlike many white women, their claims to womanhood were treated as dubious. As Evelyn Higginbotham argues, "Gender, so colored by race, remained from birth until death inextricably linked to one's personal identity and social status. For black and white women, gendered identity was reconstructed and represented in very different, indeed antagonistic, racialized contexts."[14]

This racialized context was also one that regulated the public attitude and behavior of blacks. During U.S. slavery and until the 1960s in the South, blacks could not exhibit linguistic agency, nor could they initiate verbal interactions with whites under the threat of death.[15] Submission to white supremacy demanded nonverbal communication as well. Thus, while the place of black women in the legal history concerning women's rights is truly disturbing, control and surveillance were relentless and occurred within all aspects of black life, especially in terms of day-to-day interactions. Since discursive practices of all black people were regulated by white supremacists, all black communication with whites in general was performed as powerless, agentless, childlike, and thus feminine. Interaction styles included nearly every conservative, overly polite verbal and nonverbal expectation of women's speech, such as: use formal address when speaking to a white person, do not speak unless spoken to, do not speak assuredly (use hedges), do not make statements (overuse tag questions), and so on. The discursive requirements also included nonverbal rules such as stepping aside when a white person approaches, keeping one's head lowered, and not looking someone directly in the eye. Thus linguistic and conversational cues of subservience and dependence were necessary as performatives to corroborate the defense for slavery, and later Jim Crow segregation.

While the speech of all blacks was monitored to address the needs and demands of white patriarchy, this was true for white women's speech as well. White women's speech has historically been relegated to subservient status in the role of servant or sex object.[16] The "normal" woman's speech was thus described as less informal and more standard and conservative than men's. This designation did not result in equality in conversation. Instead, white women were treated to more interruptions from males and the frequent use of back channels (urging others to continue). Rather than initiating conversations on their own, they focused on helping others keep their turn at talk. In contrast to stereotypes of the dominant, subversive, emasculating, uncaring black woman, feminist psychology and linguistic theory portrayed middle-class white women as indiscriminate "people pleasers," concerned with harmony and with being accepted in life and in conversation. Signifying, loud-talking black women simply didn't stand a chance.[17] Rejecting the cult of the good woman who speaks without agency, hip-hop women have chosen a discourse style that is not only independent of patriarchal censorship and control but also freely critiques the loss of power and responsibility of the good woman.

## I Say a Little Prayer

The power of women to discursively claim a space and challenge both patriarchy and feminism was born during the discursive struggles of the black power movement. While many identify the black power movement as the beginning of collective black pride, it was also the end of discursive compliance with white supremacy. The civil rights movement employed the polite and nonconfrontational discursive style of the middle class in order to construct the image of the equal, worthy, intelligent citizen. Once the black power movement reframed the struggle for civil rights as one that demanded the same entitlements as whites, a discourse style was ushered in that did not simply address, confront, and resist compliant African American discourse. The new discourse annihilated the old and considered it a symbol of a slave and self-hate mentality. Suddenly, to speak in a deferential manner marked one as a lackey of white supremacists (an Uncle Tom). The new discourse style confronted white supremacy and neither complied nor demanded rights within it. Instead, the discourse style asserted a black presence on its terms, one that reflected a different consciousness and a sense of entitlement. As a result, African American speech in white-dominated contexts went from childlike, feminine, overly polite, and self-effacing to aggressive, impolite, direct, and in-your-face threatening.

Black women found themselves caught in the crevices of the movement from powerless and feminine discourse to a powerful one symbolizing not simply masculinity but a powerful black masculinity that challenges, threatens, and competes with white masculinity. To assert equal entitlements meant negotiating both feminine and masculine discourses, with racist and sexist baggage embedded in both. Thus, while this discursive space is potentially a powerful one, it is also one of unending contestation and mediation. This space was occupied not only by black women after slavery but also by the women of the blues, who in singing about women's realities introduced their strategies and methods for change and representation. Their only alternatives were to portray or defend cultural values about accurately describing people and treating them fairly and equally. It is not surprising that at the core of black communities are women who were prepared and compelled to confront racial, class, and gender injustice. There are rewards for women who are adept at handling discourse concerning these subjects, and there is punishment for those who are naive and fail to recognize the power they and those in power have over their words. As a result, there are two intertwined themes throughout African American women's discourse. One is associated with representing individual and group identity and the other with representing racial, gender, and class injustice. Consequently, any critique of gender hegemony is also a critique of race.

## Respect

> Your revolution will not happen between these thighs
> Will not happen between these thighs
> Will not be you shaking
> And me [sigh] faking between these thighs
>
> Because the real revolution
> That's right, I said the real revolution
> You know, I'm talking about the revolution
> When it comes
> It's gonna be real
> It's gonna be real
> It's gonna be real

When it finally comes
It's gonna be real.[18]

While hip-hop women are committed to representing their lives and compete equally with men, their quest is not without peril and retaliation. On October 1999, Sarah Jones's recording of "Your Revolution" was played on public radio station KBOO-FM, in Portland, Oregon. Before that date, it was considered by college radio to be a creative and important response to misogynistic representations of women in male-MC popular hip-hop lyrics. Soon after the program aired, the FCC informed the station that it had broken decency laws and would be fined. On May 17, 2001, the FCC penalized KBOO for playing the recording, fining them $7,000 for indecent language. The FCC's ruling states: "The rap song 'Your Revolution' contains unmistakable patently offensive sexual references. We have considered the KBOO Foundation's arguments concerning the context of this material. Specifically, the KBOO Foundation asserts that the rap song 'Your Revolution' cannot be separated from its contemporary cultural context . . . [and] is 'a feminist attack on male attempts to equate political "revolution" with promiscuous sex' and as such, is not indecent."[19]

Both Sarah Jones and the station argued that not only was the feminist perspective necessary to respond to misogyny in some male performer's lyrics, it is appropriate within hip-hop's tradition of lyrical battle. They also argued that the FCC had lost previous rulings regarding hip-hop radio play.[20] Though the FCC eventually reversed its ruling, it remains disturbing that they focused on a female spoken-word and hip-hop artist who defended herself in male terms. Moreover, their malfeasance not only exposed the nature of patriarchal control; it also educated many women on inequities in the application of power and authority.

While the FCC may protect America from women speaking their minds, the agency also expects black women to fend for themselves against unfettered misogyny. For example, some students at Spelman College, a prominent black women's college in Atlanta, successfully pressured the rapper Nelly to cancel an appearance at their school because they found his song "Tip Drill" and its accompanying video offensive.[21] Their protest resulted in a public dialogue that highlights many of the vexing issues that complicate hip-hop's interpretive framework. The dialogue occurred within a complex contestation of realities. First, the "Tip Drill" video played late night on BET, the only national cable station in the United States with a format directed toward African Americans.[22] Second, Nelly's music, as well as that of other artists who use misogynist lyrics, is regularly played at dance clubs frequented by students from the area, including the Spelman women. Some of the women in the video are purported to be students at colleges in Atlanta. Not only did the incident involve a black performer and business, but Nelly was visiting the campus in order to educate African Americans about the need for marrow and blood-stem-cell donors among minorities! All of these facts are significant in terms of the specificities of hip-hop as both an African American and popular product. By rejecting Nelly's appearance, the women of Spelman also argued that though they regularly participate in all forms of hip-hop music, and though they watch and support the only major black-themed cable station, and though they consider the bone marrow drive important to the health of their community, these were not sufficient reasons to accept the offensive representation of black women.

The contestation, with its multiple twists and entanglements in terms of race, gender, and sexuality, are common for women in hip-hop culture.[23] Women have consistently protested and complained about sexual exploitation in lyrics and videos—though they dance to many of these same songs in clubs. Hip-hop artists both dance and protest as cultural participants and innovators. They use their skills and constantly embody and reframe feminist identity. They do so within a move to incorporate the range of emotions that they encounter within hip-hop. They do not leave the game; rather, they play and critique it as members while constantly raising the stakes on race and gender.

### Call Me

As discussed earlier, music is part of the fabric of African American culture and serves as the backdrop for virtually every ordinary and important event. It is constantly played and heard. It often serves as a call to home where African traditions (and tales of African traditions) provide a strategy for how to deal with family, ancestors, threats, culture, and power.[24] Works detailing the use of song to inform slaves of locations of the Underground Railroad are legend, as are songs that signify on white supremacy and act as a way to exercise some sense of agency during Jim Crow.[25] African American music provides information and knowledge by telling indirect and embedded stories about life and injustice in America. Early blues and jazz artists performed during periods of rampant white supremacy. The

mere existence of these performers, as well as their performances and recordings, provided lessons and confirmation of a black reality for those who
wanted to hear the truth. Daphne Harrison describes the importance of
these musicians' roles: "The blues artist speaks directly of and to the folk
who have suffered pain and assures them that they are not alone." They
present a story that says, "We have been through that too."[26]

While there are many writings on the women who developed both jazz
and the blues in America, the women of the blues have received most of the
academic attention. This is largely due to their role in presenting an identity
that included working-class realities as well as one that suggested agency
regarding sex, knowledge of both the white and black world's attitude and
treatment of women, and complicity as well as critique of life for a black
woman. The lives of these artists provided essential information about the
world and black life that was not available to most of the black population
until the late 1960s. They were living proof that bad luck and trouble could
be survived if you were Ma Rainey, Dinah Washington, and Bessie Smith. It
could also take you down if you were Billie Holiday. These performers' mere
existence was witness not to what *could* happen to you if you were a black
woman, but what *did* happen to you with regularity. Blues singers took the
old saying "All you have to do is stay black and die" and provided the deeply
layered meanings and webs of irony, betrayal, bitterness, and longing that
comprised staying black in America.

Thanks to their bawdy and brilliant language use and perspective, blues
women were able to engage in romantic, sexual, and political rhetoric. As
Angela Davis writes, "That their aesthetic representations of the politics
of gender and sexuality are informed by and interwoven with their representations of race and class makes their work all the more provocative."[27]
The blues emerged from ex-slaves who participated in and experienced the
slave spiritual as the religious symbol for freedom, representing the collective need and desires of the enslaved. The end of slavery was also the
beginning of the expression of individual and emotional needs and desires
of African Americans. As Davis argues, "The birth of the blues was aesthetic
evidence of new psychological realities within the black population" (5). The
blues performance world was a man's world, and they sang of loss, injustice, irony, power, heartbreak, and the need to keep moving away from their
bad, hard luck and trouble. They sang about being a black man in a white
man's world—and it was a man's world, indeed. Women blues singers, and
later jazz singers, sang about a man's world where they tried to please their

men who were subjugated and who also left them regularly. They knew their men's notion of a better world did not include women's equality. Blues women chronicled the evidence of patriarchal ideology with accounts of physical and sexual abuse and financial ruin. They were often audacious in their depictions of a woman's life, where romantic love was the equivalent of abuse and heartbreak and the only happy ending was getting out with a little dignity and "some of what you came with."

Hip-hop performers took their cues from the blues and jazz women who preceded them. As black people began to exercise their voice, the blues represented the "real" world of hardworking black people who knew their only chance to succeed (make it) was to work and try to protect oneself from the uncontrolled power of white supremacy. The often-heard refrain "If it wasn't for bad luck, I wouldn't have no luck at all" is part of the irony of being black in the land of the free. It is not surprising, then, that the discourse of women in hip-hop includes a critique of the clueless and naive woman who lacks agency; does not speak up or examine patriarchy or respect her own sexuality; does not recognize patriarchy; and does not value class, race, or culture. Hip-hop artists build from the blues and then broaden their notion of womanhood to incorporate hip-hop's female science. While both the blues and jazz have been dominated by men, the women performers have not only demonstrated remarkable talent but also negotiated woman-hood in a man's world. Likewise, hip-hop artists value lyrical skill and make a conscious effort to provide a full assessment and critique of racism and sexism, while offering alternatives that explicitly explore social class as well as desire, emotion, power, and patriarchy. Blues women often focused on cheating lovers, relationships, domestic violence, and what Davis calls the "ephemerality of many sexual partners" (3). While women of hip-hop focus on similar topics, they also articulate a position that is both individual and related to the collective good.[28] Talented hip-hop women toil alongside men when they want or need to—whether the men like it or not—and challenge both patriarchy and prescribed notions of feminism. Medusa proudly and brazenly demonstrates that she has the skill and power of the word: "I'm the mouth almighty, I got tongue everlasting. . . . Rhymes like these invented the phrase 'next level.'"[29] Hip-hop women represent the spiritual, the blues song, and the drum. They construct knowledge, intelligence, and emotion as connected and demand that they be heard.

## Chain of Fools

The right to talk and represent oneself and one's community is a fundamental aspect of citizenship. Black women in particular have worked to reframe family, womanhood, relationship, and sexuality to guarantee their right to represent women within the American life. Yet no matter what image or ideology a hip-hop woman represents, she operates within an adolescent world where identities, roles, and status are constantly being explored and where participants are convinced that everything is at stake and everything is about them. The hip-hop nation's insistence on noncensorship and representation of frank honesty and realism means that virtually any activity or opinion that exists can be reflected and/or critiqued. Within this system, silencing is an unacceptable practice, since ideological censorship is viewed as the work of hegemonic forces attempting to co-opt and corrupt hip-hop. But the hip-hop community does not provide a platform for all views, since it can be fanatically heterosexist. This is exacerbated by the conflicts and excesses that result from negotiating adolescent desire (and rejection), emerging and conflicting gender identities and roles, and racism in a society that produces, avoids, and silences public discourse on sex and sexuality and the objectification of women in general. The misogynist representations of male desire—where any woman who does not support or like a man who likes her is by definition dishonest, scheming, unfaithful, or a lesbian—is one outcome of this situation. It is within this fully charged context that women in hip-hop forge an identity and presence that is consistently feminist, progressive, passionate, and sexual.

Considering the powerful language of male discourse and the overall protection that it receives, it is not surprising that research on teenage girls' identity finds that adolescent girls unselfconsciously rejected constructs of feminism in favor of "benign versions of masculinity that allowed them to be 'one of the guys.'"[30] It is also predictable that they are conflicted regarding the expression of sexuality that is not exclusively dependent on men and society's notion of the good woman. As Audre Lorde explains, "The erotic is a measure of our sense of self and the chaos of our strongest feelings."[31] At the same time that the erotic may represent power and joy, it can also be objectified and represent a loss of power through voyeuristic fantastic reinterpretations. The tension created by unbridled male adolescent sexual exploration and the desire of young women to represent themselves honestly and unashamedly creates an energizing space for young women, one where all hip-hop artists gain membership through artistic skills and where audiences and crews insist that their lives—including contradictions—be represented.

## Baby, I Love You

It is common for hip-hop women to say that they support men and at the same time want to be respected and in control of their bodies. Supporting men recognizes race and class hypocrisy and does not mean that men make decisions for women. Rather, irrespective of who is leading, women and men support their relationship, critique racism and classism, and respect each other. For example, the ultimate queen of hip-hop, Queen Latifah, began her recording career as an alternative to the male construction of the scheming, disloyal woman by situating herself as a woman of royalty who chooses her sex partners, is not interested in a man who needs to control her, has superb rap skills, and is committed to educating her community. Her proclamation not only claims her personal identity but reconfigures the black nationalist notion of the man-dependent Queen Mother to one who is independent of men for her identity.

> You asked, I came
> So behold the Queen
> Let's add a little sense to the scene . . .
> From Latifah with the Queen in front of it
> Droppin' bombs, you're up in arms and puzzled
> The lines will flow like fluid while you guzzle . . .
> 'Cause it's knowledge I'm seekin'
> Enough about myself, I think it's time that I tell you
> About the evil that men do.[32]

Though artists like Queen Latifah can proclaim a strong identity as a woman of power, that is not to say that hip-hop operates with fairness regarding gender. Successful female MCs are constantly besieged with gossip regarding their sexuality, a form of gossip not summarily directed toward men. Mainly because they insist on respect for and the safety of women, they are often rumored to be lesbian and bisexual. Women MCs often address their own sexuality in reference to their own desire and knowledge of society's desire for them—whether male or female. Some women are openly bisexual, simultaneously lesbian and intensely heterosexual. While some artists consider it important to talk about their sexual prefer-

ence, overwhelmingly they argue that feminism and sexuality do not determine their skill as artists and their determination to say it the way they see it.
They insist on performing with their sexuality intact and want to be judged
by their skills and ability to represent all aspects of their lives. Consequently,
while men's lyrics often reflect male adolescent desire, women MCs reflect
a multiplicity of perspectives and discourses about relationship, sex, desire,
and friendship—the issues facing young women.[33]

The method for supporting and critiquing sexually assertive female rappers was established in the early 1990s with two female rap groups: Hoes
wit Attitude (HWA) and Bytches with Problems (BWP). HWA considered
their group a copy of gangsta and sex-obsessed groups like NWA and 2 Live
Crew, but absent of lyrical skills. They presented themselves as sexual
objects from a gangsta's perspective and were never seriously considered
true hip-hop. Their performances were sexually explicit.[34] BWP, on the other
hand, argued that they were a progressive and educational response to the
misogyny that persisted in hip-hop in the early 1990s.

> You finally reach a point when you say, "It's not working. Let me just
> come down to your level for a minute." I know how to go back up when I
> want to . . . the music women have been doing is, "Oh, my man cheated
> on me, and he left me. But I'll be strong. I'll love him, and he'll come
> back." I want to hear, "Fuck you, muthafucka! I don't need you!" That's
> why we came up with this concept. It's time for raw music like that.[35]

BWP insisted that they sold reality and not sex and cited seven problems
that concerned them: men who cheat on their girlfriends and wives; men
who preach positive messages and then leave their families and don't pay
child support; men who beat women; men who talk about how great they
are in bed but can't live up to it, even for two minutes; date rape; women who
get their period and take it out on everyone else; and female rappers who
get ahead by putting down other female rappers.[36] When hip-hop women
address explicit concerns of young women, they consistently construct a
fully developed context that includes working-class realities, relationship
issues, and a variety of women's issues. Another instance of this is artists' attempts to use the word *bitch* to discuss issues of physical and sexual
abuse, jealousy, power, and the reality of life for strong young women. In
"U.N.I.T.Y.," Queen Latifah spells the word and contrasts a community need
to act as one unified group against racism and sexism by considering the dis-
respect of women as a factor that renders the black community less power-

ful. She both asks for romantic and platonic love from men and criticizes them for disrespecting women. In turn she asks for sisterhood from women and criticizes those who don't respect themselves and their families and do not critique misogyny.

> U.N.I.T.Y.
> U.N.I.T.Y., that's a unity
> U.N.I.T.Y.
> U.N.I.T.Y., that's a unity
> U.N.I.T.Y., love a black man from infinity to infinity
> Who you callin' a bitch?
> Here we go. We got to let them know.
> U.N.I.T.Y., love a black woman from infinity to infinity
> You ain't a bitch or a ho

Similarly, early in her career, MC Lyte considered herself hard-core and argued that any viewpoint that exists in the community should be allowed in hip-hop. In her work she introduced prochoice themes, AIDS awareness, and antidrug messages consistently in a style that was unsentimental and powerful. Even though she supported positions often viewed as feminist, she was not comfortable with the label.[37] When asked if the term *bitch* should be used toward women in general, she responded: "I've been called a bitch. And I have no problem with being called a bitch if you know me. If you don't know me then no! You don't have the right to call me that."[38] Years later, women are still being called "bitch," and Missy Elliott explains exactly what MC Lyte meant by "if you know me." For Missy Elliott, *bitch* indicates that the speaker, the one who uses that name, is a loser who can only resort to name-calling as a sign of loss of social face.[39] She extends this meaning to include the notion of the proud woman with skills who cannot be stopped.

> "She's a bitch"
> When you say my name
> Talk mo' junk but won't look my way
> "She's a bitch"
> See I got more cheese
> So back on up while I roll up my sleeves
>
> "She's a bitch"
> You can't see me, Joe

Get on down while I shoot my flow
"She's a bitch"
When I do my thing
Got the place on fire, burn it down to flame.[40]

This is also true for Rah Digga, whose *Dirty Harriet* release is introduced with the acknowledgment that she is a strong, bad bitch:

Rah Digga, the Harriet Tubman of hip-hop, has returned, baby! C'mon!
I be that bitch niggas wantin' in the lab
Rhymes comin', rhymes goin' like I was a dollar cab
Fingerin' the man tryin' to tap into his feelings
A misguided soul so ain't checkin' for the lyrics
Many different players, only one hold the ball
Ghetto-fabulous chick, go against the protocol
With the grittiest lingo, still such a little sweetheart
Book-educated with a whole lotta street smarts
Follow me now, as I build my fan base.[41]

## Think

The passion in hip-hop for a "fresh" representation of womanhood is not focused exclusively on the inclusion of young African American women. It is part of the "world economy of passion"[42] and proposes to reframe feminism to acknowledge and incorporate aspects of all women's lives. Yet this passion is about not only emotion and desire but also the emotional connection that one has to aesthetics, culture, memory, and others.[43] Hip-hop women argue that the desire to be included as a woman in society is the passion to be accepted as a product of all of their experiences. Furthermore, as Bennett argues, this desire and passion has political implications in that it makes "the most private of interactions culturally and socially meaningful."[44]

Hip-hop women practice and perform desire: the desire for love; the desire for revolution, for respect, for fulfillment, for politics; the desire for a feminist ideology that includes all women and privileges none. Desire is a powerful, deep, unending force that exists through reason, war, love, and pain. Desire shreds the veil. Instead of hip-hop aggressively putting "bass in your face," it places race and class in your face—as well as the womb, the clitoris, the family, the ancestors, and Bessie Smith. Because they focus on women's responsibility for their own lives and bodies, women in hip-hop consistently explore feminism, the intersections of race and class, and gender marginalization and oppression. They also express their support of African American men, the male friends and family members who are routinely targeted by the state. As Gwendolyn Pough explains: "When you call someone your sister or brother, or comrade in the struggle against racism, a bond is created. In that bond there is love. Rap music therefore offers space for public dialogues about love, romance and struggle in a variety of combinations."[45]

Most successful female MCs are building bridges and shredding veils and refashioning them to wear in their hair and around their waists. They recognize that for them there are more than two worlds, and the only place where they can negotiate race, class, gender, and sexuality with relative freedom is the hip-hop world. It is not an ideal space, but it is one populated by those searching for discourse that confronts power. Everyone in that world expects to be respected. Young feminists are watching as hip-hop women develop their skills, represent their communities, and demand respect from and for their brothers who, along with the rest of society, are slowly and reluctantly losing their hostility and ambivalence about showing solid respect for them. They accept their turn at being "the problem" with a refreshing, kick-ass fierceness that encourages women everywhere to discuss their lives openly.

## Notes

The idea for this article developed during a seminar series at Harvard University titled "Gender and Sexuality in African America" chaired by Evelyn Hammonds, Lani Guinier, and Evelyn Higginbotham. I would like to thank all those who participated for their comments and encouragement.

  1  See Paula Giddings, *When and Where I Enter: The Impact of Black Women on Race and Sex in America* (New York: William Morrow, 1984); Hazel Carby, *Reconstructing Womanhood: The Emergence of the Afro-American Woman Novelist* (Oxford: Oxford University Press, 1987); Barbara Smith, ed., *Home Girls: A Black Feminist Anthology* (New York: Kitchen Table/Women of Color, 1983); Smith, "Toward a Black Feminist Criticism," in *The New Feminist Criticism: Essays on Women, Literature, and Theory*, ed. Elaine Showalter (New York: Pantheon, 1985), 168–85; and Leith Mullings, "Images, Ideology, and Women of Color," in *Women of Color in U.S. Society*, ed. Maxine Baca Zinn and Bonnie Thornton Dill (Philadelphia: Temple University Press, 1994), 265–89.

  2  W. E. B. Du Bois, *The Souls of Black Folk* (1903; Chicago: A. C. McClurg, 1990).

  3  W. E. B. Du Bois, *Dark Water: Voices from within the Veil* (1920; Millwood, NY: Krauss

International, 1975), 172. I would like to thank Leith Mullings for first introducing me to this quote.

4 See Angela Davis, *Women, Race, and Class* (New York: Vintage Books, 1981); Giddings, *When and Where I Enter*; and Patricia Hill Collins, *Black Feminist Thought: Knowledge, Consciousness, and the Politics of Empowerment* (New York: Routledge, 1990).

5 See Bonnie Thornton Dill, "Fictive Kin, Paper Sons, and Compradrazgo: Women of Color and the Struggle for Family Survival," in *Women of Color in U.S. Society*, ed. Maxine Baca Zinn and Bonnie Thornton Dill (Philadelphia: Temple University Press, 1994), 149–69.

6 See Mullings, "Images, Ideology, and Women of Color," 265.

7 The phrase *hip-hop women* refers to those who assert that they grew up in hip-hop culture and are a product of it. Though misogyny in hip-hop continues to be a major issue, the focus of this article is women's voices and their agency within the male-dominated genre of hip-hop. This article is also an attempt to participate in what Marta Savigliano, in *Tango and the Political Economy of Passion* (Boulder, CO: Westview, 1995), calls the "world economy of passion." She uses passion to analyze the contestations around race, class, sexuality, nation, and the tango.

8 C. Delores Tucker was chair of the National Political Congress of Black Women and Chair of the Democratic National Committee Black Caucus. In the 1990s, she participated in a national campaign against violent lyrics in rap music. In 1997, she and her husband sued the estate of Tupac Shakur for $10 million over lyrics in which Shakur rhymed her name with an obscenity. Her lawsuit alleged, among other things, that her husband, William Tucker, had suffered loss of "consortium."

9 See, for instance, bell hooks, *Outlaw Culture: Resisting Representations* (New York: Routledge, 1994).

10 Angela Davis, *Blues Legacies and Black Feminism: Gertrude "Ma" Rainey, Bessie Smith and Billie Holiday* (New York: Pantheon, 1998); Michael C. Dawson, *Black Visions: The Roots of Contemporary African-American Political Ideologies* (Chicago: University of Chicago Press, 2001); Tricia Rose, *Black Noise: Rap Music and Black Culture in Contemporary America* (Hanover, NH: Wesleyan University Press, 1994); Dionne Bennett, "The Love Difference Makes: Intersubjectivity and the Emotional Politics of African American Romantic Ritual" (PhD diss., University of California, Los Angeles, 2003).

11 Medusa, "My Pussy's Gangsta."

12 The performers invoking these names include Medusa, Lauryn Hill, Lil' Kim, MC Lyte, Rah Digga, and more.

13 See Evelyn Brooks Higginbotham, "African-American Women's History and the Metalanguage of Race," *Signs* 17 (1992): 251–74.

14 Ibid., 8. Thus while Butler (1990) interrogates the meaning of women within historical and political contexts regarding sexuality, Harris (1996) is concerned with when the legal status of black women moved from "property" to "woman." Judith Butler, *Gender Trouble: Feminism and the Subversion of Identity*(London and New York: Routledge, 1990); Cheryl L. Harris, "Finding Sojourner's Truth: Race, Gender, and the Institution of Property," *Cardozo Law Review* 18 (1996): 306–409.

15 Marcyliena Morgan, *Language, Discourse, and Power in African American Culture* (Cambridge: Cambridge University Press, 2002).

16   Robin Lakoff, *Language and Woman's Place* (New York: Harper & Row, 1975).

17   These, of course, are references to African American verbal genres. See Morgan, *Language, Discourse, and Power in African American Culture*; Claudia Mitchell-Kernan, *Language Behavior in a Black Urban Community* (Berkeley, CA: Language Behavior Research Laboratory, 1971); Geneva Smitherman, *Talkin That Talk: Language, Culture and Education in African America* (London: Routledge, 2000).

18   Sarah Jones, "Your Revolution," 1999.

19   According to the FCC, "The KBOO Foundation cites a case decided under Florida's criminal obscenity statute as support for its argument that material with artistic merit is not indecent. The court's determination that a lower court had not properly applied the tripartite obscenity standard of *Miller v. California*, 413 U.S. 15 (1973), does not control our indecency analysis here." *Luke Records, Inc. v. Navarro*, 960 F.2d 134 (11th Cir. 1992), *cert. denied, Navarro v. Luke Records, Inc.*, 506 U.S. 1022 (1992).

20   Ibid., 3, n. 2.

21   In a tip drill, basketball players line up and throw the ball against the backboard. The exercise is designed to develop timing and jumping ability for rebounding. In hip-hop, *tip drill* refers to a woman with a beautiful body and an unattractive face. In the music video, various strippers in thongs are filmed from the back as they gyrate their buttocks and simulate sex. The final shot is of Nelly swiping a credit card down the buttocks of a gyrating woman.

22   According to its corporate statement, BET was founded by Robert L. Johnson, chairman and chief executive officer, in 1980. A subsidiary of Viacom, it is the leading African American–owned and –operated media and entertainment company in the United States. BET runs twenty-four-hour programming that targets African American consumers, reaching more than 65 million U.S. homes and more than 90 percent of all black cable households.

23   See Gwendolyn Pough, *Check It While I Wreck It: Black Womanhood, Hip-Hop Culture, and the Public Sphere* (Boston: Northeastern University Press, 2004); Cheryl L. Keyes, *Rap Music and Street Consciousness* (Urbana: University of Illinois Press, 2002); Joan Morgan, *When Chickenheads Come Home to Roost: My Life as a Hip-Hop Feminist* (New York: Simon & Schuster, 1999).

24   See Lawrence Levine, *Black Culture and Black Consciousness: Afro-American Folk Thought from Slavery to Freedom* (Oxford: Oxford University Press, 1977); and Roger Abrahams and John Szwed, *After Africa: Extracts from the British Travel Accounts and Journals of the Seventeenth, Eighteenth, and Nineteenth Centuries Concerning the Slaves, Their Manners and Customs in the British West Indies* (New Haven, CT: Yale University Press, 1983).

25   See, for example, Levine, *Black Culture and Black Consciousness*.

26   Daphne Duval Harrison, *Black Pearls: Blues Queens of the 1920s* (New Brunswick, NJ: Rutgers University Press, 1988), 8.

27   Davis, *Blues Legacies and Black Feminism*, xv.

28   See Rose, *Black Noise*.

29   Medusa performs this song at concerts but has not yet recorded it.

30   For studies of teenage girls' identity, see Michelle Fine and Pat Macpherson, "Over Dinner: Feminism and Adolescent Female Bodies," in *Gender and Education*, ed. Sari Knopp

Biklen and Diane Pollard (Chicago: University of Chicago Press, 1993), 126–54; Bonnie J. Ross Leadbeater and Niobe Way, eds., *Urban Girls: Resisting Stereotypes, Creating Identities* (New York: New York University Press, 1996); Deborah Tolman, *Dilemmas of Desire: Teenage Girls Talk about Sexuality* (Cambridge, MA: Harvard University Press, 2002).

31 Audre Lorde, "Uses of the Erotic: The Erotic as Power," in *Writing on the Body: Female Embodiment and Feminist Theory*, ed. Katie Conboy, Nadia Medina, and Sarah Stanbury (New York: Columbia University Press, 1997), 277–82.

32 Queen Latifah, "The Evil That Men Do," 1989.

33 These two approaches parallel the typical discourse styles of teenagers, where males often play verbal games focused exclusively on skill and women focus on verbal practices that require both skill and determining the nature of friendship (see Morgan, *Language, Discourse, and Power in African American Culture*).

34 The women were similar to the professional strippers that appear with some of the acts from the "dirty South" (e.g., 2 Live Crew and Luther Campbell).

35 Michael Small, *Break It Down: The Inside Story from the New Leaders of Rap* (New York: Citadel, 1992), 51–53.

36 Ibid.

37 See Rose, *Black Noise*.

38 MC Lyte, 1991.

39 A hater who has lost social standing by not demonstrating (Goffman).

40 Missy Elliott, "She's a Bitch" (Background Records, 1999).

41 Rah Digga, "Dirty Harriet" (Elektra Records, 1999).

42 Savigliano, *Tango and the Political Economy of Passion*. See also Dorinne Kondo, *About Face: Performing Race in Fashion and Theater* (London: Routledge, 1997).

43 See Zora Neale Hurston, *I Love Myself When I Am Laughing . . . and Then Again When I Am Looking Mean and Impressive: A Zora Neale Hurston Reader*, ed. Alice Walker (New York: Feminist Press, 1979).

44 Bennett, "The Love Difference Makes," 14.

45 Pough, *Check It While I Wreck It*, 86.

Nichole T. Rustin

"Mary Lou Williams Plays Like a Man!"
Gender, Genius, and Difference in
Black Music Discourse

**M**usic is work. The work ranges from the
daily practice sessions to the unending nights
traveling and performing to the recording sessions to the composing. The work extends to
the emotional reach of sound, the politics of
race and nation. Buried under layers of narra-
tives about genius is this fundamental quality of
work. We have but to remember the phoenixlike
reemergence of Charlie Parker after a disastrous performance in Kansas City at the High
Hat. Shamed on stage, Parker "went home and
cried and didn't play again for three months."[1]
Parker kept returning to the woodshed, master-
ing his horn, a jazzman achieving, Ralph Ellison explains, "his self-determined identity."[2]
Myths about black musicians' genius include
likening them to superheroes, preachers, revo-
lutionaries, and powerful voices speaking to the
need for truth and equality. They are black men
embodying ideals of manhood (that is, they
are self-determining) and masculinity (such as
their capacity for expressing emotional or meta-
physical states like being cool, or spiritual, or
defiant).

Herman Gray argues that black jazzmen
"enacted a black masculine that not only chal-

The *South Atlantic Quarterly* 104:3, Summer 2005.
Copyright © 2005 by Duke University Press.

lenged whiteness but exiled it to the (cultural) margins of blackness—i.e., in their hands blackness was a powerful symbol of the masculine. . . . As a 'different' sign of the masculine he was policed as much as he was celebrated and exoticized by white men and women alike."[3] Here Gray draws attention to how thinking about jazz has created blackness, or race, as a metalanguage[4] through which gender, specifically the feminine, drops out of view. Men's experiences within jazz culture, as performers, producers, and consumers, predominate in popular and critical discussions about the music and its history. Gray's reading of the ways in which the "black masculine" figures as a sign of difference, as well as a marker of genius, pleasure, and oppositionality, leaves open the question of what kind of "black feminine" black women enact in jazz culture.

I am a black woman who works in jazz. My work in music centers on historical and theoretical questions about gender, race, nation, and cultural practice. Of late, my focus has been on black women's work in jazz, specifically that of instrumentalists such as pianist Hazel Scott, who saw their performances, whether in concert halls, at political rallies, or in their homes, as a profound expression of their voices as race women, musicians, lovers, faithful, radical, modern. Black women making a living as instrumentalists in the 1950s were indeed a small percentage of jazz performers in the United States. Some, like pianists Sarah Vaughn and Carmen McRae, also performed as singers, gaining their fame in this capacity. Some, like trombonist Melba Liston, supplemented their incomes through their other musical activities, including arranging, composing, and teaching. When asked about being an exceptional woman, Melba Liston dismissed the entire concept, focusing, as I do, on the work. "All the time I don't think about being the only—Because I had my work to do, you dig? I don't ever talk about [being] the only female."[5] Despite the sometimes overwhelming struggle to find and maintain work, the women's desire for creative lives pushed them to continue pursuing the sounds that challenged and rewarded them intellectually and emotionally. As pianist and composer Mary Lou Williams once said, "It's difficult for a creative artist to live; there are all kinds of obstacles. But as long as you keep your music broad in its scope, fresh in its ideas and experimental, you'll make it."[6] To render visible the contexts in which these women created roles for themselves and their art in black communities and national stages of the 1950s is to think differently, and comprehensively, about work, genius, and music. Farah Jasmine Griffin offers the following definition: genius is a "special quality of mind and aptitudes that some individuals have innately for specific tasks or kinds of work." Created from her readings of the philosophers Kant and Lewis Gordon, Griffin emphasizes the requirements of talent, intelligence, and discipline, willing as well to offer "brilliance" as a less "loaded" term for genius.[7] How do black women work in jazz? What work does black women's music do aesthetically, culturally, racially, historically? Why is it important to have models of black female genius in black music discourse generally, and jazz specifically?

There are few, if any, myths of black female genius. Unlike those of black male jazz musicians, discussions of black women in jazz, particularly singers, have tended to obscure both the myths and the realities of their genius. Griffin suggests it is because the black woman's voice is represented in such a way as to have the effect of "a hinge, a place where things can both come together and break apart."[8] "The black woman's voice" has "given us a sense of ourselves as a people beyond the confines of our oppression." Additionally, this voice "is representative" of the human condition and a "nation's longing for an idealized vision of itself" (120). Griffin emphasizes the spectacular as well as the aural, or myths of the aural—those that become structures of historical narrative, that become myths "of a black nation, where the originary voice is rendered as female but represented by males" (105). Highlighting the distance between the sound and the image, Griffin reveals how we are often once, even two or three times removed from hearing the voice. We listen through the mediated images of black men who emerge as creative subjects through their experiences listening to or witnessing the sound of an unnamed and disembodied voice. The myth of origin ("identify a moment of hearing that voices as an epiphany: a moment that leads suddenly to insight, understanding, and a hearing of the potential of one's own artistic voice" [112]) is one that requires interpretation, whether through prose or poetic image or musical instrument.

Recent attention given to the role of black women in jazz history and culture has focused on establishing these women's credentials as intellectuals and, in fact, exploring how ideas about genius can be refined by looking at their examples. For instance, black feminist scholars and new jazz historians have increasingly reexamined Billie Holiday's image, seeking to explain how we might understand Holiday as an intellectual, as an artist concerned with politics and protest, and as a woman making choices about career and personal life. Rather than appearing as the victimized singer of torch songs, Holiday emerges in these accounts as a complex individual negotiating a number of discourses and social limitations. "Strange Fruit," a song written by Abel Meeropol, a.k.a. Lewis Allan, seems to mark a crossroads in Holiday's career. By choosing to sing the elegiac about the lynching of a black person in the South, Holiday, as recent scholars insist, draws upon a tradition of protest within black musical practice and effects a new "stylization" in her performances, thereby revealing the extent to which jazz singing requires as much "thought" and "art" as the music mostly created by male instrumentalists does.[9] Holiday's career is one example of the ways in which culture and politics meet in the jazz world, and her example points further to the trouble black women present to the neat categories around genre, genius, and authenticity that have so dominated approaches to jazz histories and studies. Reviewing Holiday's decision to make "Strange Fruit" a permanent part of her repertoire also allows us to begin analyzing the discourse of a "democratic aesthetic" emerging in postwar discussions in jazz culture. This aesthetic reveals a worldview in which, among other constituencies, black women, Jewish intellectuals, protest, and the practice of jazz art overlap. Further, black women artists' autobiographies written during the postwar period, those such as Ethel Waters's *His Eye Is on the Sparrow* (1950), Lena Horne's *Lena* (1950), and Billie Holiday's *Lady Sings the Blues* (1956), reveal the women's understanding of the relationship between black urban identities and the democratic experience, the politics of sexuality (in many ways integrated and transgressive), and conceptions of performance as art and work. Despite problems associated with autobiographies, especially those that are coauthored as these are, they remain instructive and demand attention. The worldview reflected in these women's experiences lead to suggestive rearticulations of their identities as "jazz men."

*Jazz men* is a term I use both to query and to describe gender roles and experiences within jazz culture in the postwar period. The project considers how jazz, as a music and a culture, is gendered by musicians and participants within jazz culture, and it considers how these ideas shape individuals' conceptions of themselves as gendered beings. In the particular example of Mary Lou Williams, I am intrigued by the ways in which she reconciles impressions of her performance as "masculine" with her clear-eyed perspective about being a woman, in the city and on the road. I suggest we view Williams's experiences as a disruption of the masculine confines of jazz performance and discourse. Mary Lou Williams embodies "female masculinity" in that she "refuses the authentication of masculinity through maleness and maleness alone, and . . . names a deliberately counterfeit masculinity that undermines the currency of masculinity."[10] In Williams's specific experiences, and those of jazz musicians generally, the tensions constructing the relationship between work, art, and gender are often hidden in critical histories and biographies. This is a preliminary effort at marking where the tensions are most visible. I draw attention to two key dynamics in Williams's career that introduce several fruitful avenues of research within jazz studies. The first section elaborates on Williams's ideas about music, performance, and composition, while the second section raises questions about race, vulnerability, and gender.

### As Good as or Better Than the Man

In 1957, British pianist Marian McPartland interviewed Mary Lou Williams for *Down Beat* magazine. McPartland combined working the jazz scene in New York with freelance work as a jazz journalist. Taking place shortly after Williams's semiretirement from performing in the mid-1950s, the interview covered the usual territory of the jazz press—recent gigs, style, comparisons with other musicians, performance résumé, repertoire (including Williams's own compositions). And, as McPartland wrote, "Naturally, our conversation drifted to the subject of women musicians." Mary Lou Williams responded regularly to questions about being the exceptional female. She would say, "People ask me how it is to be a woman musician. I don't think about it so much, and I guess that is because I am first of all a musician." She also noted that "there have never been any problems performing because I was a woman. You just have to be as good or better than the man is. And if you get carried away in your work you really don't know if you are a woman or a man." Williams's response had been given many times before; this time she added a bit more to her reactions. "You've got to *play*, that's all. They don't think of you as a woman if you can really play. I think some girls have an inferiority complex about it, and this may hold them back, but they shouldn't feel that way. If they have talent the men will be glad to help them along. Working with men, you get to think like a man when you play. You automatically become strong, though this doesn't mean you're not feminine."[11] Williams recognizes that her authority as a performer is located within her physical prowess rather than her gendered self. To "play" is to give oneself over to the embodied work of music, learning and sharing through the physical experience of making music.[12] Broaching "the subject of women musicians" was as much about critiquing the male-dominated jazz scene as it was about the issues related to actually working as a woman in the jazz world. Williams's attention to aspects of "play" emphasizes the inaccuracy of gender stereotypes as well as the significance of technique, discipline, feeling, and thought. Williams, who had been performing ever since she was a toddler, spoke from the experience of a long career working in predominantly male bands for which she often provided the arrangements, original compositions, and stunning musical talent that anchored the other band members. Williams also hit upon a key aspect of the success or failure of female instrumentalists during a period when gender conventions were becoming increasingly conservative even as racial ideas were becoming increasingly liberal[13]—the idea that young girls are taught their proper social roles, which certainly did not include working as a jazz musician. Singers dominated the respectable place of women in popular music; female instrumentalists were much harder to find. However, despite their general avoidance of performing with women, many male musicians, including Thelonious Monk, Gerald Wiggins, and Bud Powell, were trained by and played with women. Williams, in fact, spent most of her career and life tutoring musicians.

In her discussion with McPartland, Williams reiterated advice she had proffered nearly a decade earlier in an article, "Music and Progress," penned for *Jazz Record*. Speaking to an audience of aspiring musicians, Williams stressed the importance of self-confidence, goal setting, and patience in one's development as an artist and in the development of the art as well. "If we are to make progress in modern music, or, if you prefer *jazz*, we must be willing and able to open our minds to new ideas and developments. If we decide that a new trend is real music we must work with that new trend and develop it to its peak of perfection. When it has reached this so-called 'peak,' it is really only the beginning, for then we build the new ideas on top of the old." Williams considered herself an experimenter and a thinking musician, meaning that she imagined her role as an artist to include being a student of musical ideas, thinking them through in performance and composition, while also learning from other musicians. Williams believed that the performer, like the art, must be in continual development. She claimed, "Once a composer or a musician stops being aware of what is going on around him his music also stops."[14] For Williams, style was a way of working in and thinking about music—what it tried to communicate, how it could communicate, and the process of communication.

Williams, confident in her musicianship, suggests a way of thinking about her genius. "What happens to many good pianists is that they become so stylized they can't break out of the prison of their styles and absorb new ideas, new techniques. Some of them play the same things the same way, night after night—something I just couldn't do. . . . Actually I'm the only pianist who can play with anybody." Relying on her discipline and the practice of music enumerated the qualities any working modern musician should have. Williams had definite ideas about what makes music modern. For Williams, deeply involved in the postwar music scene, bebop was an example of the new and deeply influential modern music. A musician, according to Williams, is ever observant, engaging the music that surrounds her—it is this continual interplay between observation and performance that makes a musician modern. Williams argues that the way in which a musician learns from new musical styles is significant and will affect her own compositions. She suggests not that people copy or mimic different styles, but rather that they internalize them. Often, as she explained, it is an unconscious process. She writes, "I have watched [bebop] grow from its infancy and in fact I recently discovered that I unconsciously used many of its sounds and chords in my own 'Zodiac Suite' which was written before I knew there was such a thing as Be-bop" (23).[15]

Mary Lou Williams composed and arranged her own music, and that of others, for small groups and big bands. She considered herself and her music modern, meaning that they kept growing intellectually. "Modern music is not only limited to small groups of musicians. . . . One of my greatest ambitions will be realized when I am called to present some of my work at a concert with the New York Philharmonic or the Boston Symphony" (24). With her first long-form composition, *The Zodiac Suite* (1945), Williams accomplished that. Turning our attention to Mary Lou Williams and her efforts to work in long form opens up a variety of questions about gender, jazz, and genius. Williams's experiences and the critical reception of her music as a composer and performer present a useful opportunity for thinking through her career as an instrumentalist and tropes about genius, gender, and genre. How do the compositions of a self-taught, black female prodigy exist within the context of theories about the production of "works of art"? How does her work communicate? What new worlds does her work represent or reveal to us? How does jazz composition, especially an extended piece such as *The Zodiac Suite*, exist both as the representation of work and as a work of art? These questions, addressing a variety of issues from narratives of self-construction, debates about modernity and race, performance and gender, are emblematic of the way a black woman could *work* and *play* "like a man" in the world of jazz.

Duke Ellington, while now celebrated as a composer of long forms, was criticized for his first forays into suites. Most of the white jazz critics writing about Ellington in the 1930s and 1940s praised his compositions—his "tunes" like "Mood Indigo." When he began working with longer forms, such as his 1943 *Black, Brown, and Beige*, critics hurled vitriol at him, decrying his perversion of jazz, which, according to the conventional wisdom of the time, was most properly a music of improvisation and short in duration. The idea that jazz was authentically and primarily an improvised music suggested that it could not be composed, and certainly not composed into a long form. Because he was known as "a brilliant miniaturist," Duke Ellington's foray into the extended form was seen as overreaching his talent and ideas.[16] The premier of the forty-five-minute long *Black, Brown, and Beige: A Tone Parallel to the History of the Negro in America* at Carnegie Hall also marked Ellington's debut at the hall. Though other jazz artists, like Paul Whiteman and James Reese Europe, had already performed at the hall, Ellington was the first black composer presenting original music there. The week before Ellington's *Black, Brown, and Beige* concert was dubbed "Ellington Week" in New York City, the concert its culminating event. Two years later, Mary Lou Williams debuted *The Zodiac Suite* at Carnegie Hall. Like Ellington's, Williams's work as composer tended heavily toward shorter pieces. *The Zodiac Suite* recordings of 1945 marked a new stage in her work.

Williams created *The Zodiac Suite* because, she wrote, "I have always thought of astrology and the study of the stars as understanding one of the influences that molds man's destiny, and I have given the Signs the musical interpretation which I feel they warranted." For each sign, Williams drew inspiration from the personality of a musician, actor, or dancer whom she knew personally and with whom she had some experience working. Williams further explained that *The Zodiac Suite* was her first step on the road to her goals as an artist: "As a composer and musician, I have worked all my life to write and develop serious music that is both original and creative."[17] The musicians, actors, dancers, and critics Williams depicted in the suite ranged from Billie Holiday to Leonard Feather to Lena Horne to Benny Goodman to Pearl Primus to Art Tatum to President Roosevelt. We should note that Williams did not sift through her acquaintance to find individuals under each sign and then decide to compose music accurately depicting the personalities of those individuals. The relationship between influence, creativity, and composition does not involve quite so pedestrian a process. Williams explains, "The personalities of those influenced by the stars have been interpreted freely, so that I could achieve the scope and effect I wanted in each case." When Williams began composing the suite in 1943, questions about modernity, music, and technology shaped much of the critical and professional discussion about music, from classical to jazz. The increasing popularity of using recorded music on radio stations, building on the impact of sound technology in film, reduced the number of work opportunities available to musicians. During the 1940s, the American Federation of Musicians organized two recording bans, prohibiting musicians from making records. The bans were hoped to alleviate radio's reliance on recordings and extend opportunities for live performances to musicians. The development of *The Zodiac Suite* grew out of her individual composing, and the live collaborative work done with her bassist and drummer over the course of thirteen weeks performing live on the radio, an arrangement facilitated by Barney Josephson while Williams worked at his Café Society Uptown.[18]

Reviews of the suite—from the compositions to the recordings by Williams and her accompanying drummer, Jack Parker, and bassist, Al Lucas, on Asch Records to the orchestral performances at Carnegie Hall and the New York Philharmonic—were largely positive. In the *Record Review*, the reviewer noted her skill at combining "the harmonic and rhythmic sequences of jazz" and "the scales and chords used so effectively in modern symphonic composition. . . . We have long been looking for something in jazz revealing outstanding creative talent. Here it is!"[19] Williams further elaborated on the role of the musician as performer and colleague when she explained to Marian McPartland, "Musicians should try to help each other, not talk about each other. If you feel good inside, you can change people and make them feel it, too, and that goes for audiences. You can really change an audience. If you're relaxed and you're sincere, they'll know it, and they'll start to feel the same way." In fact, she continued, "I really play best when I play for myself. . . . I get such strong vibrations from an audience. If they're noisy or not paying attention, that's when I'll play the slowest, softest tune I can think of, and it works."[20] Striking here at the heart of the dilemma facing the performing artist, Williams indicated that though she recognized she worked as an entertainer, her main priority was to balance that aspect of entertainment with her musical ideas. Like other musicians working in small venues like nightclubs, the most accessible performing space during the postwar period, Williams noted the casual air some audiences exuded toward musicians, seeing them as background noise to their entertainment. And, like other musicians, Williams developed her own strategies for turning the audiences' attention back to her and what she was trying to say. "If the crowd is noisy, or I don't feel so good, I just play some of my old arrangements and get out. If I feel like it and the crowd is good, then I just settle back and maybe do a little composing right on the spot."[21]

## The Little Piano Girl of East Liberty

Born Mary Elfreida Scruggs on May 8, 1910, in Atlanta, Mary Lou Williams moved with her mother, sister, and other family members to Pittsburgh in 1915. Like other black migrants urged north and to urban centers during World War I and after, Williams's family sought work and escape from the harsh realities of black life in the South in the era of Jim Crow. However, arriving in northern urban centers such as Pittsburgh and its neighboring townships did not mean that migrants had arrived at a promised land. Racism and color prejudice on both sides of the color line often marked new migrants' experiences. Additionally, the waves of European immigrants and the unions' strangleholds on jobs made it difficult for unskilled black laborers to find employment. The story of black migration is also a story of the performing arts. Though the Harlem Renaissance plays a prominent role in our understandings of black cultural life in the early part of the twentieth century, the experiences of black artists in cities such as Pittsburgh deserve consideration as well. Through routes of musical experiences, including the vaudeville circuit, and through the political engine of the *Pittsburgh Courier*, Mary Lou's hometown was a vital locus for black entertainment and political circles. Like Los Angeles's Central Avenue, Pittsburgh had its own "Little Harlem," the center of black entertainment during segregation and its own segregated local of the American Federation of Musicians.

Williams's biography as a performer is forever linked to the narrative of her precocious genius, the talent that enabled her at three (an age sometimes related as four, five, or six) to sit on her mother's lap and play the piano in a storefront church in Atlanta. According to various sources, this was perhaps the most precious memory Williams had of her mother; they were estranged during Williams's adulthood. After moving to Pittsburgh, Williams, known as the "little piano girl," was soon earning a living playing at college parties, brothels, her neighbors' homes, elite homes, and the like to crowds intrigued by her skill and her youth. Her career seemed almost over before it began when she broke her arm and had to have it reset twice before it healed properly. Her mother had no idea about her reputation or activities. "Not seeing me, the neighbors came to our house and asked why I hadn't been around to play for them. Not realizing it, my little visits had changed the entire scene."[22] The player piano her stepfather, Fletcher Burley, bought led to the further development of her skills. She used the player piano to learn classical music, Irish ballads, waltzes, light operas, the blues, and boogie-woogie. Burley looms large in Williams's conception of herself as a musician and as a woman. Not only did he provide her with the tools to develop as a musician; he was also a father figure who, because of his street reputation, provided her with protection in the nightclubs and rent parties she played at while an adolescent in Pittsburgh.[23] He died in 1925, leaving an emotional void in Williams's life.

After a first disastrous attempt to perform as a traveling professional in a tent show made up primarily of adolescents, Williams joined the vaude-ville show of Buzzin' Harris and His Hits 'n Bits in the summer of 1924. At sixteen, she married a saxophonist named John Williams, who joined the Hits 'n Bits near Christmas in 1924. They played the Theatre Owner's Booking Agency (TOBA) circuit.[24] His first sight of Mary made him "very disgusted" because she was female, and in his experience, "women piano players [would] be just tinkling. Women really couldn't handle it at the time—I'm not lying. And it wasn't popular for them to be doing it in the first place. Because at that time, in the teens and twenties, musicians were kind of ruffians—drinking and hanging out and staying out all night." John Williams's description of Williams echoes most other descriptions of men's introduction to women instrumentalists in early jazz history. He describes the masculine power coming from the young girl's body as well as the pre-dominantly masculine character of public performance in the teens and twenties. "She outplayed any piano player I'd ever played with. She played note for note anything that she heard, Earl Hines, Jelly Roll Morton, and heavy like a man, not light piano. At fourteen."[25] Imitation, daring, and tal-ent enabled Williams to perform like and with men. *Down Beat* columnist Sharon Pease explained that Williams "plays with the same solid touch used by professional pianists of the opposite sex. . . . The touch she employs has been developed by proper relaxation, thus getting the weight of her arms and body onto the keyboard much in the same manner as a prizefighter gets the weight of his body into a punch."[26] Another critic explained, "Her sense of musical responsibility accounts for the consistency of her playing and writing and for her steady growth from her early years with Andy Kirk to the present. No other pianist, male or female, has so steadily met the demands of the increasingly demanding art of jazz keyboard performance."[27] The loaded, gendered terms of piano performance in these various descriptions should give us some slight pause. These critics suggest shifts from ideas about the piano as a "feminizing instrument" to ideas about it as a tool for masculine expression and imply that to achieve that expression, one needed to tame the instrument, bring it into submission. Jelly Roll Morton, the "Father of Jazz," acknowledged that as a young boy he harbored an overwhelming desire to be a musician, but he hesitated about playing the piano because he did not want to be "misunderstood." He explains, "I didn't want to be called a sissy. I wanted to marry and raise a family and be known as a man among men when I became of age."[28] His career represents not only the "development" of jazz but also a concerted effort at masculinizing his instrument of choice. While on stage Mary Lou Williams's performance proved her as powerful as a man, even with her slightly built frame, offstage, the teenager needed protection. John Williams goes on to describe the circumstances of their beginning a life together:

> Mary and I started a romance pretty soon. It was around February or March in 1925 that she and I started shacking together to cut expenses and we did that until we married in '26. You'd pick your favorite and shack up. By us being in music and me being the leader and the glamour boy and the new one, well, it threw us together. It really wasn't no love, but I was lucky enough to have a real good brain and I was a father image to her. How much does a girl know, traveling around at fourteen, fifteen years old?[29]

John Williams's analysis of their relationship, that it developed out of the necessity for the girl's protection on the road, underscores the tensions between her experience as a musician and her vulnerability as a young black woman. Williams's life story, handwritten as diaries and drafts of an autobiography, presents many stories about the dangers of sex and the burgeoning sexuality of young black women in the first half of the twentieth century. On the road, as a married woman, as a headliner, Williams was subject to a myriad of experiences of potential sexual violence. Williams documented many instances of her own near rape and rape in her diaries. Whether or not she planned for these stories to be included in her memoir, Williams at least wanted to broach the subject of the sexual dangers women encountered on the road. The usual silence on this topic remains fundamentally characteristic of jazz studies, partly because of the paucity of testimonies and partly because of the insistent focus on jazz as black music, black men's music.

While she certainly regarded musicians such as Jelly Roll Morton with awe, men were not the only influence on Williams. After seeing pianist Lovie Austin, she recalled her "surprise and thrill to see a woman sitting in the pit with four or five other male musicians, with her legs crossed, cigarette in her mouth, playing the show with her left hand and writing music with her right hand for the next act to come on the stage. And was she a master of conducting music."[30] Modeling herself on Austin, Williams harbored a desire to compose during performance. In Williams's description of Lovie Austin, we see her pleasure at seeing someone like herself, one whose physical presence, legs crossed and cigarette in mouth, was certainly "unladylike," as was her performing style—the strength in her left hand allowing her to compose with her right, and her performing context, the predominantly male band.

As Williams began learning how to arrange and compose, she did not realize how vulnerable she was creatively. Despite John Williams's assertion of being a "father figure" providing her with protection, he did little to stem the exploitation Mary Lou Williams encountered as a composer and arranger. With Andy Kirk, who headlined the band she and Williams worked in throughout most of the late 1920s and 1930s, she began composing; critics described their relationship as one of master to apprentice, artist to assistant. Mary Lou Williams describes the writing process of their first recording session in 1929: "Andy knew that I had ideas. I was writing all along but I couldn't write it down. I'd give them ideas during rehearsal. Maybe they wanted to play a song like 'Singing in the Rain' and I'd say, 'Well, listen to this.' Andy would take it down real fast. . . . Never have I written so many things so quickly in my entire career, about 20 things."[31] This process of dictation did not lead to Williams receiving proper composer credits; consequently, she never earned royalties for most of the material she composed while with Andy Kirk and the Clouds of Joy. Kirk did teach Williams the rudiments of music theory and reading, which started her on the road of being able to arrange and compose on her own.

When she moved to New York in the early 1940s, after leaving John Williams and Andy Kirk and striking out on her own, Williams continued composing. Praise for her compositions were generally tempered by some variation on the "exceptional woman" theme. Sometimes the variation reinforced her masculine power at the piano; other variations sexualized Williams, attempting to discover how her femininity contributed to her musical practice. She was

> the once child prodigy of the piano and arrangement world who grew up. . . . A pianist with strong fingers and clear-as-crystal technique for a woman. . . . She does most of her music writing and thinking in a pink satin upholstered movie star bed, and smokes cigarette after cigarette as she works. Mary Lou has a velvet and rhythmical voice, smooth-as-satin skin and "manageable" hair which she curls herself. . . . Friends and agents in show business have tried unsuccessfully for years to get Mary Lou to "blossom out" by wearing daring gowns with slits and slashes and going in for "bringing out" colors, such as white and turquoise and all pastel shades. But Mary Lou insisted on being herself and allowing her talent to make up for whatever she lacked in personality. Only recently has Mary Lou donned a few gowns to cause the oohs and ahhs and she thinks she likes the "New Look."[32]

While this description feminizes Williams, describing her "pink satin upholstered movie star bed," as well as racializing her by noting her now "'manageable' hair," it also suggests Williams's having taken Lovie Austin's example to heart.

Williams converted to Catholicism in 1957. The decision to convert came after a period of intense depression and disillusionment about jazz and the culture around it. Searching for a higher spiritual purpose and direction, Williams "converted to Catholicism for peace of mind." For about three years, Williams did not touch the piano, focusing her attention on helping out musicians who were down on their luck by offering them places to stay, food, and money. She lived off her royalties during this period. During this period Williams's friends, including Dizzy and Lorraine Gillespie, viewed her as vulnerable and in need of protection. They were alarmed by her intense devotion to Catholicism, her seemingly obsessive prayer sessions, and her fear of the "demons" she believed were associated with the jazz music scene.[33] They were concerned about her sublimation of her music to her vision of her mission to aid drug-addicted musicians. Her developing friendship with a priest (introduced to her by good friend and convert Lorraine Gillespie) led her back to the music she had kept silent for so long.

In 1964, Williams composed her first religious song, "Hymn in Honor of

St. Martin de Porres." Much of the scholarship written about Williams as a composer focuses on her religious compositions and her "sanctification of jazz." Because of this work, comparisons are most frequently made between Williams and Ellington, for he was, at approximately the same time, also focusing his energies on religious masses. Echoing Amiri Baraka's philosophical musings about the "quality of soul" ("let us think of soul as *anima*: spirit [*spiritus*, breath] as that which carries breath or the living wind"),[34] Ellington described Williams's music as retaining and maintaining a "standard of quality that is timeless. She is like soul on soul."[35] According to Williams's biographer Tammy Kernodle, the ease with which Ellington gained access to churches to perform his masses was a source of bitterness for Williams. Williams felt that she had been writing her compositions long before Ellington's turn to the spiritual and that despite all of her efforts to create a relationship with the Catholic Church to perform them, she was continually thwarted.

## Beginnings

This brief overview of Williams's theories about her authority as a performer, composer, and teacher illustrates her acceptance of a form of female masculinity, one that allowed her to acknowledge the dominant ways of thinking about the music (that it is for men, that women are novelties) and subvert that way of thinking through her own descriptions of her masculine style, both as a performer and a composer. We note throughout her lack of discussion of the male body as relevant to performance or the music. Rather, her attention is focused on the mental work of music, with emphasis placed on "masculine" characteristics such as discipline, strength, experimentation, and endurance. Even, however, as we work through seeing Williams as exemplifying characteristics of female masculinity, we cannot ignore the realities of her experiences as a woman in a wide-ranging set of performing contexts. Indeed, turning our attention to those contexts reveals themes of precocity, relations of sex and protection, and the power dynamics embedded within intraracial contexts, such as all-black bands. This tension between her "female masculinity" and her "black womanhood" reveals the ways in which race shapes our discussion of gender in jazz; the specificity of her experiences as a black woman and a black female genius cannot occur within discussions of jazz. Jazz is shaped by the metalanguage of race; jazz is a "black music" performed by black men and those seeking to celebrate or exoticize them. Women like Williams are possibly only "masculine"; rarely are they seen as black and feminine. Turning from the interracial to the intraracial jazz context allows us to see, as Farah Jasmine Griffin illustrates in her essay "When Malindy Sings," the gendered relations of power within black music practice.

Mary Lou Williams's experiences allow us to think more inclusively about the presence of women within jazz culture. Perhaps more important than recovering absent presences is the work of understanding the myriad ways women contributed to the intellectual and artistic discourses and practices of jazz culture. In thinking about how I work in jazz, I looked to Williams to conceptualize three areas of investigation for a gendered study of the postwar jazz scene. The first concerned understanding that any analysis of the work of performing includes analysis of the conditions of performance. Race and gender affect the music and ways musicians come to think of their performances, shaping the language and authority they deploy in discussing or representing their experiences, as well as the ways women and men relate to one another through their work as musicians. Second, thinking through questions of youth and shifting ideas about protection and vulnerability offers one vantage point from which to see through the metalanguage of race to the specificity of black women's experiences. Third, the "difference" represented by female instrumentalists within jazz demands that we complicate our ideas about genius and "blackness" by exploring the possibilities that these women offer for "exiling" masculinity, or conventional notions of authority, authenticity, and brilliance, to the margins of race. Exploring these types of questions enables us to delve more deeply into how musicians cross lines of race and gender to make meaning about jazz and black music. If, as Williams argued, music is everything you are, then we who investigate the music should engage musicians' ways of thinking and talking about their experiences and their music when we think we know what genius is.

### Notes

I wish to thank the intellectual and collegial support and criticism of the Sister Scholars in the Ford Foundation's "Meanings and Representations of Work in the Lives of Women of Color" Research Seminar, and also John L. Jackson, Grant Farred, Robin D. G. Kelley, Farah Jasmine Griffin, Desiree Yomtoob, Cheryl Hicks, Audrey Petty, Karima Rustin, and Marlin D. Paschal.

   1   Charlie Parker, *Hear Me Talkin' to Ya!* ed. Nat Hentoff and Nat Shapiro (New York: Dover, 1955), 355.

2   Ralph Ellison, "Living with Music," in *Living with Music*, ed. John F. Callahan (New York: Modern Library, 2002), 61.

3   Herman Gray, "Black Masculinity and Visual Culture," *Callaloo* 18 (1995): 401.

4   See Evelyn Brooks Higginbotham, "African American Women's History and the Meta-language of Race," *Signs* (Winter 1992): 251–74.

5   Melba Liston, Smithsonian Oral History Collection, Washington, DC, p. 38.

6   Barry Ulanov, "Mary Lou Williams," *Metronome*, July 1949.

7   Farah Jasmine Griffin, *If You Can't Be Free, Be a Mystery: In Search of Billie Holiday* (New York: Free Press, 2001), 15–16.

8   Farah Jasmine Griffin, "When Malindy Sings," in *Uptown Conversation*, ed. Robert O'Meally, Brent Hayes Edwards, and Farah Jasmine Griffin (New York: Columbia University Press, 2004), 104.

9   See Angela Davis, *Blues Legacies and Black Feminism: Gertrude "Ma" Rainey, Bessie Smith, and Billie Holiday* (New York: Random House, 1999), especially chapters 5 and 6, which focus specifically on the sexual politics of Holiday's "love songs" and the social critique embedded within "Strange Fruit." Griffin, *If You Can't Be Free*, and the documentary *Strange Fruit* (California Newsreel, 2002) explore a number of these concerns as well. Eric Porter's discussion of Abbey Lincoln's growth as a singer examines how Billie Holiday's aesthetic choices shaped Lincoln's vision of what was possible as a singer and composer, revealing as well how Holiday's choices are given meaning as black feminist praxis.

10  Judith Halberstam, "The Good, the Bad, and the Ugly: Men, Women, and Masculinity," in *Masculinity and Feminist Theory: New Directions*, ed. Judith Kegan Gardiner (New York: Columbia University Press, 2002), 345.

11  Marian McPartland, "Mary Lou: Marian McPartland Salutes One Pianist Who Remains Modern and Communicative," *Down Beat*, October 17, 1957, 12.

12  See Vijay Iyer, "Exploding the Narrative in Jazz Improvisation," in O'Meally, Edwards, and Griffin, *Uptown Conversation*, 393–403. Iyer offers a compelling analysis of the kinesthetic and sonic dimensions of musical practice.

13  Ruth Feldstein explores this dynamic in her book *Motherhood in Black and White: Race and Sex in American Liberalism, 1935–1965* (Ithaca, NY: Cornell University Press, 2000).

14  Mary Lou Williams, "Music and Progress," *Jazz Record*, November 1947, 23–24.

15  In 1948, Williams presented a lecture on "the development of Be Bop," drawing on her suite for examples of the influence of bebop experiments in harmony. See also Ulanov, "Mary Lou Williams." He quotes her saying, "I was trained to play with everyone and to play everything. I grew up around older musicians and I listened to a lot and I learned. I listened to how a pianist pushed, like Count Basie, and I pushed. I broadened, I moved, I experimented. That's what I've always taught the kids who come to me. You've got to keep going. There's only one reason, really, to stop. That's to take account, to get new sounds, to get the sounds you're not hearing." Ulanov concluded, "So fully has she made it, that one can almost measure the success or failure of the music of her time by her music. So fully has she made it, that in discussing her work one almost forgets that she is a woman. Ah, but that's another story."

16  See John Edward Hasse, *Beyond Category: The Life and Genius of Duke Ellington* (New York: Simon & Schuster, 1993), 263. Paul Bowles's review in the *Herald-Tribune* ("Duke Elling-

ton in Recital for Russian War Relief," January 25, 1943; reprinted in Mark Tucker, ed., *The Duke Ellington Reader* [New York: Oxford University Press, 1993], 166) illustrates the mixed reaction to the composition. Celebrating Ellington's proven talents at conducting, arranging, and performing, Bowles approved of Ellington's ability to keep to the integrity of early jazz. However, Bowles found *Black, Brown, and Beige* "formless and meaningless . . . a gaudy potpourri . . . corny . . . trite. . . . The whole attempt to view jazz as a form of art music should be discouraged." John Hammond wrote that Duke Ellington "unfortunately . . . took to heart" the praise of "serious composers" who decried the restrictions placed on his talents by "dance tempo and the thirty-two-bar form." *Black, Brown, and Beige* suffers from incoherence, according to Hammond. "It was unfortunate that Duke saw fit to tamper with the blues form in order to produce music of greater 'significance'" ("Is the Duke Deserting Jazz?" *Jazz*, May 1943, 15; reprinted in Tucker, *The Duke Ellington Reader*, 172).

17  Mary Lou Williams, "Why I Wrote the *Zodiac Suite*," liner notes to *The Zodiac Suite*, Smithsonian reissue.

18  Tammy L. Kernodle, *Soul on Soul: The Life and Music of Mary Lou Williams* (Boston: Northeastern University Press, 2004), 108–9.

19  *The Record Review*, 1947, 24.

20  McPartland, "Mary Lou," 41.

21  "Land of OO-bla-dee," *Time*, December 12, 1949.

22  Mary Lou Williams, quoted in Linda Dahl, *Morning Glory: A Biography of Mary Lou Williams* (Berkeley: University of California Press, 2001), 23. Kernodle's *Soul on Soul* is a phenomenal addition to the critical literature on Mary Lou Williams.

23  Kernodle, *Soul on Soul*, 20–29.

24  John Williams, quoted in Dahl, *Morning Glory*, 43. For more on the Theatre Owner's Booking Association, also known as "Tough on Black Asses," see Ted Vincent, *Keep Cool: The Black Activists Who Built the Jazz Age* (London: Pluto, 1995).

25  John Williams, quoted in Dahl, *Morning Glory*, 44.

26  Sharon Pease, "She Has a Touch Like a Man!" *Downbeat*, date unknown, scrapbook 17, Mary Lou Williams Papers, Institute of Jazz Studies, Rutgers University, hereafter cited as MLW.

27  Article, source and date unknown, scrapbook 17, MLW.

28  Alan Lomax, *Mister Jelly Roll: The Fortunes of Jelly Roll Morton, New Orleans Creole and Inventor of Jazz* (1950; reprint, New York: Pantheon, 1993), 6.

29  John Williams, quoted in Dahl, *Morning Glory*, 45.

30  Ibid., 29.

31  Mary Lou Williams, quoted in ibid., 73.

32  Dolores Calvin, "'New Look' Pleases Swing Pianist," source and date unknown, scrapbook 17, MLW.

33  Kernodle, *Soul on Soul*, 195.

34  LeRoi Jones (Amiri Baraka), "The Burton Green Affair," in *Black Music* (New York: William Morrow & Company, 1970), 136.

35  Duke Ellington, *Music Is My Mistress* (New York: Da Capo, 1973), 169.

Elizabeth Alexander

## The Negro Digs Up Her Past: "Amistad"

Whenever I teach fiction or poetry that could be called historical, I always ask my students, why then? As Ishmael Reed engages 1920s Harlem in his novel *Mumbo Jumbo* to ask questions about the new New Negro politics of the early 1970s in which the book was written, the possibilities and limitations of racialist thinking in the Black Arts era are well served by considering the changing same (to borrow Amiri Baraka's phrase) in the 1920s. Of Toni Morrison's *Beloved*, an interesting question might be, Why did this particular envisioning of slavery meet its zeitgeist moment in 1987? Yes, Morrison is a majestic writer, but clearly that book was born at the right time. Why is *Beloved* seen as more "historical" than *Sula* or *Song of Solomon*, which appear to be equivalently researched and detailed regarding everyday life in time and place? And so forth.

I live in New Haven, Connecticut. One day several years ago I was pushing my then-baby in the stroller and stopped in front of the New Haven Historical Society. Why hadn't I ever been inside? I thought, so in we went. The society has a more or less permanent *Amistad*

The *South Atlantic Quarterly* 104:3, Summer 2005.
Copyright © 2005 by Duke University Press.

exhibit on display. Of course, I have long known the story of the *Amistad* rebellion, but there at the historical society I saw things new to me: the letter the young boy Kale wrote to thank his Christian benefactors, newspaper clippings with detailed physical descriptions and silhouette illustrations of the captives, accounts of how they were let out to exercise on the New Haven Green during their long incarceration in the city while awaiting trail, and much more. A million questions grew from this story, which is such a centerpiece of African American history. Children on the *Amistad*? I only ever thought about Cinque. Kale's letter was in English cursive. Who taught him English, and how? What is the relationship between the Mendeland of 1839 and Sierra Leone of today? What became of the three little girls on board? How does a community survive without grown women? What was the role of Yale University professor Josiah Willard Gibbs, whose rudimentary translations helped the captives tell their story in court, and his Yale students? What did the New Haven Green I daily cross look like in the mid–nineteenth century? These were the kinds of very basic material questions about time, place, and people that led me to research more. What really happened to Cinque? I scrutinized Nathaniel Jocelyn's beautiful, quietly idealized portrait of the rebellion's storied hero and thought harder. Who was he and who was he not? What might he think of what's been done in his name? There is Cinque, and there are the many ideas of Cinque-as-Negro-Hero. A poem felt like the only way to explore all these questions simultaneously.

The more I learned—at the New Haven Historical Society and at other archives and libraries—the more I was able to take the imaginative leap into the poem. And I was able to think about the ground on which I walk every day, and what happened there. Now that we have come through the historical revisions of several black arts movements, and now that the academic field of history as such has expanded to give us a more readily available accounting of those stories, how might we imagine differently? Need we still be reverent toward our Negro heroes, or might we imagine their complexities and flaws? Are we able to hold on to all of our history, or is writing the continual reminding of what we once knew but need to repeat in order to continue knowing? Even the word *ancestor* has a heft to it, an unassailable gravitas, a stentorian demand. But I wanted to write a black history poem that was not just about stoicism. I also wanted to explore the past in the face of the aggressive ahistoricity that plagues and misnames this nation and is a tool for misleading the people.

One of the obvious predecessors of "Amistad" is Robert Hayden's short epic "Middle Passage," which he first published in 1943 and continued to publish in revision as late as 1962. He researched the poem extensively in the 1930s and early 1940s, both at the Schomburg Collection (then known as the Harlem Branch of the New York Public Library) and in his capacity as a researcher for the Federal Writers' Project in Michigan. "Middle Passage" was first published in *Phylon*, the preeminent journal W. E. B. Du Bois founded in 1939. The poem calls on archival materials to imagine life aboard those slave ships during the Middle Passage and features the character "Cinquez."

In his great 1940s sonnet "Frederick Douglass," Hayden meditated on the utility and shortfalls of heroism. The poem is about love, as the sonnet has always been, but of a love profounder than the romantic variety. Hayden is interested in the kind of difficult love of community that is not about answers, per se, and not about heroes, solely, but rather about the hard processes of living, facing struggle, and imagining strategies, the kind of heroism that is not about pedestals. Poetry is always implicitly enacting, "I don't want to forget this," which in the end works the same as the grander "This must be remembered."

In 1925 in *The New Negro*, the great collector Arthur Schomburg published the essay "The Negro Digs Up His Past." His opening still resonates: "The American Negro must remake his past in order to make his future." That's what the old folks say, and I think it is still true. Never have we had more material to work with, more archival sources and resources with which to explore and then imagine the past. And the imagination, in the history poem, can take up where written history stops. If we measure out Linda Brent's crawl space and let ourselves imagine seven minutes, let alone seven years, in such confines; if we contemplate the *Amistad* as a ship without mothers, the utter absence of mothers in a violently formed society; if we wonder what people dreamed in their captivity, we might begin to understand what they lost, what it took to build themselves up again, and what it might take to move forward. It is the unique potential of poetry to be able to locate and activate what is in the imagination. Art takes us to knowing that may have no other way of being found, and that is one of the very things we need in order to move more intelligently forward.

## Amistad

### *Beginning*

After the tunnel of no return
After the roiling Atlantic, the black Atlantic, black and mucilaginous
After skin to skin in the hold and the picked handcuff locks
After the mutiny
After the fight to the death on the ship
After picked handcuff locks and the jump overboard
After the sight of no land and the zig-zag course
After the Babel which settles like silt into silence
and silence and silence, and the whack
of lashes and waves on the side of the boat
After the half cup of rice, the half cup of seawater
the dry swallow and silence
After the sight of no land
After two daughters sold to pay off a father's debt
After Cinque himself a settled debt

After white gulf between stanzas

the space at the end
the last quatrain

### *The Blue Whale*

swam alongside the vessel for hours.
I saw her breach. The spray when she sounded
soaked me (the lookout) on deck. I was joyous.
There her oily, rainbowed, lingering wake,
ambergris print on the water's sheer skin,
she skimmed and we skimmed and we speeded
straight on toward home, on the glorious wind.

Then something told her, Turn (whales travel
in pods and will beach themselves rather than split) —
toward her pod? — and the way she turned was not
our way. I begged and prayed and begged for her
companionship, the guide light of her print,
North Star (I did imagine) of her spout.
But she had elsewhere to go. I watched
the blue whale's silver spout. It disappeared.

### Absence

In the absence of women on board,
when the ship reached the point where no landmass
was visible in any direction
and the funk had begun to accrue—
human funk, spirit funk, soul funk—who
commenced the moaning? Who first hummed that deep
sound from empty bowels, roiling stomachs,
from back of the frantically thumping heart?
In the absence of women, of mothers,
who found the note that would soon be called "blue,"
the first blue note from one bowel, one throat,
joined by dark others in gnarled harmony.
Before the head rag, the cast-iron skillet,
new blue awaited on the other shore,
invisible, as yet unhummed. Who knew
what note to hit or how? In the middle
of the ocean, in the absence of women,
there is no deeper deep, no bluer blue.

### boy haiku

the motherless child
rests his hand on a dead man's
forehead 'til it cools.

### Poro Society

Without leopard skin, leather,
antelope horns, warthog tusks,
crocodile jaws, raffia muffs,

without the sacred bush,
the primordial grove,
our ancient initiations,

we will find a way
to teach the young man
on board with us.

We contend
with the forces of evil
in the universe.

Aggressive magic
addresses the need for control
in an imperfect world.

### Approach
With shore in sight, the wind dies and we slow.
Up from the water bobs a sleek black head
with enormous dark eyes that question us:

Who and what are you? Why? Then another
and another and another of those
faces, 'til our boat is all surrounded.

The dark creatures reveal themselves to be
seals, New England gray seals, we later learn.
They stare. We stare. Not all are blackest black:

Some piebald, some the dull gray of the guns
our captors used to steal and corral us,
some the brown-black of our brothers, mothers,

and two milky blue-eyed albino pups.
Albino: the congenital absence
of normal pigmentation. Something gone

amiss. Anomaly, aberration.

### Connecticut
They squint from shore
at scarlet-shirted blackamoors.

The battered boat sails in:
White sky, black sea, black skin,

a low black schooner,
armed black men on deck

in shawls, pantaloons,
a Cuban planter's hat—

Parched, starved,
dressed in what they found

in the dry goods barrels,
the Africans squint

at trees not their trees,
at shore not their shore.

### Other Cargo
Saddles and bridles,
bolts of ribbon,
calico, muslin, silk,
beans, bread, books,
gloves, raisins, cologne,
olives, mirrors, vermicelli,
parasols, rice, black bombazine.

### Education
In 1839, to enter university,
the Yale men already knew Cicero,

Dalzel's *Graeca Minora*, then learned more Latin prosody,
Stiles on astronomy, Dana's mineralogy.

Each year they named a class bully
who would butt heads with sailors in town.

"The first foreign heathen ever seen,"
Obookiah, arrived from Hawaii in '09

The most powerful telescope in America
was a recent gift to the school

and through it, they were first to see
the blazing return of Halley's comet.

Ebeneezer Peter Mason
and Hamilton Lanphere Smith

spent all their free time at the instrument
observing the stars, their systems,

their movement and science and magic,
pondering the logic of mysteries that twinkle.

Some forty years before, Banneker's
eclipse-predicting charts and almanacs

had gone to Thomas Jefferson
to prove "that nature has given our brethren

talents equal to other colors of men."
Benjamin Banneker, born free,

whose people came from Guinea,
who taught himself at twenty-two (the same age

as the graduates) to carve entirely from wood
a watch which kept exquisite time,

accurate to the blade-sharp second.

### The Yale Men

One by one the Yale men come
to teach their tongue to these
caged Africans so they might tell

in court what happened on the ship
and then, like Phillis Wheatley,
find the Yale men's God

and take him for their own.

### Teacher

(Josiah Willard Gibbs)
I learn to count in Mende one to ten,
then hasten to the New York docks to see
if one of these black seamen is their kind.

I run to one and then another, count.
Most look at me as though I am quite mad.
I've learned to count in Mende one to ten!

I shout, exhausted as the long day ends
and still no hope to know the captive's tale.
Is any of these black seamen their kind?

I'd asked an old Congo sailor to come
to the jail, but his tongue was the wrong one,
I learned. To count in Mende one to ten

begin *eta, fili, kian-wa, naeni.*
I spy a robust fellow loading crates
Is this the black seaman who is their kind?

He stares at me as though I am in need,
but tilts his head and opens up his ear
and counts to me in Mende one to ten,
this one at last, this black seaman, their kind.

### Translator
(James Covey)
I was stolen from Mendeland as a child
then rescued by the British ship *Buzzard*
and brought to Freetown, Sierra Leone.

I love ships and the sea, joined this crew
of my own accord, set sail as a teen,
now resupplying in New York Harbor.

When the white professor first came to me
babbling sounds, I thought he needed help
until *weta*, my mother's *six*, hooked my ear

and I knew what he was saying, and I knew
what he wanted in an instant, for we had heard
wild tales of black pirates off New London,

the captives, the low black schooner like
so many ships, an infinity of ships fatted
with Africans, men, women, children

as I was. Now it is my turn to rescue.
I have not spoken Mende in some years,
yet every night I dream it, or silence.

To New Haven, to the jail. To my people.
Who am I now? This them, not them. We burst
with joy to speak and settle to the tale:

*We killed the cook, who said he would cook us.*
*They rubbed gunpowder and vinegar in our wounds.*
*We were taken away in broad daylight.*

And in a loud voice loud as a thousand waves
I sing my father's song. It shakes the jail.
I sing from my entire black body.

### Physiognomy

> Monday, September 16, 1839
> *Another of the captured Africans named Bulwa (or Wool-*
> *wah) died on Saturday night. This is the third who has*
> *died in this city, and the thirteenth since their leaving*
> *Havana. One more remains sick in this city, the others*
> *having been removed to Hartford on Saturday, to await*
> *their trial on Tuesday the 17th. Several are still affected*
> *with the white flux, the disease which has proved fatal to*
> *so many of them.*
> — *Daily Herald*, New Haven

Kimbo, 5 feet 6 inches, with mustaches and long beard,
in middle life, calls himself Manding. Very intelligent,

he counts thus: 1. eta, 2. fili, 3. kian-wa, 4. naeni,
5. loelu, 6. weta, 7. wafura, 8. wayapa,
9. ta-u, 10. pu.

Shuma, 5 feet 6 inches, spoke
over the corpse of Tha
after Reverend Mister Bacon's prayer.

Konoma, 5 feet 4 inches with incisor teeth
pressed outward and filed, with large lips
and projecting mouth, tattooed on the forehead.

Calls himself Congo (Congo
of Ashmun's map of Liberia,
or Kanga, or Vater)

They are represented by travelers as handsome.
They are supposed to be more ancient of the soil than Timmaris.
Their language, according to Port Chad, is distinct from any other.

Biah, 5 feet 4½ inches with remarkably pleasant countenance
with hands whitened by scars from gunpowder.
Calls himself Duminah (Timmari).

Counts also in Timmari.
He counts in Bullom thus:
He counts in Manding like Kwong.

With face broad in the middle
With sly and mirthful countenance (rather old)
With full Negro features
With hair shorn in rows from behind
With permanent flexion of two fingers on right hand
A mere boy, calls himself Manding
With depression of skull from a wound from the forehead
Tattooed on breast
With narrow and high head
With large head and high cheekbones
Marked on face by the smallpox
Stout and fleshy

Teme, 4 feet 3 inches, a young girl
calls herself Congo but when further interrogated
says her parents were Congo, she a Manding.

Observe that in this examination
no one when asked for his name
gave any other than an African name.

No one when asked
to count counted in any
language other than African.

There was no appearance in any of them,
so far as I could judge,
of having been from Africa more than two or three months.

### Constitutional

Mary Barber's children beg their mother
to take them into town each day to see
the Africans on the New Haven Green
let out of their cells for movement and air.

A New York shilling apiece to the jailer
who tucks away coins in a full suede purse.
The children push through skirts, past waistcoats,
to see the Africans turn somersets.

In the open air, in the bright sunlight,
the Africans chatter, and sound to
the children like blackbirds or cawing gulls.
The Africans spring. The Africans do not smile.

### Mende Vocabulary
they
my father
our father
your father
my mother
our mother
my book
his house
one ship
two men
all men
good man
bad man
white man
black man

I eat
he eats
we eat
they sleep
I see God
did I say it right?
we sleep
I make
he makes
they have eaten
this book is mine
that book is his
this book is ours
I am your friend
here
now

that
there
then

### The Girls

Mar-gru, Te-me, Ke-re,
the three little girls onboard.
In Connecticut
they stay with Pendleton
the jailer and his wife.
Some say they are slaves
in that house. The lawyer
comes to remove them,
but they cling to their hosts,
run screaming through the snow
instead of go. Cinque comes
and speaks in their language
with much agitation.
Do you fear Pendleton? *No.*
Do you fear the lawyer? *No.*
Do you fear Cinque? *No.*
Who or what do you fear?
*The men,* they say, *the men.*
The girls will become Christians.
They will move to Farmington
with the Mende mission
and return to Sierra Leone.
One will return to America
to attend college at Oberlin.
They will be called Sarah,
Maria, and Charlotte.

### Kere's Song

My brother would gather the salt crust.
My grandmother would boil it gray to white.

My mother boated in the near salt river,
grabbed fat fish from the water with bare hands.

Women paint their faces with white clay and dance
to bring girls into our society, our

secrets, our womanhood, our community.
The clay-whitened faces of my mothers

are what I see in my dreams, and hear
drum-songs that drown girls' cries after

they have been cut to be made women.
If someone does evil, hags ride them

all night and pummel them to exhaustion.
Hags slip off their skins and leave them

in the corner during such rambles.
At my grandmother's grave, cooked chicken, red rice,

and water to sustain her on her journey.
I was learning the secrets of Sande

when they brought me here, before my dance,
before my drum, before my Sande song.

### Judge Judson

These negroes are *bozals*
(those recently from Africa)
not *ladinos*

(those long on the island)
and were imported
in violation of the law.

The question remains:
What disposition shall be made
of these negroes?

Bloody may be their hands
yet they shall
embrace their kindred.

Cinqueze and Grabeau
shall not sigh for Africa
in vain

and once remanded
they shall no longer
be here.

### In Cursive
Westville, February 9, 1841

Miss Chamberlain and others,
I will write you a few lines
because I love you very much
and I want you to pray to the great God to make us free
and give us new souls and pray for African people.

He sent his beloved son into the world
to save sinners who were lost. He sent
the Bible into the world to save us
from going down to hell, to make us turn from sin.

I heard Mr. Booth say you give five dollars
to Mr. Townsend for African people. I thank you
and hope the great God will help you and bless you
and hear you and take you up to Heaven when you die.

I want you to pray to the great God make us free
and go our home and see our friends in African Country.
I want the great God love me very much and forgive all my sins.
All Mendi people thank you for your kindness.

Hope to meet you in heaven. Your friend, Kale

### God
There is one God in Farmington, Connecticut,
another in Mendeland.

None listen.
None laugh, but none have listened.

We will sail home carrying Bibles
and wearing calico.

The journey this time
is seven weeks.

If we find our mothers,
children, fathers, brothers,

sisters, aunties, uncles,
cousins, friends,

if we find them,
we will read to them

(we read this book)
the God stories in our Bibles.

That is the price for the ticket home
to Mendeland

for us the decimated three years hence.

### Waiting for Cinque to Speak
Having tried,

having tried, having failed,

having raised rice
that shimmered green, green,
having planted and threshed.

Having been a man, having sired children,
having raised my rice, having amassed a bit of debt,
having done nothing remarkable.

Years later it would be said
the Africans were snatched into slavery, then,
that we were sold by our own into slavery, then,
that those of our own who sold us
never imagined chattel slavery,
the other side of the Atlantic.

Having amassed debt, I was taken to settle that debt.
(Not enough rice in the shimmering green.)
Better me than my daughter or son. (I was strong.)
And on the ship I met my day
as a man must meet his day.
Out of the Babel of Wolof and Kissee
we were made of the same flour and water, it happened,
on the ship, I met my day.

### The Amistad Trail

The Amistad Trail bus
leaves from the commuter parking lot,
exit 37 off Highway 84.
There is interest in this tale.

See where the girls lived while waiting
for the boat to sail home, see Cinque's room,
the Farmington church where they learned
to pray to Jesus, Foone's grave.

Good things: Eventual justice, John Quincy Adams,
black fighting back, white helping black.
Bad things: the fact of it, price of the ticket,
the footnote, the twist, and the rest—

Done took my blues
Done took my blues and

—the good and the bad of it.
Preach it: Learn. Teach it: Weep.

Done took my blues.
Done took my blues and gone.
The verse will not resolve.
The blues that do not end.

### Cinque Redux

I will be called bad motherfucker.
I will be venerated.
I will be misremembered.
I will be Seng-Pieh, Cinqueze, Joseph,
and end up CINQUE.

I will be remembered
as upstart, rebel, rabble-rouser, leader.
My name will be taken by black men
who wish to be thought RIGHTEOUS.
My portrait will be called "The Black Prince."
Violent acts will be committed in my name.
My face will appear on Sierra Leonean currency

I will not proudly sail the ship home
but will go home, where I will not sell slaves,
then will choose to sail off
to a new place: Jamaica, West Indies.
In America, they called us "Amistads."
The cook we killed, Celestino, was mulatto.
Many things are true at once.

Yes I drew my hand across my throat
in the courtroom, at that cur Ruiz
to hex his thieving, killing self.
Yes I scuffled here and there instead of immolate.
Yes I flaunted my gleam and spring.
No I did not smile.
No I never forgot the secret teachings
of my fathers. No I never forgot

who died on board, who died on land,
who did what to whom, who will die
in the future, which I see
unfurling like the strangest dream

### The Last Quatrain

and where now
and what now
the black white space

**Brackette F. Williams**

## Getting Out of the Hole

> If a man does not keep pace with his companions, perhaps it is because he hears a different drummer. Let him step to the music which he hears, however measured or so far away.
> —Henry David Thoreau

**D**eakie Boy was different. He was not like those old winos, hanging out in front of the company store or squatting on makeshift chairs in front of one- and two-room adobe huts, always just waiting—waiting and playing dominoes. Deakie Boy played dominoes, and by age eight he could hustle the oldest players, and he knew to wait and roll the others when, drunk, they went to take a crap. Deakie Boy was going places. He always knew he was going places. Had him some plans, he did. By age ten, his brain was a road map. Every road on it led out of Arrowhead Camp, affectionately known as the Head.

The Arizona desert, with its buttes and cacti and miles of irrigation ditches and cotton fields, was nowhere near big enough to hold Deakie Boy. He was not only different, he was big, real big, and he knew it. He had only one problem. He could not wash off the smell of Tokay Rose. It clung to him, stinking like a bad Saturday night

The *South Atlantic Quarterly* 104:3, Summer 2005.
Copyright © 2005 by Duke University Press.

held over for replay on Monday afternoon, when the sweat rolled off the old winos like flash-flood water through an arroyo. Deakie Boy swam in the irrigation ditches. He washed off in the cow troughs. The smell clung to him, even after he took the obligatory Friday baths. It followed him around as he made his big plans to escape the trap his parents and their parents had fallen into when they took that first migrant labor bus up from Lu'zana. His parents were gone, dead since he was nine.

—————

The year of the tadpoles was the year he started to put his plans into action. That year it had rained so much that even with the irrigation pumps off, ditches remained full. The Camp was overrun with frogs. First they were real small and cute. Deakie and the other boys caught them and used them to frighten the stupid girls, stuffing the frogs down the front of their blouses. Deakie Boy did what the other boys did, but he was not having fun. He was making plans and practicing his escape. That year he hooked up with Bubba Joe. Bubba Joe was not different. Like all the old winos, Bubba Joe had what the folks on the Camp called loose character. It sort of hung about Bubba Joe's shoulders, never really settling onto his puny frame. Loose character wasn't the sort of thing to be confused with personality. Bubba Joe had no personality. None of the old winos had personality; they had loose character, a way of being that was loose because it could be played any which a way those different, like Deakie Boy, wanted to play it.

Deakie Boy wanted to play everything fast and loose because that suited his plans. He did not know where the plans came from or what motivated them, and he did not care. At first Bubba Joe wasn't having any of Deakie Boy or his plans. He did not like Deakie Boy and he let everyone know it. Whenever Deakie Boy tried to take the lead in a game, Bubba Joe called him on it. There was no low that Bubba Joe had not visited. He tattled, he lied, he stole, and he peeped.

Stealing, lying, and even cheating was a forgivable act on the Head. Peeping was a hanging offense. People tried to protect themselves from peepers by hanging curtains to mark their space. The houses were little but the people were big. To proclaim their respect for one another's privacy, they cut their eyes and swore on Bibles and all manner of things, like mamas' graves and stillborns' umbilical cords. Bubba Joe peeped and everyone knew it. He knew they knew and didn't give a damn. Deakie Boy knew Bubba Joe had looser character than was acceptable, even on the Head. His plans counted on using that fact one day when it served his purpose.

That time came in the year of tadpoles. Bubba Joe and Deakie Boy were thirteen. They had spent most of each of their thirteen years on the Head. Time spent had not been continuous because migrant labor time was a cycle. Each year for the length of the cotton harvest they came back to ground zero—the Head. If everyone had been paying attention to the tadpoles, they would have understood the importance and danger of that year, but they were too busy heeding general superstitions that encouraged them to ward off the warts they thought they would get from contact with the frog piss that was all over the place that year. Deakie Boy did not give a damn about frog piss. It was not that he did not believe it caused warts. It was just that he had never seen a wart and he did not waste time worrying about what troubled loose-character people. He was different and he was going places and the road maps on his brain were pointing the way. Like his plans, he did not know how the road maps came to be there and he did not care.

---

The year of the tadpoles also was the year Pretty Black got her hole. Like Bubba Joe and Deakie Boy, for most of her nearly sixteen years she had come to the Head with her parents to do the chopping, thinning, and harvesting of cotton. Like them and all other kids, she had ducked in and out of the consolidated regional school system. She had done her Roman numerals, multiplication tables, and fractions just like everyone else. It was during one of those other years that she had got her name. In the years since her first visit to the Head, she had gone from being Lula Belle from Lu'zana to become Pretty Black. Folks called her that because that's what she was— pretty and black. Some said she was part 'Pache and part patched black-and-white Creole, like all them Lu'zana folk. Deakie Boy figured it did not matter what the whole was that, as loose-character folks, they thought made up her pretty black parts. What mattered to Deakie Boy and to Bubba Joe, who despite his initial dislike had become Deakie's sidekick, was that the year of the tadpoles was the year she got her hole and Deakie Boy taught her how to work it into his plans.

The year of the tadpoles Pretty did not come to the Head with her parents. She arrived with Sissy Mae and Joenella. They were her close friends; all of them were kicking down the door of sweet sixteen. Learning to work her hole into Deakie Boy's plans was not easy, but it was quick. As far as anyone would ever know, for Pretty Black, use of the hole was no sooner learned than forgotten. Deakie Boy would remember and repeat the lesson. This too was a fact that the folks of the Head were not to know.

=====

That day by the time Deakie Boy stopped by the house Bubba Joe shared with his deceased parents' friends, Sarah Lee and Day Stump Ross, Big Red had rose high in the sky on what seemed to be a normal fall day. Deakie Boy, Bubba Joe, and Day Stump headed for the field, leaving Sarah Lee behind because she had cramps and was staying in bed. Day Stump was pissed at her illness. He needed her hands to help him pull enough cotton to make a good day's pay. Sarah figured she would improve and promised she would join them to work by noontime. Like Deakie Boy, Day Stump stank of Tokay Rose. He had the smell of it in his pores because he drank his share of it from quitting time, Saturday noon, to time to quit, late Sunday night. Deakie Boy smelled of Tokay Rose though he never touched the stuff. It touched him. It was the essence of the Head that seeped into his pores and gave him the only reason he needed for being different, for pursuing his plans.

Working in his usual indifferent and slow way, that day Deakie Boy managed to pull eighty pounds of cotton. It was a pitiful showing for a boy of his age and size, for he was not a frail pail like Bubba Joe. For his age and height, Deakie Boy was well formed and stout, so folks said. "Gonna be a lady-killer one day," some said. Others disagreed, even though they noted that his face was not ugly. In fact, they agreed it showed real promise of a better future. No, his face was not ugly. It was scary. It was not scary because it was misformed but rather because it was sort of pretty until one looked close at the eyes and mouth. These features were like light to a moth—they drew attention to themselves only to leave those drawn wishing they had been repelled.

At the day's end, Day Stump, Deakie Boy, Bubba Joe, and Sarah Lee, who had managed to make it to the field by noon, came home with all the other hands. It was a bountiful crop they were working. Everyone had made a good pulling, putting them in the happy mood that outcome produced. They walked lightly and sang along with the cacophony of different tunes playing on the many pocket transistors that were tucked in their fellow workers' breast and hip pockets. Sam Cook, Otis Redding, Waylon Jennings, Johnny Cash, and the like entertained the hands and shared in their celebration of a day well made. Deakie Boy did not own a transistor; he listened to others' tunes and, like his indifferent work habit, he was more concerned with watching the others, especially Pretty, than he was in participating in work and play. He had plans and they required keeping an eye on Pretty Black and her hole. Two days earlier she had shown him her hole. One look and Deakie began to think about how he could teach her to work it into his plans.

═════

At the edge of the Camp, behind the rows of abode huts, before heading home at the end of the workday, the men stripped down to their underwear to wash off the day's dirt, sweat, and raw funk. Those who drank during the week, rather than waiting for the week's end, and that was a goodly number of them, pulled the fifths of Tokay Rose out of their hiding places and began the other ritual of washing away the day's labor pains. Soon, all around the Head the clank of dominoes on the board and the rank talk that made them fall properly could be heard as the male sounds accompanying the clanging of pots and pans made by the womenfolk getting supper started. For the women, the smell of overused cooking grease intensified their body odors. They would eat with the day's stench and these odors clinging to them, waiting to wash the dishes and then themselves long after Big Red and the children were well bedded down.

When finally the women settled down for some much-needed sleep or a less-needed tussle with their old men's Tokay Rose–embalmed bodies, Deakie Boy watched Pretty Black head out across the field. He smiled to himself even if it looked like he was smiling at Bubba Joe, who was looking right at him but did not see the point. At least he didn't that night, distracted as he was thinking about the old bachelors who, like the many camp dogs that fed on the scraps of scraped-together suppers, were slinking off to curl up to the sounds of their own rumbling bellies. Deakie Boy did think about the bachelors. He no longer saw them because he knew he was never going to end up like them—eating tuna fish, pork and beans, and Vienna sausages out of cans opened with little turn keys and heated on refuse oil drums. Deakie Boy knew he was different, with plans that would take him places beyond the cycle of migrant-labor time.

At nightfall, Bubba Joe slunk away to the spot he used to peep at Sissy Mae and Joenella. That night, like many other nights, as they found comfort in one another, his greatest joy was watching Sissy Mae cum. People on the

Camp called her Dummy because she could not talk. When she came her scream couldn't be heard, and that allowed Bubba Joe to participate: imagining that he screamed for her, lending her his voice in her time of need and passion. Bubba Joe liked to be useful.

The next day started like any other day. Except for Pretty Black's sneaking away, as had become her habit, no one noticed anything remarkable. Still, Pretty Black did sneak away that evening, and unlike on other evenings, she was not carrying a hammer, nails, boards, or anything. These facts made that evening the beginning of something that proved quite remarkable. Her empty hands brought a smile to Deakie Boy's face because he knew the day's end was a beginning, even if everyone else thought it was a day like any other day on the Head.

Deakie Boy played dominoes that evening. He did so to keep himself from following Pretty Black. He did not care whether he won or lost, but when all the shit talking was done, he was three dollars richer. More important, his view of the road maps in his brain were clearer, the pathways more defined. Now it had mileposts marking the timing of his departure from the Head.

Grit under his fingernails usually bothered Deakie Boy, disturbing his sleep as he chewed on his fingers, trying to dislodge it and rubbing his hands to ease the pain of cuts from the sharp cotton bolls. That night, all the more convinced that he was going places, Deakie Boy drifted into an untroubled sleep. The grit and cuts could come along for the ride.

———

Several weeks passed and October showed itself. The crop had been good, and some folks had managed to save enough to think about heading home, back to points south from which they had come west. Maybe they would even make it as far as visits with relatives in Oklahoma, Texas, or with those all the way down in Lu'zana. They had hopes; the cotton was high, the prices good, and the row boss had been fair. They had made the year and thought they might survive to see another one. That was how everyone, except Deakie Boy and Pretty Black, was thinking.

The second weekend after that fall day when Pretty Black had first sneaked away across the field, the man everyone called Suspenders was found in one of the irrigation ditches behind the houses. He had been stabbed through the back of the neck, three times. His body had bloodied the irrigation water, but the crops still used it and the tadpoles did not seem to care that for a short time they swam in blood. Each day there were new frogs.

The ambulance that came for Suspenders's body provided a moment of excitement for the children on the Head. The killing had made the adults nervous, but their nerves stretched tighter, pulling at their loose character, as the sheriff's department sent men to investigate the crime. They asked a lot of indifferent questions. To folks on the Head questions were like peeping with a mouth instead of eyes. In their khaki and brown uniforms, for several days the men were like a thick, wet khaki blanket spread all over everyone's good times and hopes. They shoved the Head's men around, calling them names too dirty to print. They spat a lot of tobacco juice on good compacted ground, made smooth by the women who swept it daily, trying to make it act like concrete. For the officers, their actions were like aspirins, meant to rid themselves of a headache. For the folks on the Head they were like a bad meal, giving them heartburn.

One afternoon, a few weeks after they first visited the Camp, the officers returned and took away Mae Jo Taylor, leaving behind a rumor that she had stabbed Suspenders to death over an unpaid debt. Nobody bought it. Even those with only loose change for brains knew better than to cash in on that one, knowing as they did that Mae Jo never made enough money to have any to loan. Fat as a hog at killing time, she could not pull much cotton, and given her love of food, at weigh-in time, all her earnings moved right pass her outstretched hands into those of the company store owner, to whom she was always in debt. They also knew that even Ole Hog Butt, the name most folks called Mae Jo when they weren't calling to her, was not big enough fool to loan Suspenders a tick off a dead dog. The old bachelor, a bag of bone that would have blown away with the first big wind except for being anchored by extra-large feet, ate little because his mouth was full of giveme after spending his earnings on drinking and whoring. Still, the khaki blanket had its woman, and the Head was left with its rising fears because Suspenders *was* dead. *Someone* had killed him. They talked the matter to death, trying to settle on another suspect before finally shutting up to conserve their energy, as their fears dictated, to try and grow eyes in the backs of their heads.

Deakie Boy also talked loud and long only to hush his mouth when others clamped theirs shut. He did not need rear eyes; like the rest of him, his eyes were different and focused on what Suspenders's death contributed to his plans. Each night, his eyes followed Pretty Black's moves. If the people of the Head had been paying attention, the way they should have been, they would have noticed Deakie Boy's eyes. They would have thought more carefully about how it was his eyes more than his mouth that made his otherwise pretty face scary.

---

Waddie Mack, Pickle, and Dodo Poo came to the Camp together that year in a 1950 Ford pickup, fifteen years or so beyond its prime and hard used in the years before Waddie won it in a poker game. They left the Head three days after Suspenders was killed, traveling to nearby Florence in the hope of hanging there for a little bit, maybe picking up some yard work, then going on to Phoenix, and maybe down to Tucson. As it turned out, they did not go nearly far enough.

Like the other young Head men, working at rapidly shedding their boyhood, they took to hanging around Donnie's Down Home Bar, just outside of Florence, when they had no yard work and still had a few dollars to spend on bad whiskey and good Tokay Rose. The three had scraped up money before leaving their hometown in Texas, intending to follow Waddie Mack's plan to work the harvest and then settle out of the stream—to quit migrant labor—and start a yard-work business. Camp folks always had a plan for how to settle out, but their plans had a way of settling in over the years to just become parts of a life lived. Maybe if Waddie Mack, Pickle, and Dodo Poo had gone farther faster, their dream too may eventually have become nothing more than a way of settle in. They didn't, and instead their truck and yard-work tools wrote their death warrants.

Deakie Boy was not going to settle out by settling in. For Deakie Boy, it was good that Waddie Mack, Pickle, and Dodo Poo had small plans, because that was why they were hanging out at Donnie's the night in the year of tadpoles when Deakie Boy and Bubba Joe arrived at Donnie's. For anyone who was paying attention, what Deakie and Bubba were up to was not all that hard to figure, even if later it proved too hard for the khaki blanket, so long in the habit of not really trying to figure until thinking no longer counted. By that time Deakie Boy had taught Pretty Black how to make her hole part of his plans. To Deakie Boy, Pretty Black's hole had been there waiting for him and his purpose. To others it was a hole left behind from some agricultural task that was beyond their concerns. For Deakie Boy, holes always needed to be filled, and bodies, to his way of thinking, were as good as any filler. At least that was how Deakie Boy summed up the matter when he explained to Bubba Joe and Pretty Black how the hole would fit into his plans.

━━━━━

Donnie's Down Home Bar was jumping that night, as the sound of mariachi music slid into the rhythm and blues with Dyke and the Blazers praising funky, funky Broadway. The dance floor picked itself up and the night dusted itself off with the caterwauling of Johnny Cash, Charlie Pride, and Waylon Jennings, all moaning well-understood country misery. Clanking pool balls added to the staccato rattle of a dying breed of nickel-and-dime craps hustlers, rattling the bones at one another for lack of richer prey. Women in seductive paints and skimpy dresses joined cowgirls and good ole boys wearing jeans tight enough to strangle thighs and squeeze butts into unnatural contours. Deakie Boy was in his element. Sitting at the bar, tossing back watered-down whiskey and eagle-eyeing the patrons, he waited. He suppressed an ironic smile as the jukebox switched to Wilson Pickett, because he took the lyrics admonishing him to "Wait 'til the Midnight Hour" personally. In point of fact, it was well after 1 a.m. and the last call for rounds had been given when the men Deakie Boy had been unknowingly waiting for came in. They wore the casual look of people out of place, people looking for the pleasures they thought were to be found in out-of-the-way places. Donnie's Down Home Bar was the kind of out-of-the-way joint in which the men expected to find those pleasures. Sighting them, Deakie Boy took it as a solemn responsibility that they should not be disappointed in their quest.

Sliding off the barstool, he walked slowly (no need to rush a good thing) across the room to stand near the two newcomers. If they noticed his move, they gave no indication. Snickering like little boys determined to be bad, they commented to each other about the quality of what they took to be available ass. As Deakie Boy stood listening and planning, Bubba Joe, who also smelled the scent of good fortune and right timing, interrupted his thoughts.

"'Ey man, what's doing?" Bubba had figured the wait was over when he noticed Deakie Boy eyeing the city Marks. For more than a month now they had waited. Bubba was primed for action, any action, but also knew Deakie's script and had learned well the lines of script Deakie had given him as his role in it.

"Wipe the hungry off your mouth, boy," Deakie Boy hissed, just loud enough for Bubba Joe to hear. "You want to give up the dime before we can make the call?" Deakie Boy's anger was contained beneath his usual outer calm. He was determined that Bubba Joe would not spoil what he had waited for all night. Keeping his eyes trained on the Marks, he moved in closer and cleared his throat to get their attention.

"Sey, you boys looking for goods to go?" He thought that sounded about right. The men turned and eyed him, but neither spoke. Unlike himself and Bubba Joe, probably they had not rehearsed their parts in the little drama in which they wanted to participate. So they played it by ear.

"Could be, if the package is wrapped right and tight." The tallest one, gangly, yet reasonably well built, spoke the words, but it was the short, stocky one who nodded with enough energy to provide Deakie Boy the clue he needed to measure the depth of the men's wants. Several nights and several tries the previous month had taught Deakie Boy that not all Marks had wants deep enough for his purposes. Those with shallow needs were satisfied with parking-lot bouts with old birds too tough to need Deakie Boy's pimping intentions. These two were different, looking for tender heifers on the hoof, and because Deakie Boy was different he easily recognized their desire.

Right on time and the way he was supposed to, Bubba Joe piped in, "We right good at packing. Had lot of 'sperince doing that kind of work."

Deakie Boy kept his head slightly down, his eyes now well hooded as he waited for Bubba Joe to deliver his next line from the script.

"If'n ya'll gen'man a step outside, I 'specks we could wrap you a deal or two." He smiled broadly, neoning his face, trying to control his hungry mouth.

Without further words the four left the joint to gather in the parking lot behind it. The smell of raw piss puddles assailed them. Deakie Boy looked down in time to step over a puddled mixture of whiskey and rib sandwich a patron's stomach had decided not to take home. He cursed under his breath at the same time he took it as sign of why he would be moving on.

Bubba Joe, not so lucky, cursed as he looked around for one of the scattered patches of goat burr plants that were the only grass in the otherwise hard-packed dirt surface of the parking lot. He cleaned the mixture from his shoes and, rejoining Deakie Boy and the Marks, noted that Deakie Boy had already delivered his next line. The Marks now knew that for the right price they could attain the kind of packages they wanted. As the men made to get into their small green sports car, Deakie Boy stopped them.

"The road we gon' travel is a mite rough for that baby. Whyn't ya'll leave her here and us'll get you there and back."

Deakie Boy listened to the crickets and frogs across the way in one of the ever-present irrigation ditches. He thought they might be trying to croak in time with the Bobby Blue Bland tune that was dishing up canned blues for the straggling customers who were still holding down bar stools and chalking pool cues in Donnie's. For a moment, as the Marks disagreed on whether to accept the offer of transportation, Deakie Boy saw his own blues coming at him if the Marks made the wrong choice. He neither needed the trouble of trying to get rid of a car nor the loss of time it would take to walk across the field from the road. To get the job done, they would need every moment of darkness before the dawn.

Inside, where it did not count, Deakie Boy was furious, thinking that yet again he might have wasted his time and resources. He had paid an old whore well for a little of the drug she used to put johns to sleep long enough for her to rob them of a supplement to the funds they were willing to pay for her services. Deakie had used it to slip Waddie Mack, Dodo Poo, and Pickle mickies tonight. He had been that certain this was to be the night. Waddie and his sidekicks were sleeping it off on the bar stools back in Donnie's. He would have their truck back in the parking lot by the time they woke up the next morning. Donnie, accustomed to allowing the trio to sleep off their drunks in the bar, would close up and leave them undisturbed. Usually, they slept through the night, leaving the next morning with the door locking automatically behind them, but Deakie, attuned to difference and the difference it made, was taking no chance that this night they might awake and go looking for their truck before he could return it.

Watching the Marks, Deakie Boy held his breath, wanting to just roll the sonzabitches and forget the drama, but he knew that would not get him what he wanted. He held in a scream and he stroked his face to assure himself that, yes, his smile was still in place. The Marks stopped arguing and came back to him; the moment of terror was over.

"How far is the place we are going?" Mark One, as Deakie Boy had named the tall one, asked. He and Bubba Joe had that question covered. The script, as he had written it in his mind, was playing out.

As he was scripted to reply if asked, Bubba Joe answered, "It's justa piece down the road. As the crow flies, we'll be there afore you can get your zipper down." Deakie Boy said nothing. He was moving toward Waddie Mack's old truck. The back of the truck was filled with spades, posthole diggers, and other gardening tools that Waddie and his buddies were storing up for their new venture that now would serve well Deakie Boy's plan. Like the puddled mixture, the availability of Waddie Mack's truck Deakie Boy took as a sign of the necessity and righteousness of his escape plans. He hopped into the truck. He had the key, having lifted it earlier from Waddie, while pretending a drunken slip that resulted in a silly tussling match. He started the engine. It loped to life with the cries and screams characteristic of old engines that once had massive horsepower but were now long past the moment when they should have been put out to pasture. The Marks crawled in on the passenger side, as Bubba Joe scrambled into the back. Deakie Boy backed out slow and careful. Until they were on the highway heading for Arrowhead and the field beyond it, no one said anything. Then one of the Marks, the stocky one, Mark Two in Deakie's mind, spoke.

"This better be great. For the price of a few grunts, we could have copped some pretty good stuff back there." Knowing this was not true, Deakie saw no reason to comment, and instead, he kept his mind on his driving and his future. What the Marks really thought Deakie Boy neither knew nor cared. The script was playing itself out nicely, and, soon, very soon, he would be moving on.

The foursome arrived at the Head, and Deakie Boy slowed to make the turn onto an access road leading into the field. Then he veered off it to cross the cotton field on a path he had walked to determine whether the truck could make it without stalling out or getting stuck. He continued to drive silently as the old Ford bumped and grumbled its way across the ups and downs of the newly cut cotton rows. When they were near the center of the field, Deakie Boy slowed it to a stop and cut the engine. He left the lights on as he told the Marks to get out. The Marks looked nervous. They kept quiet, though they looked as if they wanted to say something, to ask some more questions. Maybe they knew it was too late, although for certain they did not know for what it was too late.

Deakie Boy instructed Bubba Joe, who already was on the ground. "Take them on over, I'll keep the lights on for a little bit until y'all git firm on the path, then I'll follow." Although the instructions were a known part of the script, Bubba Joe nodded and led the two Marks into the cotton field. Through the stubble of the dead plants, at the far boundary of the field, Bubba Joe saw the light coming up from the bottom of the hole. With only the dim truck lights to make a path, the trio moved as steadily as could be expected through the field to the other light that beckoned the Marks to their desired pleasures in an out-of-the-way place.

The Marks struggled to keep pace with Bubba Joe. One of them, the tall Mark, kept cussing under his breath and wondering about the wisdom of being in the middle of a cotton field in Goddamn-Near-Nowhere, Arizona, at such a godforsaken hour. He thought about the fact that he could have been in bed with his wife. The thought was enough to keep him moving forward. He would be back in California, and back in that hell soon enough. Why not have a little fun? So it was a bit weird, all the better for a memory to look back on. These were young boys, he concluded, how dangerous could they be? Likely, he told himself, they also worked with young girls and that would make the trouble worthwhile. Preoccupied with these thoughts, he smiled in the darkness. The smell of his sweat mingled with the acridness of defoliants that had been used on the plants before they were cut, all of which soon, but for only short time, would be masked by the smell of his and his fellow Mark's blood and guts.

When Deakie Boy figured, more than saw, that they were nearing the hole, he shut off the truck lights, and ran sure-footed to join them at the rim of the hole. Moving past, he dropped to his knees and tapped on one of the sheets of corrugated tin that partially covered the hole, which was about eight feet in diameter, the walls formed by a tube of corrugated tin.

Mark One spoke. "What the fuck? You expect me to go into some damn hole in the ground?"

Neither Deakie Boy nor Bubba Joe responded. There was nothing in the script and nothing needed saying. As the Mark's words died, from inside the hole, a stick pushed back the sheet of tin, followed a few second later by the tips of a wooden ladder that was precariously leaned against the side of the hole. Deakie Boy grabbed the ladder and positioned it firmly against the rim. With a grand gesture, he motioned for Mark One to get onto the ladder. The Mark turned his back and craned his neck around as he positioned his foot on the first rung of the ladder. The second Mark started to follow, but Deakie motioned for him to wait. In less than a minute after the Mark's feet were heard hitting the ground of the hole's floor, the trio at the top heard a deep guttural sound, followed by a final bubbling gurgle. Slit throats have their own rhythm.

"Whaat . . . ?" It was the beginning of a question from the second Mark, as the rock Deakie Boy had secreted near the hole for this purpose smashed into the side of his head, making a large gash and rendering him unconscious, dropping him to the ground faster than Deakie Boy could toss the rock aside.

Yelling down into the hole, he asked, "You got that one good, Pretty?"

"Yeah, he is done. Get your ass down here, and I mean now!"

Seeing Bubba Joe staring at Mark Two, whose head was oozing blood onto the ground, Deakie Boy kicked his foot, "Come on, you know what to do," he screamed. Coming out of a near trance, Bubba Joe whirled around and ran, stumbling, toward the truck, where he grabbed a canvas. While riding in the back, he had, as the script required, wrapped into it two spades, a posthole digger, a bag of lime, and two axes. The package, as he had promised, was wrapped right and tight, but it was still hard for a person of his size to rapidly and efficiently move it across the field. There had been no opportunity to practice this move, though Deakie Boy had not been overly worried about it, so Bubba Joe figured his effort and timing were of no real concern. The lime had been Pretty Black's contribution to the script. After all, she said, the hole was her home and she still wanted to be able to live there until she left the Head to go back home. The lime, stolen from the shit-houses on the Camp, where it was stored for use in keeping the smell of the houses tolerable between cleanings, would mask the smell of the rotting corpses, to be buried beneath the floor of her home. The lime, like the hole and the lesson it provided, Pretty and Bubba would soon forget, while Deakie Boy again would find use for all three.

While Pretty Black and Deakie Boy worked, first stripping off Mark One's clothing, then chopping him up at the bottom of the hole with one of the axes and some knives Pretty kept in the "kitchen" of her hole, Bubba Joe got to work at its rim, using the second ax to chunk up Mark Two. His first ax chop had finished the job the rock started. The scene was bloody and more gruesome than either Pretty or Bubba could have imagined if they had bothered to try, which neither of them had done. Deakie Boy, who had conceived the possibility years before while watching a hog killing, had neither the need to imagine nor the interest in being bothered by knowledge.

Bubba Joe cursed at the nausea and the spinning in his head. He struggled to keep his hands steady and get on with the work. At the bottom of the hole, Deakie and Pretty were engaged in their own struggles. The meat and muscle that made up Mark One's body were not so easily cleaved. The bones were hard to break. The head stayed stubbornly connected because the tight space in which they worked did not give them much room for solid ax whacks. Deakie Boy silently promised himself a short-handled hatchet if he were to do this kind of job again in tight space. Despite the difficulty of the task, in little more than an hour they had reduced the Marks to chunks of a size that they could bury by stacking them in the deep hole they had dug, with the spades and posthole digger, in the floor of the hole that was Pretty Black's home. Except for the slap and splatter sounds it made, the work seemed, to Deakie Boy, much like the wood chopping he had done from time to time, though with less enthusiasm than that to which he now applied his skill. To the extent that he needed something to get his Self through the task, Deakie Boy concentrated on the sounds, and neither knew nor cared what assisted Pretty Black and Bubba in getting done what had to be done.

The digging of the hole was made easier and more rapidly completed because each night of the weeks that passed after Deakie Boy had laid his plan, in the floor of her hole Pretty Black worked to dig another hole that when it was finished was to be three feet wide and five feet deep. The hole she worked on was not unlike that the Camp's men dug each Fourth of July for pit barbecuing. Working long into each night, Pretty had made good progress, but still there was a need to deepen the hole so that finally they could use it the way Deakie Boy had taught them it could and should be used to become part of his plan. When the body had been chunked up properly, Deakie sent Pretty Black out of the hole. He called for Bubba Joe to come down with the spades and posthole digger so that they could finish the job Pretty had started. Though the folks on the Head had not noticed, over the weeks she also had moved most of her few worldly goods back to the space Sissy Mae and Joenella shared on the Camp. Even if they had noticed, they would have thought that she, like everyone else, was merely packing up to get ready to leave at the end of the harvest. With her few remaining goods pushed to one wall of her home, the boys made as much space as possible for digging and made short work of finishing the grave at the bottom of the hole, into which they carefully layered the chunks of body. Between coverings formed with the two Marks' clothing, they layered generous quantities of the lime.

At one point, Deakie Boy looked up and saw tears streaming down Bubba Joe's face. The sight angered him enough to stop what he was doing and counsel Bubba.

"You can't let them tears fall, Bubba. If'n you do, they'll be like glue. In your sleep they will put the pieces of these bodies back together and you gon' see them like some great big Frankenstein every time you try to sleep. A body can't function proper in this world without a good night's sleep. Now, you know I'm right. Get holt of yourself." Deakie said these words quietly, lacing them with only enough of a snarl to pull them tightly together, to make the little sense Bubba Joe needed to get through the balance of a well-planned task.

Like smoke pulled by a draft, Bubba Joe's loose character wrapped itself around Deakie Boy's words, making itself comfortable there, slowing and easing the spinning of Bubba Joe's mind. Bubba Joe would have liked to wipe the tears from his face as a sign to let Deakie Boy know how much he understood and appreciated his wisdom, but his hands were a bloody mess, so he stilled them before they could mess up his face. It did not occur to him that the splattering of guts and the bloody back-spray from his ax strokes already had made quite a mess of him, face and all.

Looking onto the scene from the rim of her hole, Pretty Black too listened to Deakie Boy's words and took comfort from them. Still, she was angry over having to share her hole with the likes of Deakie Boy and Bubba Joe. One mistake, she thought, and the whole world of shit comes tumbling down on you. She had not intended to kill Suspenders, she simply did not want to fuck him and she did not want him following her to her hole with that expectation, the way he had done the night before she had killed him. She did not doubt that he would have returned every night, taking her as a free fuck, a chance to save his whoring money for more drink. She had put an end to his plan by putting an end to him.

It was just her luck that Deakie Boy had seen enough that he could give her up to the khaki blanket, making it necessary for her to cut a deal with him for the sake of his goddamn plans. She almost laughed at the ugly, unintended pun, as she looked down at her feet and spied a small piece of stray meat from a chunk of Mark Two. Now she wondered what would become of her, how she would get on with her future plans with Deakie Boy and Bubba Joe entwined in her present, and these buried corpses tainting her past. She would have to think carefully, but for now, she would simply get this job done. Maybe Deakie Boy would keep his word and he and Bubba Joe would settle out by moving on. Maybe, she knew, was one of the longest damn words in the English language—two feet longer than a useful *if* and a yard beyond the length of a reasonable *hope*.

With Bubba Joe controlling himself and working steadily, he and Deakie were soon setting about the task of covering the last of the lime by refilling the hole with the dug-out dirt. They smoothed and patted the surface with the spades. They carefully spread dirt at the rim of the hole to absorb the puddles and splatterings of blood there. Pretty Black covered the newly compacted earth with the horse blanket she had been using for a rug. On top of that she placed, end to end, the two tomato crates she had acquired for use as a coffee table. Deakie and Bubba helped her put the rest of her meager goods back into place. It would do for the brief time she had left to call the hole home.

Pretty was insistent that they not stop the work until she was satisfied with the cleanliness of the interior of her hole. Deakie Boy was compliant because he knew she was within her rights. It was her home, and it wasn't right to fuck around with someone's home. He smiled to himself as he worked, thinking that Pretty was an all right gal, and he told himself that he would not have threatened to dime her out on Suspenders's death if she had not had something he needed. Suspenders, just another loose character, an old bachelor, was nothing to him. No one was anything to Deakie Boy, and he was not inclined to think about who might be something to someone else.

Day was breaking when Deakie Boy and Bubba Joe returned Waddie Mack's truck to the parking lot behind Donnie's. Deakie left the keys in the ignition. He knew Waddie Mack would simply kick himself and tell everyone that he had been a dumb enough ass to leave his keys in his truck. Everyone would laugh, and some would probably joke about how nobody with any self-respect would be caught dead stealing the likes of Waddie Mack's truck. Deakie Boy smiled and the nervousness he had held in around what to do with the keys eased back. There was no problem there.

He and Bubba Joe both looked at the little sports car, waiting for owners who would never return. They felt bad about that. They thought for a minute of taking it. They even walked around it, making note of the California tag. In the end, they decided taking it would not be a good move because neither of them had a driver's license.

Finally, Bubba Joe broke the passenger side window and eased open the door. Deakie took over, rapidly but thoroughly searching through the glove compartment. He smiled when he discovered two wallets. These explained why they had found only a total of two hundred and ten dollars in the two Marks' pockets. The wallets contained far more—a bit over five hundred dollars combined. Deakie removed the cash and replaced the wallets. He had offered to split thirds with Bubba and Pretty, but she refused. She had told him her debt was paid and she wanted nothing more than to get to her bed, knowing that she had seen the last of him and Bubba Joe. Deakie Boy would have settled for a third of what they took off the bodies. Any grub stake was better than none, but more important than size of the initial grub stake gained was getting his plans under way. Money would always come to those who showed the Fates that they had the courage to follow the convictions of well-made plans.

═══

After Deakie Boy and Bubba Joe split the money from the Mark's pockets and wallets, they shook hands and headed off in opposite directions along the highway leading away from the Head. Each was thinking to hitch a ride to the beginning of a new life. Neither minded that probably it would be several hours before there was enough traffic to give any hope of copping a lift. Each had washed carefully in the irrigation ditches before returning the truck, but neither was foolish enough to think that the smell of blood and raw human flesh did not still cling. Both counted on the fact that the intense morning sun, for which Arizona was justly famous, would dull the odor as it dried their skin and the fresh clothes they donned. Deakie Boy patted the satchel he carried, which contained his blood-splattered garments. Like dirt that he was unable to remove from beneath his nails, for a while they too would come along for the journey.

Neither the path that Bubba Joe would take, nor the fact that Pretty Black would remain for awhile on the Head, bothered Deakie Boy. Unlike Pretty and Bubba, he had sufficient imagination to count on the khaki blanket to take care of the small details of any evidence left behind, in the same way it had solved Suspenders's murder. When first he had dared to dream, the events of that night in the year of the tadpoles had not been part of his dream. Now, as he walked away down the road from the Head, he could only shake his head and broaden his smile as he thought about how limited his imagination once had been. That night's events had opened in his mind new vistas, bright sparkling vistas. Deakie Boy wondered, but only briefly, if ever again his path would cross those of Pretty Black and Bubba Joe.

He felt better than he had any day since age nine, when both his parents had died in a car crash and he began to drift with migrant laborers. Now, at thirteen, Deakie Boy knew he was different. He was free. He had over three hundred dollars in his pocket, but it was not the money that gave him freedom. No, he knew it was his willingness to follow a well-made plan that was destined to take him to places beyond the cycle of migrant time.

Deakie Boy lifted his forearm to his nose, taking in the smell of the moss- and tadpole-laced irrigation water in which he had washed. The odor was mixed with the coppery smell of fresh blood. He smelled as well of the faint scent of frog piss—or was it frog sex? He smiled. The distinction was beside the point. What mattered was that there was no smell of Tokay Rose. When the odor returned, and Deakie Boy did not doubt that it would, it would be the sign. The sign that would foretell the next step in his plans, pointing out for him those loose-character folks that he would use or remove to get to the next milepost on the road map of places he was fated to visit. As a teacher had once told him it was written, he was going places that could be visited only by those who heard and stepped to the measure of a different drummer. Deakie Boy heard a tune playing in his head and mouthed the lyrics he thought accompanied it: "Zippity do-da, zippity yeah, fun, fun, fun, what a wonderful day!"

———————

[In the decades to follow, chronicled in the forthcoming novel from which this story is excerpted, Deakie Boy and his coconspirators would rampage across the Southwest, amassing fortunes and producing a generation destined to discover the legacies that had made possible their families' wealth. Their discoveries would set off a scramble to hold on to their ill-gotten gains while avoiding the consequences of a history of other hideous deeds that linked their parents' killings on the Head to intersecting ancestral trails of murderous enterprises stretching back to slavery and across to contemporary Africa.]

**Text by Amiri Baraka**
**Collages by Theodore A. Harris**

Our Flesh of Flames

The *South Atlantic Quarterly* 104:3, Summer 2005.
Copyright © 2005 by Duke University Press.

Dis is THE CAPITAL of HELL

H. Box Brown
 Was how I found
 Out this mammy jamma
 Was upside down.

Like H. Rap later
 Box had to split
  From the subjugator
      & they slavery shit

God called Box
Allah called Rap

Told both of them
      To get they hat

"Yall cant be around
 this slave—master rat

              "Hate Good     Love Evil
              Think They God     When They the Devil!"

That's why
      Everything
            Turned around!

They got the whole
      World
      Upside
      Down!
            FREE MUMIA!

Remember Eric Smith (1999)

What street is this?
What this is that?
Oh greed is not just a cry
It leaved him to fly

The Beast name 666
Rules the world
With Billion Karats
A Billion sticks

But if you see
& ask the question
Elegba
Put you on
The
Good
Foot

You got Brother Malcolm's
Multiplying history
Like the river you cross
Is signed
With a kiss

(to celebrate
the Death
of Dis!)

Meditations for Betty Shabazz (1998)

THAT'S NOT HITLER!

The American Word
For *Nazi*
Is *American*!

Our Bones Have Numbers on Them (2000)

Theodore A. Harris

Hunted Everywhere: Collaging the Capitol,
a Manifesto

*This was the house of liberty, and it had been built by
slaves. Their backs had ached under its massive stones.
Their lungs had clogged with its mortar dust. Their bodies
had wilted under its heavy load-bearing timbers. They had
been paid only in the coin of pain. Slavery lay across
American history like a monstrous cleaving sword, but the
Capitol of the United States steadfastly refused to divulge
its complicity, or even slavery's very occurrence.*
—Randall Robinson, *The Debt: What America Owes to
Blacks*

I'll begin by discussing my use of one of the
symbols of our republic, the United States Capitol Building, and the effect poetry has had on my
work. When people ask me why I turn the image
of the U.S. Capitol Building upside down in my
collages, as if it were a bomb, my short answer is:
"It's upside down because they're upside down."
As an example of this upside-downness, I can
easily point to the 2000 presidential election
of George W. Bush by the Supreme Court and
NOT THE PEOPLE! (I can't think of anything more
upside down than that.) But before I could make
these kinds of statements in my work, there
were visual artists such as Charles White, Diego
Rivera, Howardena Pindell, John Abner, Melvin
Edwards, Picasso, Romare Bearden, Elizabeth

The *South Atlantic Quarterly* 104:3, Summer 2005.
Copyright © 2005 by Duke University Press.

Catlett, John Heartfield, Leroy Johnson, Reginald Gammon, Charles Al-
ston, Vincent Smith, Hans Haacke, Juan Sanchez, Leon Golub, Pat Ward
Williams, Jacob Lawrence, and Adrian Piper and writers such as Sonia Sanchez, Lamont B. Steptoe, James Baldwin, Gwendolyn Brooks, Audre Lorde,
Comrade Askia M. Toure, Amiri Baraka, Pablo Neruda, Ernesto Carde-
nal, Haki Madhubuti, Frank Chipasula, Dennis Brutus, and David Diop.
Through their work, these artists taught me how to use metaphor and content in a powerful way, enabling the viewer to go beyond the surface and
look deeper.

Diop, a poet writing in the time of the Negritude literary revolution, wrote
in a stanza from his poem "For a Black Child":

> In the land where houses touch the sky
> But the heart is not touched
> In the land where hands are laid on the Bible
> But the Bible is not opened.[1]

Sounds like he's dis-scribing the Religious Right, but Diop wrote these
clear-visioned words in response to the lynching of fifteen-year-old Emmett
Till, who was killed in Money, Mississippi, in 1955 by two white men—Roy
Bryant and his stepbrother, J. W. Milam—for wolf whistling at Bryant's wife.
Neither murderer ever served a day in jail for the crime.

Professor Clenora Hudson-Weems has written a detailed account of the
Till case in *Emmett Till, the Sacrificial Lamb of the Civil Rights Movement*.
While reading the book, I came across a photograph that is what I'd call the
perfect picture of irony. It is of Mamie Bradley, Till's mother, with relatives
and a bishop climbing the steps of the Capitol Building, pointing at it, with
looks of hope on their faces.

These seekers of justice and democracy must not have known that America still has not outlawed lynching! My point is that most great artists, such
as David Diop, record the time in which they live, and I aim to do this with
visual art, to make social commentary in a visual language.

Whenever I'm watching the news on television being reported from the
nation's capital, the reporter and the U.S. Capitol Building are consistently
in the frame, as a backdrop, set design, in the theater of white supremacy
(and conquest). As I watch, I hear the words from a Sonia Sanchez poem
titled "right on: white America":

> this country might have
> been a pio

neer land
once.
  But.    there ain't
no mo
     indians       blowing
custer's mind
      with a different
image of america.
            this country
might have
        needed shoot
outs/ daily/
     once.
        but. there ain't
no mo real/ white/    allamerican
          bad/ guys.
just.
  u & me.
       blk/ and un/ armed.
this country might have
been pion
      eer land.   once.
           and it still is.
Check out
     the falling
gun/ shells     on our blk/ tomorrows.[2]

After reading this consciousness-raising poem, I felt as if I was being hunted everywhere. I had to check out my surroundings: where was I being hunted, why was I being hunted, for how long? What I found out early on was that our blood is the mortar, and the bricks of our black and red bones built this country's capitol and its capital.

From then on, I knew I had to strike back with the only weapon I have— art. With my pen or scissors I would avenge the senseless deaths of my ancestors, I would indict America in the courtroom of my own opinion, HERE IN THESE UNITED-AGAINST-US STATES WHERE INTERROGATION ROOMS NEVER CLOSE, POLICE AT THE MT. CALVARY CORRECTIONAL FACILITY PUT SILENC-ERS ON CRUCIFIXION NAILS, BEAT US INTO INTERSTELLAR SPACE WITH WET TELE-

PHONE BOOKS, GIVE RECTAL EXAMINATIONS WITH TOILET PLUNGERS IN THEIR
PRECINCT BATHROOMS!

When I look at the history of this country and our involvement in it as
African Americans, I see us always struggling to get out from under the
slave ships, the whips, the chains, the prisons, the nightsticks, the Patriot
Act police, and Campus Watch, which aid in "the nazification of America,"
according to Toni Morrison,[3] by detaining independent thinkers in jails
of character assassination, rulers with bombs and bullets of imperialism
aimed at unarmed protesters fire-hosed with the slobber of barking dogs!
It is because of this I became a confrontational collagist, engaged in visual
warfare, decolonizing the mind through collage. For my question is, who
is going to fight in the visual arts or literature against the mayor-gargoyle
Giulianis of the world, who have made it clear that our vetoed dreams don't
count? As Amiri Baraka said: "Every day what becomes clearer and clearer
is the desperation of this system. The United States bourgeoisie reminds
me of a man running away from a lion, who keeps throwing out pieces of
meat until finally his little bag is empty and the only piece of meat left is
himself."[4] Or, in the words of Ngugi Wa Thiongo: "Art is more powerful
when working as an ally of the powerless than it is when allied to repression. For its essential nature is freedom. While that of the state is restriction
and regulation of freedom."[5] Both points are further illustrated in the April
2003 issue of *Harper's Magazine*, which reported, "On January 27, 2003, a
tapestry of Pablo Picasso's epic painting Guernica that hangs at the entrance
of the Security Council of the United Nations in New York City was deemed
an inappropriate background for press briefings about the possibility of a
war in Iraq. It was therefore draped." These actions by the state only confirm to me that I'm aiming my combative collages in the right direction. I
now see my work functioning as visual poetic essays.

When folks view my work, I want them to come away with the strength
to keep on, holding on to these fraying ropes of struggle. I hope that what
I'm creating is purposeful for people to use in this racial and class struggle,
as a weapon in this fight Lamont Steptoe labels a "low-intensity war" (personal communication with author) in which we battle every day for our
lives and the lives of our children, living under a government of dangerous
philistines. In my most recent work, to further articulate how America is
imploding on itself, I have inverted the Pentagon building, turning it into
a wounded guillotine.

For my aim as an artist is to reflect the reality of our lives, the exiled from exile.

## Notes

1 David Mandessi Diop, "For a Black Child," in *Hammerblows and Other Writings*, ed./trans. Simon Mpondo and Frank Jones (Bloomington: Indiana University Press, 1973).

2 Sonia Sanchez, "right on: white america," in *The Poetry of Black America, Anthology of the Twentieth Century*, ed. Arnold Adoff (New York: HarperCollins, 1973). Reprinted by permission of Sonia Sanchez.

3 Toni Morrison quoted by Amiri Baraka, lecture at Haverford College, Spring 2002.

4 From Charlie Reilly, ed., *Conversations with Amiri Baraka* (Jackson: University Press of Mississippi, 1994).

5 Ngugi Wa Thiongo, *Penpoints, Gunpoints, and Dreams: Toward a Critical Theory of the Arts and the State in Africa* (New York: Oxford University Press, 1993).

2 a.m. Sept. 11 (2001)

Appeal to the Secretary of the Lower Intestine (2003)

On the Throne of Fire after "Somebody Blew Up America" (for Amiri Baraka) (2003)

Police .45 666 Shooter (2004)

The Pentagon Is a Wounded Guillotine (2004)

They Put Silencers on Crucifixion Nails in the Theatre of Conquest
(for Paul C. Harrison) (2004)

Tess Chakkalakal

"Making a Collection": James Weldon Johnson
and the Mission of African American Literature

### Anthology Theory

In the preface to the second edition of the
*Norton Anthology of African-American Literature,*
the general editors—Henry Louis Gates Jr. and
Nellie McKay—come out as "un-theoretical."[1]
Although several of the anthology's eleven editors were still engaged with theory during the
mid-1980s, they explain that the process of actually editing the anthology helped them to realize theory's irrelevance. Their position against
theory pits their project against the established
realm of literary studies: "We were embark-
ing upon a process of canon formation," they
acknowledge, "precisely when many of our poststructuralist colleagues were questioning the
value of the canon itself" (xxx).

Of course, it quickly becomes apparent that
theory does inform the formation of the anthology. To simply put various texts written in
different times, spaces, and genres together in a
single book would not demonstrate the connections between them; it would not satisfactorily
constitute African American literature. And that
is the project. For the editors view the construction rather than the deconstruction of a literary

The *South Atlantic Quarterly* 104:3, Summer 2005.
Copyright © 2005 by Duke University Press.

canon as "essential for the permanent institutionalization of the black literary tradition within departments of English, American Studies, and African American Studies" (xxix).

This essay is an attempt to illuminate this claim by the editors of the *Norton* not by analyzing the texts that the editors select for inclusion, but by considering both the impulse to collect various literary texts to form a single entity called "African American literature" and its impact on our understanding of literature as such. I will thus compare the claims of the *Norton Anthology of African-American Literature* with the structure and process by which the first African American literary anthology was brought out by James Weldon Johnson in 1922. While the differences between these two anthologies are certainly significant, both make claims for the anthology as satisfying a growing interest in African Americans themselves. What interests me here is the relationship between literature and African Americans both anthologies maintain.

In their anthology, Gates and McKay are advocating a tradition (and specifically a literary tradition) that should be taught and studied. They see "broader access" to African American literature as a sign that African Americans are full and equal members of American democratic institutions—and are afforded all the rights and privileges that go along with such membership. American democracy, in this literary formulation, is not simply a form of government and the process of choosing political leaders; it also, as the line I just quoted demonstrates, recognizes the representation of African American literature as part of college and university curriculums. As the editors suggest, the scores of African American literary anthologies produced before the *Norton* were also interested in canon formation, but few make the case that the African American literary anthology is a vital component of American democracy. Johnson's anthology, however, does make the same case. There he argues that the recognition of an African American literary tradition will end racism in the United States and allow all Americans to enjoy the rights of living in a democratic nation. By examining the striking similarities in the purpose behind Johnson's anthology and that of the recent *Norton*, I hope to suggest some of the ways in which the African American literary anthology understands itself as standing in for the voice of African Americans—a voice that has essentially been stifled. Before turning to my discussion of Johnson's anthology, and its connection to the *Norton*, I will pursue further the *Norton*'s claims for "institutionalization."

The overwhelming popularity of the *Norton Anthology of African-American Literature* has helped to highlight the importance of the anthology to our general understanding of African American literature. The editors insist that "its sheer scope and inclusiveness enable readers to trace the repetitions, tropes, and signifying that define the tradition" (xlv). And readers seem to value what the *Norton Anthology* offers. This anthology, as the editors explain, has had a far greater and wider appeal to consumers of literature than previous anthologies with similar objectives: "To our surprise, the anthology was widely reviewed in both trade and academic publications. . . . Within the academy, 1,275 colleges and universities worldwide have adopted the anthology since publication in 1997" (xxx).

The use of the anthology in so many classrooms "worldwide" is, at least in part, a result of the favorable reviews it has received. Manning Marable, an editor of another recent African American anthology, writes that "by any standard, it is a remarkable work of scholarly endeavor and cooperation."[2] Indeed, the *Norton* is distinct from other anthologies because it is, Marable says, "the most comprehensive." This mark of distinction, among others, leads Theodore O. Mason to claim that "more so than any predecessor, this anthology stands as a communal statement about the intellectual and cultural foundations of African American writing."[3] What is the nature of that statement and, more to the point, what does such an anthology say about African American writing? Unlike previous anthologies of African American literature, this one derives much of its significance from being the most inclusive. Indeed, the second edition is considerably larger than the first; it has added a number of new selections by authors included in the first edition and introduces several "new voices." Some of these are from the distant past, while others are contemporary. The point of the expansions and additions is to maintain the anthology's commitment to inclusion.

There is nothing wrong with the commitment to collecting texts for the purpose of making them more accessible for students of African American literature or profiting from such a literary venture. Yet that rationale for anthologizing would shift the significance of the works included to the *idea* of the anthology itself. The editors' commitment to the project of inclusion is linked to a belief in what they believe literature can do for the role African Americans play in American democracy.

As Mason points out, and as is clear to all those familiar with Gates's earlier work, the idea for the *Norton* is "inspired profoundly by Gates's work in *The Signifying Monkey: A Theory of Afro-American Literary Criticism* (1988) and *Figures in Black: Words, Signs, and the Racial Self* (1987)."[4] Gates's earlier theoretical ventures (rather than that of his coeditors) can be seen as providing a ground for the collaborative task of editing an anthology. Gates's status as both a maker and disseminator of African American literature provides the link between the multiple editors and the literary works they choose for inclusion. Gates's theory insists on a relationship between authors and texts that arises not from similarities between them but rather from the differences or revisions that each text is seen as exhibiting. In this theory of African American literature, the substantial differences between the writing of, say, Toni Morrison and Frederick Douglass are precisely what connects them. While Morrison and Douglass write during different times and in different forms, their work, when read within the context of the same book, reveals a certain thematic continuity that qualifies them for participation in the anthology—and, ultimately, in the community of African American writers and readers.

Most of Gates's work has helped to clarify the formal properties of African American literature through close readings of individual texts. What Gates found through his investigation of writings by people of African descent was the repetition of a number of tropes and narrative conventions that formed the basic structure for a separate literary tradition. With its roots in the Fon and Yoruba cultures of Benin and Nigeria, the African American literary tradition was created and expanded with a singular purpose: "To demonstrate that persons of African descent possessed the requisite degrees of reason and wit to create literature, that they were, indeed, full and equal members of the community of rational, sentient beings, that they could, indeed, write" (xxxviii). The *Norton Anthology* provides the evidence that substantiates Gates's claim.

The *Norton*, however, also does more than simply prove that men and women who can trace their genealogy back to Africa possess the requisite degrees of reason to create a lasting and meaningful literature. It claims that the works found within this anthology count as "literature" that will prove essential to furthering the democratic goals of the institutions that adopt it as such. Few have been as successful as Gates in giving African American literature such a vital purpose. Perhaps only James Weldon Johnson in his 1912 novel *The Autobiography of an Ex-Coloured Man* and in his prefaces to his own anthologies, *The Book of American Negro Poetry* and *The Books of American Negro Spirituals*, makes as persuasive a case for using a literary anthology to widen the borders of American democratic institutions to include African Americans.

In the early twentieth century, however, the task of "institutionalizing" African American literature confronted a different set of challenges. Rather than questions concerning the inclusion of African American literature in various college departments, questions concerning the form and function of American democracy dominated the literary scene in the early twentieth century. It was in this environment that Johnson started to write fiction and poetry. By the time he wrote his preface to *The Book of American Negro Poetry*, American literary anthologies were standard fare. But his anthology claimed to do something that other such anthologies did not do, for his "has a direct bearing on the most vital of American problems."[5] Johnson's *Book of American Negro Poetry* sets out to complete the task his protagonist in *The Autobiography of an Ex-Coloured Man* abandoned in order to pass for white. I want to suggest here that collecting individual texts to produce a single, collective body of African American literature is an important but neglected feature of Johnson's fiction and broader racial project that has come to shape our notion of African American literature today. The emphasis, however, on the passing plot of the *Autobiography* has left other aspects of the novel and Johnson's anthologies virtually unexamined. Johnson's anthologies, produced in the 1920s, still stand as a milestone in the making of an African American literary tradition; the form and critical apparatus of his anthologies have a direct bearing on the most recent African American literary anthology. Anthologizing African American writing, seen today as a necessary and standard literary practice, was still a novel idea when Johnson, with the help of his literary editor, J. E. Spingarn, decided to produce one.

Completed in 1922, *The Book of American Negro Poetry* stands as the first anthology of African American literature. Although nowhere near as comprehensive as the recent *Norton*, Johnson's work's lengthy preface, its selections, and its terms of classification tell us a great deal about the African American anthology form that, for the first time in literary history, has achieved the recognition of the English and American anthologies. By analyzing the way the first African American literary anthology was produced and the collective effort behind this singular achievement, this essay argues that a central objective of producing an African American literary anthology is to make African Americans essential to furthering the project of American democracy.

Such an objective differs somewhat from the standard definition of the anthology form. In her study of British anthologies produced during the eighteenth century, Barbara Benedict draws upon the etymology of the term. The Greek term *anthology* refers to a collection of flowers, not litera- ture. When it is used to refer to literature, however, Benedict finds that the term describes choice and distinction as well as unity of contents.[6] Anders Olsson, in his recent study *The Anthologization of "American Literature,"* develops Benedict's analysis, suggesting that texts selected to be included in an anthology "are decontextualized to become recontextualized."[7] Bene- dict's focus on British anthologies and Olsson's on American anthologies help us to understand the national character of the literary anthology form, but neither author mentions the racial content of the enterprise. Johnson's project to collect poems and songs by different authors written at different times under the rubric "Negro American" brings a distinctly racial element to the anthology form, the consequences of which I begin here to theorize.

## A Novel Anthology

Considered primarily a book about passing, Johnson's novel *The Autobiog- raphy of an Ex-Coloured Man* is informed by a theory of literature clarified in his preface to *The Book of American Negro Poetry*, published a decade later. In the *Autobiography*, Johnson introduced to readers a protagonist who fails to fulfill his racial mission after witnessing the lynching of a black man in the South. This event shifts the course of the story and brings it to an abrupt end. Before this event, the protagonist had committed himself to collect- ing and reproducing "themes and melodies . . . trying to catch the spirit of the Negro in his relatively primitive state" so that "Negroes themselves" and others might value the "heritage of the American Negro."[8] The novel ends with the project incomplete, as the protagonist is unable to overcome the "shame" of belonging "to a race that could be so dealt with; and shame for my country, that it, the great example of democracy to the world, should be the only civilized, if not the only state on earth, where a human being would be burned alive" (187–88). The flagrant disregard for black men and women living in the United States contradicts the democratic principles that the nation claims to stand for. Until this condition is remedied, the protagonist suggests, the idea of American democracy cannot be realized.

The protagonist's inability to fulfill his mission despite the shame he feels is, for recent readers, a sign of his moral failure.[9] Such an understanding of the novel affirms what we already know about its unnamed protagonist: he lacks character. But it is also the case, as Kenneth Warren has more recently argued in his provocative discussion of Ralph Ellison, that "Johnson's novel reveals itself as a text that was written only because the quest to create a text of 'classic' expression had to be abandoned along the way."[10] Although the project to create a text of classic expression is abandoned in the *Autobiography*, as Warren suggests, Johnson would return to his fictional protagonist's project, taking on the burden of completing the work of collecting "Negro themes and melodies" himself.

Johnson would later disavow any autobiographical connection between his own life and that of his unfortunate protagonist. In 1927, with the help of Carl Van Vechten, he brought out a new edition of the book. The new edition included the name of the novelist, although the protagonist remained unnamed. Van Vechten explained the disjunction between the novelist and protagonist in his introduction to the second edition, a fact not difficult to recognize since Johnson was well known for leading a high-profile campaign against lynching as secretary of the National Association for the Advancement of Colored People. Although Johnson would again disavow any connection between his life and the ex-colored man's in his own autobiography, *Along This Way* (1933), he does explain how aspects of his fiction were crucial to introducing African American literature to those who had not yet been touched by it. The unknown "authorship of the book excited the curiosity of literate colored people, and there was speculation among them as to who the writer might be."[11] The "literate colored people" who expressed interest in the *Autobiography*, however, are the same as "the educated classes" who Johnson's protagonist points out "are rather ashamed of" the "old slave songs" (143). By collecting these old slave songs in the form of a book, Johnson asserted that they merited pride rather than shame.

Johnson's protagonist turns to collecting original songs and lyrics of former slaves and their descendants while touring Europe with his patron, known throughout the novel only as "the millionaire." The protagonist's tour of Europe ends in Berlin, where he witnesses a friend of the millionaire's reverse the musical process that he had mastered: "This man had taken ragtime and made it a classic" (142). As a result, the protagonist feels "stirred by an unselfish desire to voice all the joys and sorrows, the hopes and ambitions, of the American Negro, in classical music form" (147). This desire is "unselfish" in the protagonist's terms, because documenting the hopes and ambitions of the American Negro to create a single classic text will "help those I considered my people." The conversation between the ex-colored man and the millionaire raises key issues over the function of literature in national life that Johnson, at the time of writing the *Autobiography*, had become increasingly interested in through his own conversations with his literary mentor, Brander Matthews. Johnson met Matthews in 1902 when he moved to New York from Jacksonville to pursue, with his brother Rosamond and their partner Bob Cole, a successful career as a lyricist for a number of popular musicals. But Johnson soon found his interests diverging from the stage to the page, which is how he and Matthews became friends.

In outlining his genealogy in his autobiography, *These Many Years*, Matthews presents himself as the son of the millionaire Edward Matthews, who had made and lost his fortune trading and speculating.[12] Lawrence Oliver, a recent critic of Matthews's life and works, traces Matthews's intellectual journey from "Professional Millionaire" to "Literary Fellow" in his book *Brander Matthews, Theodore Roosevelt, and the Politics of American Literature, 1880–1920*.[13] In it, he "aims to restore Matthews to his rightful place in American literary and, more broadly, cultural history" (xv). Matthews occupies a singular place in Johnson's literary career that is tied to the contentious position he occupies in American literary history.[14]

Johnson makes only a brief appearance in Oliver's account of Matthews. But Oliver's account of the relationship between Matthews and Johnson is the most detailed one. Oliver suggests that Johnson "sought out Matthews, whose writings on the drama had attracted his attention" (52). But Johnson was interested in more than just Matthews's writings on drama; he also admired the convergence between literature and politics that Matthews forged through his life and work.

Well-known for his crusade to protect American authors through his founding of and membership in a number of organizations including the American Copyright League and the Modern Language Association, Matthews also led a political crusade to increase literacy in the United States by simplifying spelling. Such political crusades were always connected to his literary pursuits, which ranged from writing plays, novels, and short stories to criticism on a variety of topics both literary and political. The warm reception Johnson describes Matthews as giving him indicates the extent of his respect for him and a certain affinity between the two men that came as something of a surprise to Johnson, who had grown accustomed to the separation of people from different social and cultural groups. When he decided to go up to Columbia University to talk with Matthews about enrolling in his courses, Johnson was flattered to find

> that Professor Matthews knew of my work in musical comedy, a phase of the theater that he followed and studied closely. My reception was extremely cordial. As soon as the greetings were over and I had taken a seat, he produced his cigarette case and offered me a smoke. For the life of me, I could not prevent the inculcated inhibitions of my years at Atlanta University from rushing out in full force upon me. I accepted the cigarette and smoked it, but it was difficult for me not to feel that I was breaking school rules. Of course, I had smoked constantly since my graduation from Atlanta, but to be smoking with a professor in his office on the university grounds struck me for the time as being not only incongruous but slightly unholy.[15]

Johnson may have been particularly surprised by the camaraderie Matthews exhibited toward him because of the latter's exalted status as professor of dramatic literature at Columbia University and as America's foremost literary critic. Matthews counted Theodore Roosevelt, Mark Twain, and William Howells among his closest friends, yet Johnson found this highbrow intellectual easier to talk with than many of the black intellectuals he encountered while a student at Atlanta University in the 1890s. Matthews, in offering Johnson a cigarette and talking with him about his work in the theater, allowed him to become, almost immediately, one of the "old boys."

This encounter, as Johnson goes on to explain, "was the beginning of a warm and lasting friendship between Brander Matthews and me. He talked to me a great deal about the musical comedy stage and the important people connected with it." Matthews, not unlike the role the millionaire plays for Johnson's protagonist, introduces Johnson to a whole new world, the result of which is the beginning of his literary career. Aside from Oliver's discussion of Johnson's association with Matthews, none of Johnson's readers have seriously engaged how the friendship between the two may have influenced the course of African American literature. This is due, in part, to the diminished role Matthews has come to play in the history of American literature. Strongly associated with the "genteel tradition" of American literary criticism, Matthews fell out of favor with the literary establishment before his death in 1929. But for Johnson he remained one of the greatest teachers he had ever encountered and pivotal to his move away from writing lyrics for show tunes and toward a life dedicated to broadening the scope of American literature. For this reason it is pertinent to sketch Matthews's views on literary matters, particularly those related to the definition of American literature that led Johnson to enroll in his courses.

In his answer to the question "What is American literature?" Matthews dwells upon the French writers who, unlike English writers, have not discriminated against authors on the basis of "nativity or citizenship . . . or of any political separation which may have taken place between the several peoples who possess that language in common."[16] The separation between American and English literature, however, is based on the fact that "certain American poets and certain American prosemasters are important to us Americans, even if we are well aware that they may be less important to our kin across the sea" (73). While Americans of today, according to Matthews, "are still English . . . they are in no wise British"—a distinction that the editors of the *Norton Anthology* extend to their definition of African American literature. To substantiate this principle, Matthews returns to the history of French literature which, to his mind, has managed to evaluate the literary merits of texts written in that language most fairly. Quoting favorably a line from Ferdinand Brunetière's history of French literature, Matthews puts forward a principle of literary value that departs from "the universal and permanent standards": "Every race is the judge—and must be the only judge—of its own poets" (73–74). Recognizing American literature "as an integral part of English literature," Matthews saw it as adding something different to our understanding of literature written in the English language that allowed it to stand on its own. Turning to another non-English source, the "Spanish author-diplomat—Don Juan Valera," Matthews substantiates his belief in an American literature that possesses " 'a certain cosmopolitanism and affectionate comprehension of what is foreign, which is as broad as the continent that the Americans inhabit and which forms a contrast to the narrow exclusiveness of the insular British' " (77). Matthews's version of literary cosmopolitanism as emphasizing the distinction and hierarchy that exists between nations and cultures is one reason, according to recent critics, why his literary criticism has fallen out of favor in later accounts of American literary history.

Susannah Ashton's account of the "literary collaborations" Matthews initiated in the late nineteenth and early twentieth centuries deems his view of literature "proudly elitist and by extension racist, sexist, and classist."[17] This list of accusations against Matthews discounts his association with Johnson and, by extension, the role he played in institutionalizing American and

African American literature. Matthews's *Introduction to the Study of American Literature* was one of the first textbooks used for the study of American literature at the college level. Intended to assist the student in grasping "vital points" concerning American literature, Matthews explains in his prefatory note that "all dates and all proper names, and all titles of books not absolutely essential have been rigorously omitted." Those he calls "more important authors" are each discussed in a chapter of their own, while the "writers of less consequence" are "discussed briefly in a single chapter."[18] Needless to say, not a single woman or African American author is named as one of the "more important authors."

Matthews's rationale for deciding which authors are most important derives from his definition of literature. For Matthews, "literature is the reflection and the reproduction of the life of the people" (9). As a result, "American literature must needs become more and more unlike British literature" (13). Those authors who write about the elusive "difference between the American and the Englishman" are those, to Matthews, who are considered to be the more important ones. What makes literature written in English American, as opposed to British, Canadian, or Australian, is that "it enables us to see ourselves and our neighbors as we really are, or at least as we seem to ourselves to be; it explains us to ourselves" (14). In other words, literature brings "ourselves" into being. This idea of how literature might explain ourselves as Americans led Johnson to enroll in Matthews's literature courses at Columbia in 1902. Matthews's theory of literature enabled Johnson to explain himself to himself and to others in order to avoid the mistake his protagonist makes.

Johnson developed the outline for his novel when he was finishing up his course work with Matthews at Columbia. He presented the first two chapters to Matthews, who read it and offered a number of suggestions in order for Johnson to pursue his literary work further. Matthews was involved at every stage of the novel's production. After Johnson sent him the entire novel in 1908 from his post at the American Consulate in Corinto, Venezuela, Matthews took care of having the manuscript typed and prepared for publication. Finally, when the novel appeared in 1912, Matthews wrote a glowing review of it in *Munsey's Magazine* titled "American Character in American Fiction." Matthews declared that the novel "has significance for all of us who want to understand our fellow citizens of darker hue" and goes on to describe it as "composed in full accord with the principle enunciated by [H. A.] Taine in one of his letters—the principle 'that a writer should be a psychologist, not a painter or a musician; that he should be a transmitter of ideas and feelings, not of sensations.'"[19] Matthews's review is noteworthy for two reasons. First, it considers Johnson's novel—published anonymously—as a work of "American fiction" and, upon expounding its virtues, reveals a fact of its composition that only one so closely associated with it would know: that it puts Taine's theory of literature (explicated most fully in his *History of English Literature*) into practice. The novel's literary value, for Matthews (and ultimately for Johnson as well), was found in its exposition of the inner lives of "citizens of darker hue." Matthews's involvement with and evaluation of Johnson's novel helped to establish Johnson's literary principle: citizens of "darker hue" could be better understood by white citizens through literature.

Johnson developed this principle in his poem "Fifty Years," which Matthews once again helped him to revise and arranged strategically to have published in the *New York Times* on January 1, 1913, to mark the fiftieth anniversary of the Emancipation Proclamation.[20] When Johnson completed his first collection of poems in 1917, he used "Fifty Years" as the title poem and turned, once again, to Matthews to write an introduction that would help its readers appreciate and evaluate its merits.[21] Matthews viewed the collection as vital to establishing the terms of a national literature that was still trying to find its place in a new century. "Literature in the New Century," Matthews wrote, "must weigh the importance of the intensifying of national spirit and of the sharpening of racial pride. And, finally, it is for us to take account also of the growth of what must be called 'cosmopolitanism,' that breaking down of the hostile barriers keeping one people apart from the others, ignorant of them, and often contemptuous."[22] Matthews saw Johnson's work as representing the literature of the new century. His public declarations of approval of Johnson's work were matched in his private correspondence with Johnson and others. Thanking him, in 1914, for an autographed copy of the novel, Matthews claimed not to have read "anything better in the past twenty four months."[23] He also sent a copy of the novel to his close friend, Theodore Roosevelt. Encouraging Roosevelt to read the novel, he wrote that "it is not exactly fact—but it is the truth. And it lets the light into some dark and curious places."[24] Matthews's correspondence with Roosevelt suggests that he sent Johnson's novel to him not merely to promote the latter's career. He hoped that the novel would help the president to sort out the racial conflicts plaguing the nation at the time. Judging from the president's reply, Matthews's description seems to have struck the right chord: "I read the autobiography that you sent me, and was much impressed by it. Ugh! There is not any more puzzling problem in this country than the problem of color. It is not as urgent, or as menacing, as other problems, but it seems more utterly insoluble. The trouble is that the conflict in many of its phases is not between right and wrong, but between two rights." [25] The novel, just as Matthews had hoped, helped to broaden Roosevelt's view of the race problem. After reading the novel he was able to perceive the problem not simply as between right and wrong (or black and white, for that matter). Instead, the race problem, as Roosevelt understood it, involved the rights of two separate and essentially incompatible groups to exist within a single nation. The novel helped Roosevelt to clarify the distinction between black and white Americans, and the impossibility of coexistence. Literature, and particularly Johnson's form of fiction and poetry, could help the president of the United States understand the distinction of African Americans but did not bring him closer to solving the racial conflict; indeed, it only cemented his belief that the problem was utterly insoluble. Roosevelt would later, again at Matthews's request, express his high opinion of Johnson's poems collected in *Fifty Years*.[26] Judging by the correspondence between the three, we can see that Matthews and Roosevelt were not simply lending Johnson's work legitimacy, as William Lloyd Garrison had done for Frederick Douglass during an earlier time. In this case, the connection between Johnson, Matthews, and Roosevelt was predicated on their common understanding of the distinction between black and white Americans and their desire to make that distinction "between two rights" a constitutive feature of American democracy as such.

In 1922 Matthews included Johnson's poem "Fifty Years" in his anthology *Poems of Patriotism*, dedicated to the memory of Theodore Roosevelt.[27] Johnson's poem was included in this anthology for its "patriotism," although it did not yet count, in Matthews's book, as a work of American literature. In that same year, Johnson completed his own anthology of poems, which he had sent to Matthews, hoping for a favorable review from his former teacher in the *New York Book Review*. Believing himself to be "unqualified" to write a review of an African American anthology, Matthews declined Johnson's request and passed the task of writing the review on to his colleague in the sociology department. Although the preeminent critic of American literature at the time, Matthews felt that he did not know enough about African Americans to write about their literature.[28] It was with this project, even more than his famous anonymous novel, that Johnson made a name for himself in African American literature, putting, in effect, Matthews's theory of literature that explains ourselves to ourselves into practice.

## The Limits of African American Literature

Johnson became secretary of the National Association of the Advancement of Colored People in 1916 at the request of Matthews's colleague in the comparative literature department, J. E. Spingarn. Although Matthews did not share the same type of friendship with Spingarn that he did with Johnson, echoes of Matthews's racialism and patriotism could certainly be heard in Spingarn's anthology *Criticism in America, Its Function and Status,* in which he included his own essays "The New Critic" and "Criticism in the United States."[29] Spingarn, like Matthews, is now a forgotten figure of literary criticism who was closely associated with Johnson and is better known today for his role in founding the NAACP. Spingarn's literary criticism has received minimal attention; nevertheless, it is difficult to imagine African American literature without taking into account the role he played in its formation.

Disillusioned with the limitations of academia and a rarefied form of literary criticism, Spingarn was dismissed from Columbia shortly after he delivered his infamous essay "The New Criticism" in 1910.[30] Although these events, as Marshall Van Deusen explains in his biography, "led Spingarn into new worlds" that resulted both in his move outside the university to the editorial board of Harcourt, Brace and Company and in his helping to found the NAACP, he continued to hold the "conviction that America's greatest practical need of the moment was to develop a capacity for the speculative life of theory."[31] Spingarn's literary theory, like Johnson's, was closely linked to his attempts to put the idea of American democracy into practice. Spingarn and Johnson were well connected through their work for the NAACP, but it was through the publication of Johnson's *Negro Anthology* that a literary connection developed between them.

In *Along This Way,* Johnson explains that he "began work on an anthology of poetry by American Negroes" so that "that part of me which was artist" would not "become entirely submerged" by his work for the NAACP.[32] In fact, just as Spingarn's literary criticism and political activism were integrally related, so too had Johnson merged his literary and political lives. Indeed, the anthology was precisely the vehicle that allowed Johnson to make such a connection. He relates in *Along This Way* how he went about forming the anthology and writing its preface.

> Before I had gone very far with the work, I realized that such a book, being the first of its kind, would be entirely devoid of background. America as a whole knew something of Dunbar, but it was practically unaware that there were such things as Negro poets and Negro poetry. So I decided to write an introduction; and the introduction developed into a forty-two page essay on "The Creative Genius of the Negro." In that essay I called attention to the American Negro as a folk artist, and pointed out his vital contributions, as such, to our national culture. In it I also made a brief survey of Negro poetry. (374)

The "forty-two page essay" that functions as the anthology's preface obviously did a good deal more than Johnson lets on in his memoir. It not only provides a historical survey of "the American Negro's contribution"; it also lays out a theory of literature closely linked to what Spingarn calls "America's greatest practical need of the moment." Johnson, unlike Spingarn, is less elusive about what, precisely, is America's greatest practical need. For Johnson, America needed to put a stop to lynching, a practice he elsewhere called "America's National Disgrace."[33] Johnson's efforts to keep "that part of me which was artist" from becoming "entirely submerged" in the campaign he led against lynching was not, as he insists in his memoir, separate from his political work for the NAACP. In fact, Johnson's anthology enabled him to join his literary and political work and focus on a single project.

When Johnson's anthology appeared in 1922, its publisher, Harcourt, Brace and Company, sent a press release to members and friends of the NAACP. Encouraging recipients of the release to purchase the book, the publishers emphasize Johnson's position within the organization, explaining that "a most important and valuable part of the book is an essay of some forty pages by Mr. Johnson. . . . No white person can read this essay and fail to feel increased respect for the Negro. Every colored person who reads it will experience new pride in his race and a new hope for the future."[34] Purchasing the book would offer readers poems by various authors in a single collection, while it would also be an endorsement of Johnson's leadership. Unlike other poetry anthologies produced at the same time in the United States, of which there were several, only this one could boast an NAACP endorsement, since the name of its most prominent leader appeared on the front page.

Aware that this anthology would have to compete in the literary market "with many anthologies that have recently been issued," Johnson devotes his essay to distinguishing *The Book of American Negro Poetry* from other poetry anthologies. Ironically, Johnson would go head-to-head with his good friend William Stanley Braithwaite, whose own poems comprise a section of the anthology. Having "a widely recognized position in the American literary world," Johnson explains in his preface, Braithwaite "stands as unique among all the Aframerican writers the United States has yet produced. He has gained his place, taking as the standard and measure for his work the identical standard and measure applied to American writers and American literature. He has asked for no allowances or rewards, either directly or indirectly, on account of his race" (43). Given this view, it is curious that Johnson would want to include him in an anthology that makes race an essential feature of his poetry. Making Braithwaite into a Negro poet by including him in the anthology would then eliminate his apparent originality so that he might stand less problematically among the other "Aframerican writers" included in the anthology.

Braithwaite himself had tried, but failed, in the early part of the twentieth century to find a publisher for his own *Anthology of Negro Authors: Prose and Verse*. As a result of this failed venture, Braithwaite, in 1906, edited *The Book of Elizabethan Verse*, which was followed a few years later by volumes of Georgian and Restoration verse. Braithwaite eventually developed a national reputation for his anthology series, *Anthology of Magazine Verse*, which began in 1913 and was issued annually for the next sixteen years. Despite Braithwaite's success as a literary anthologist, he was never able to make his dream of editing an African American literary anthology come true.[35] Although Braithwaite was a highly regarded literary editor and reviewer, he lacked the political connections to produce an African American literary anthology; instead, Braithwaite's literary anthologies were organized exclusively by generic and historic categories, rather than identity categories. Braithwaite was merely a literary man, while Johnson merged his literary projects with his political projects, using his status as secretary of the NAACP to publicize and legitimate his authority as editor of the first African American literary anthology.

Johnson's anthology proposed a new category of literature, extending Matthews's definition of American literature as a vehicle for democracy. In order for Americans "to see ourselves and our neighbors as we really are," they must first see the distinction of African Americans. Without seeing African Americans as they really are, according to Johnson, it would be impossible to distinguish American literature from other modes of writing in English. By collecting works by "Aframerican poets" to form a Negro anthology, Johnson hoped to show that African Americans were vital to making America, as Matthews had persuasively written, different.

This nation suffers, according to Johnson, from a hazardous blind spot when it comes to "matters of Negro poets and the production of literature by the colored people in this country" (9). The consequences of this blind spot are dangerous for both parties. One way to correct the nation's vision is to remove the object that obstructs its view. For Johnson, literature enables clear vision. In his words, "No people that has produced great literature and art has ever been looked upon by the world as distinctly inferior" (9). The works Johnson has collected in his anthology provide the proof that the "American Negro" has written and continues to produce "great literature," refuting all claims to the contrary. Anyone who reads the works Johnson has collected will also benefit from the explanation the anthology provides about African Americans themselves.

The poems in the collection, despite differences in theme and content, all speak, in some way, for the nameless and speechless lynching victim Johnson presents in his fiction. The anthology collects the work of forty poets whose work, taken together, helps to elucidate the silent captivity and torture Johnson's lynching victim experiences. In the fictional narrative of Johnson's novel, this man only "cries and groans." Unable to find the words to ask for help, the narrator, along with the mob, only looks blankly at "his eyes bulging from their sockets . . . appealing in vain for help" (187). The speechless victim of Johnson's novel finds the words to articulate his painful experience in the poems collected in the anthology. For this reason Johnson gives Claude McKay's poems a preeminent place in the collection. McKay's poems head the group of the new Negro poets, whose work makes up the bulk of this anthology (43). McKay's poems "The Lynching," "If We Must Die," and "To the White Fiends" set the tone of the "Negro poets today" and mark the direction for the future. The future of America, as Johnson and his cohorts imagined it, would make lynching illegal, making it virtually impossible for a race to be "so dealt with."

Johnson's literary anthology would continue the political fight against lynching that had experienced a temporary roadblock when the Dyer Anti-Lynching Bill he had so diligently lobbied for failed to gather a majority of votes in Congress.[36] Johnson's political failure left him deeply disillusioned about the possibilities of fighting for African American rights through the electoral process. The African American literary anthology, then, proved to be a viable alternative for continuing the fight against lynching. In 1931 Johnson brought out a second edition of the anthology, which included

"An Outline of Study published separately, for the use of teachers and students" that was a collaborative effort between him and the poet/critic Sterling Brown.[37] As it happened, the final years of Johnson's life were devoted not to the political work of the NAACP but to making the anthology a part of black college and high school curriculums. Leaving his political work for the NAACP behind, Johnson worked full-time on making his anthology a vital component of literature courses taught throughout the United States until his death in 1938.

## Conclusion

In his essay "Recreations of an Anthologist," published while Johnson was studying with him, Matthews writes that "however much the collector may boast of the utility of his labors, he knows perfectly well that his motive is not utilitarian. If he is honest with himself, he will admit humbly that the attraction of 'making a collection' does not lie in the ultimate value of the collection when it shall be completed (as far as that may be possible). In the immense majority of cases the beginnings of the collection were accidental and wholly devoid of purpose."[38] Heeding his professor's words in the preface to his collection, Johnson concludes by explaining,

> My original idea for this book underwent a change in the writing of the introduction. I first planned to select twenty-five to thirty poems which I judged to be up to a certain standard, and offer them with a few words of introduction and without comment. In the collection, as it grew to be, that "certain standard" has been broadened if not lowered; but I believe that this is offset by the advantage of the wider range given the reader and the student of the subject.[39]

The "wider range" of the collection has a purpose that was not part of Johnson's original idea to make a collection. The literary anthology became for Johnson the only way to explain the importance and worth of African Americans during a time in American history when it was possible to be lynched for the mere fact of being African American.

This objective for the anthology, as I've been trying to show, is not far from that of the *Norton Anthology of African-American Literature* today. The editors' insistence on the inclusiveness of the anthology is an attempt to make it into a political act, rather than merely a literary one, which makes Gates's theory of African American literature, like Johnson's and Matthews's, committed to explaining the worth of African Americans themselves. The act of reading this African American literary anthology, editors believe, translates the experience of being African American so that we can better understand African Americans and ourselves. The African American literary anthology thus functions as a speech act, providing form for African Americans themselves to speak. While producing a more inclusive anthology may be one way of learning about how the voices of particular African Americans have been stifled, reading this African American literary anthology—either inside or outside the classroom—certainly brings us no closer to knowing African Americans themselves.

## Notes

Research for this essay was supported by a grant from the National Endowment for the Humanities.

1 Henry Louis Gates Jr. and Nellie McKay, eds., *The Norton Anthology of African-American Literature*, 2nd ed. (New York: W. W. Norton, 2004), xxix.

2 Manning Marable, "The New Bible of Black Literature," *Journal of Blacks in Higher Education*, no. 19 (1998): 132.

3 Theodore O. Mason, "Mapping the Territory," *American Literary History* 10.1 (Spring 1998): 186.

4 Ibid., 189.

5 James Weldon Johnson, ed., *The Book of American Negro Poetry* (New York: Harcourt, Brace & World, Inc., 1922), 9.

6 Barbara M. Benedict, *Making the Modern Reader: Cultural Mediation in Early Modern Literary Anthologies* (Princeton, NJ: Princeton University Press, 1996), 9.

7 Anders Olsson, *Managing Diversity: The Anthologization of "American Literature"* (Uppsala: Acta Universitatis Upsaliensis, 2000), 15.

8 James Weldon Johnson, *The Autobiography of an Ex-Coloured Man* (1912; rpt., New York: Hill and Wang, 1999), 173.

9 Comparing Johnson's protagonist to Charles Chesnutt's John Walden in *The House Behind the Cedars*, SallyAnn Ferguson characterizes the former as "smug," with "a penchant for self-aggrandizement" and "an inflated psyche—not a strong African-American identity." Johnson's "cowardly, White-looking protagonist" is effectively offset by the novel's "dark-skinned" characters, who function as moral correctives ("Unmaking Blackness: The Ex-Colored Men of Charles W. Chesnutt and James Weldon Johnson," in *Critical Essays on James Weldon Johnson*, ed. Kenneth M. Price and Lawrence J. Oliver [New York: G. K. Hall, 1997], 232–46). Ferguson's reading of the novel as a racial allegory is not far from Walter Benn Michaels's reading of the novel. While disputing the irony Ferguson and others have identified in the text, Michaels reads the novel's passing plot as a moral choice between doing the right and the wrong thing (*Our America: Nativism, Modernism, and Pluralism* [Durham, NC: Duke University Press, 1995], 117).

10 Kenneth W. Warren, *So Black and Blue: Ralph Ellison and the Occasion of Criticism* (Chicago: University of Chicago Press, 2003), 36.

11 James Weldon Johnson, *Along This Way* (New York: Viking, 1961), 238.

12 Brander Matthews, *These Many Years: Recollections of a New Yorker* (New York: Charles Scribner's Sons, 1917), 21–37.

13 Lawrence J. Oliver, *Brander Matthews, Theodore Roosevelt, and the Politics of American Literature, 1880–1920* (Knoxville: University of Tennessee Press, 1992).

14 Although Johnson shared friendships with a number of other well-known literary critics, including H. L. Mencken, Johnson's association with Matthews marks the start of his literary career.

15 Johnson, *Along This Way*, 192.

16 Brander Matthews, "What Is American Literature?" in *The Tocsin of Revolt and Other Essays* (New York: Charles Scribner's Sons, 1922), 68.

17 Susanna Ashton, *Collaborators in Literary America, 1870–1920* (New York: Palgrave Macmillan, 2003), 95.

18 Brander Matthews, *Introduction to American Literature* (New York: American Book Company, 1918), 5.

19 Brander Matthews, "American Character in American Fiction," *Munsey's Magazine*, August 1913, 794–98.

20 Matthews made substantial changes to the poem, and these changes are the subject of some critical controversy. In his discussion of the poem's composition, Robert Fleming agrees with Eugene Levy, "who says that the poem is 'much closer in spirit to *Up from Slavery* than to *The Souls of Black Folk.*'" Johnson wrote multiple drafts of the poem; the changes between the first draft and the final one are especially significant, since Johnson decided to delete nine of the first draft's stanzas because, as Johnson explains in *Along This Way*, including them would have "nullified the theme, purpose, and effect of the poem as a whole" (290). Fleming reads these excised stanzas to "show that Johnson's placid exterior concealed a raging awareness of the wrongs committed against his race" (Robert Fleming, "The Composition of James Weldon Johnson's 'Fifty Years,'" *American Poetry* 4.2 [1987]: 51–56).

21 Brander Matthews, introduction to *Fifty Years and Other Poems*, ed. James Weldon Johnson (Boston: The Cornhill Company, 1917), xi–xiv.

22 Brander Matthews, "Literature in the New Century," in *Inquiries and Opinions* (New York: Charles Scribner's Sons, 1907), 4.

23 Matthews to Johnson, December 26, 1914, James Weldon Johnson Collection, Collection of American Literature, Beinecke Rare Book and Manuscript Library, Yale University; subsequent references will be to "Johnson Collection."

24 Matthews to Roosevelt, January 3, 1913, in *The Letters of Theodore Roosevelt and Brander Matthews*, ed. Lawrence J. Oliver (Knoxville: University of Tennessee Press, 1995), 199.

25 Roosevelt to Matthews, January 7, 1913, in ibid., 200.

26 Matthews to Johnson, April 12, 1918, in ibid., 218.

27 Brander Matthews, ed., *Poems of American Patriotism* (New York: Charles Scribner's Sons, 1922).

28 Declining to review the anthology himself, Matthews's reply to Johnson (March 23, 1922) indicates that he did so because he felt that he lacked sufficient knowledge on its subject matter. Instead, he arranged to have Professor Giddings, then head of Columbia's sociology department, write the article. No such review, however, appeared. See also Matthews to Johnson, March 20, 1922, Johnson Collection.

29  These essays were the subject of considerable critical controversy when Spingarn first presented them as lectures at Columbia University in 1910. See J. E. Spingarn, ed., *Criticism in America, Its Functions and Status* (New York: Harcourt, Brace and Company, 1924).

30  Besides playing a prominent role in the NAACP, Spingarn also attempted to gain a seat in Congress in 1908. Spingarn's political activities were, as Van Deusen points out in his biography, related to his views on literary criticism. Spingarn was a close ally of Johnson's; it was at his suggestion, for instance, that Johnson was chosen as secretary of the NAACP in 1916. Spingarn was responsible for the publication of Johnson's first anthology and made a number of changes to the original manuscript that Johnson readily accepted (Spingarn to Johnson, September 30, 1921, Johnson Collection). The convergence between Spingarn and Johnson's theory and practice is a subject worth considering in a separate article. See Spingarn, *Creative Criticism: Essays on the Unity of Genius and Taste* (New York: Henry Holt and Company, 1917), 3–44.

31  Marshall Van Deusen, *J. E. Spingarn* (New York: Twayne, 1971), 31.

32  Johnson, *Along This Way*, 374.

33  James Weldon Johnson, "Lynching—America's National Disgrace," in *Writings*, ed. William L. Andrews (New York: Library of America, 2004), 720.

34  NAACP press release, April 19, 1922, Johnson Collection.

35  Thanking Johnson for supporting his efforts to present a series of lectures at his alma mater, Atlanta University, Braithwaite explains to him the importance of carrying his message "to the Negro academic world." He explains, "If I can put this over to the extent I have measured for it in dreaming and brooding, and laboring to provide, I think we will have won as a Race the fulfillment of the precious heritage of this American civilization. The project is the editing of an OMNIBUS OF NEGRO LITERATURE which will be a library of literature, and the practical summation of our achievement to the present" (Braithwaite to Johnson, August 12, 1934, Johnson Collection).

36  The Dyer Anti-Lynching Bill, named after Representative Leonidas C. Dyer of Missouri, was one of two federal antilynching bills brought before Congress in 1918. In *Along This Way*, Johnson describes working with Dyer and the political lobbying he did on behalf of the NAACP. Although the bill failed to pass into law, Johnson's view of his experience is generally favorable. Besides learning a number of different political "tricks" in his attempts to gain the attention of different senators, he also claims that "the Dyer bill brought out the greatest concerted action I have yet seen the colored people take." For Johnson, the Dyer bill did succeed in bringing together divergent elements of "the colored people of the country" under a single cause (364–65).

37  Johnson, "Preface to the Second Edition," *Book of American Negro Poetry*, 8.

38  Brander Matthews, *Recreations of an Anthologist* (Freeport, NY: Books for Libraries Press, 1967), 3.

39  Johnson, *Along This Way*, 374–75.

**John Hartigan Jr.**

Culture against Race:
Reworking the Basis for Racial Analysis

The subject of race is riven with many interesting fissures. There are deep gulfs between
those who live it in a daily way as a form of sub-
jugation and those who, mostly unconsciously,
benefit from this system of social differentiation.
Wide divides, as well, separate academics who
make race the singular focus of their scholarship
and those who are steadfastly disinterested in
the subject. There are also radically different
perspectives on how race matters, depending
whether one emphasizes the enduring, deter-
ministic power of racial history or, alternatively,
the onrushing future where the nuance and
complexity of racial differentiations is intensifying and increasingly unstable. To say something
useful and coherent about race, then, requires
one to straddle these and other significant, contrary beliefs, experiences, and dispositions, at a
time when it is more important than ever to
analyze the multiple, profound ways that race
shapes our daily existence. At this challenging
moment, the concept of culture is of greater
relevance than ever before.

Race and culture, two of the most powerful
analytical fulcrums of the past century, are curiously intertwined. Each has been invoked to

The *South Atlantic Quarterly* 104:3, Summer 2005.

inscribe nefarious distinctions between peoples. Both concepts are also used to analyze and critique such practices that spuriously subdivide humanity. In addition, race and culture are each subject to periodical critical reevaluations of their conceptual coherence and relevance.[1] The concerted work of anthropologists like Franz Boas, Ruth Benedict, and Margaret Mead to critique and disrupt racial thinking hinged, in part, on articulating a counterbalancing conception of culture.[2] Indeed, to this day one of the basic starting points for a discussion of race is the assertion that it is a cultural construct, rather than a biological means of delineating inherent differences between people. But during the 1980s and 1990s, it was culture's turn to be rendered as a subject of deconstruction.[3] The self-reflexive turn in anthropology treated culture as a suspect means of conceptualizing social dynamics. In the wake of this critique, "race" came to seem a more solid basis for talking about power and inequality. But this shift in emphasis entails another set of problems, which is the subject of this essay. In such critiques, these terms are reassessed as a basis for making sense of powerful operations of social differentiation. The basic question posed today of each term is whether or not it does more harm than good. That is, do invocations of either race or culture end up reproducing an overriding belief that there are natural and essentialized forms of differences constituting distinct people?

Following criticisms of the culture concept, a reinvigorated form of racial analysis seemed poised to reorganize various fields of scholarly and activist engagements with forms of social hierarchy. But in place of this favored role for race, Paul Gilroy discerns, rather, "the crisis of raciology"—the collapse of its commonsensical and explanatory bases—and he calls instead for a "deliberate and self-conscious renunciation of 'race' as a means to categorize and divide humanity."[4] Interestingly, in this critique Gilroy both distances himself from culture and relies upon a range of invocations of culture to explain what we should be talking about instead of race. I think Gilroy's ambivalent stance toward culture suggests that this concept may well be irreplaceable when it comes to discussing race, despite the problems entailed by its invocation. In this essay—drawing upon my own and others' ethnographic research and my efforts to teach students about how and why race matters—I regard the dialectical relationship between race and culture as a basis for devising an effective means for analyzing how social dynamics shape contemporary collective identities.

A key aspect of critiques of the culture concept developed in the 1990s—critiques that fundamentally transformed the practice of anthropology and opened up new trajectories of analysis for cultural studies—honed in on the particular racial effects generated by certain uses of culture. Lila Abu-Lughod demonstrated that "the concept of culture operates much like its predecessor—race—even though in its twentieth-century form it has some important political advantages." The problem, Abu-Lughod asserted, is that *culture* is conceptually flawed, implying characteristics of "coherence, time-lessness, and discreteness" that distort more than they reveal about social dynamics. Just as troubling, though, "culture is the essential tool for making other," and in this role "the culture concept retains some of the tenden-cies to freeze difference possessed by concepts like race."[5] The solution she proffered was to "write against culture" by eschewing generalizations and the power-laden entailments of objectivity in favor of "ethnographies of the particular" that focus "closely on particular individuals and their changing relationships" (158), rather than on broad depictions of social dynamics and processes.

Virginia Dominguez furthered this critique of culture by calling atten-tion to the political impact of such invocations. Dominguez observed that "this 'thing' that anthropologists have for decades taken to be what we study, describe, decipher, and theorize about can be, and often has been, an ideological mechanism for subordination and social control."[6] Dominguez linked this predicament to what she characterizes at the problem of "cultur-alism," a form of legitimation pursued by national governments that strives for a "minimization of divisiveness" by invoking culturally defined ethni-cities. Culturalism mirrors the racial implications that Abu-Lughod found in uses of culture. "The switch from talk of races and immigrant groups to talk of ethnic groups and ethnic identity carries with it what I call the culturalization of difference," Dominguez wrote. "A public discourse that promotes intergroup tolerance employs the notion of cultural pluralism, not biological diversity, multilingualism, or class harmony" (32). These stra-tegic forms of public discourse, Dominguez argued, point to the need for analysts to refrain from deploying "culture" because of its racial impacts and to be circumspect about its use in political discourses. "We need to move away from asking *about* culture—what belongs, what doesn't belong, what its characteristics are, whose characteristics are being imposed and whose are being excluded—and toward asking *what is being accomplished socially,* politically, discursively, when the concept of culture is invoked to describe, analyze, argue, justify and theorize" (21, emphasis original). In this gesture, culture became evidence of racial thinking, rather than providing a basis for understanding how race operates.

For Dominguez, though there are conceptual problems with culture—"it is the concept of culture itself that carries in its continued discursive usage a huge social, economic, and political value" (35)—her critique primarily fixed on political effects from deploying the term.

> I worry that in conceptualizing cultural politics too substantively, empirically, or regionally or locally, intellectuals, community activists, and politicians are, even in acts of resistance against European hegemony, perpetuating the very terms—of hierarchies of differential values—that constitute the hegemony. And in the process we may well be missing the more significant phenomenon—that these struggles are taking place now not because of existing or expanding or narrowing "cultural" differences among groups of people, but because at this point in time much of the world has internalized culture as the marker of difference. (38)

Dominguez regarded an attention to culture as a means of diverting us from recognizing the important political dynamics that increasingly have come to be parsed succinctly as "racial" in the emergent lines of inquiry in cultural studies.

Developing out of these suggestions for curtailing uses of culture, some anthropologists turned instead to a revamped attention to race. One incisive statement of this view was articulated by Kamala Visweswaran, who drew upon work in cultural studies and critical race theory to underscore what she regards as the paucity of anthropological accounts of "lived experiences" of race and to stress the centrality of race to contemporary power relations. From a different angle, Faye Harrison asserted that it is more specifically racism that needs to be a central focus of anthropological research and analysis. Taken together, these two perspectives make clear the crucial concerns at stake in the dialectical interplay between these two powerful concepts, race and culture.

Visweswaran framed the problem for anthropologists by insisting that "the failure to supply an account of our own role in propagating a notion of culture that lent itself to essentializing and fundamentalist tendencies signals not only an analytical weakness but a poverty of vision as well."[7] But the problem Visweswaran diagnosed runs deeper than the tendency of culture to reproduce racial thinking; she additionally finds it inadequate to the task of making sense of contemporary race dynamics. Visweswaran asserts that "the modern anthropological concept of culture has lost any descriptive ability with regard to the construction of racial identities" (77). As a result, the relevance of anthropology to current circumstances has faded, while other analytical approaches have rushed to fill the void. "Multiculturalism and cultural studies have emerged as counterdisciplinary formations that radically foreground race and racial identity precisely because the modern anthropological notion of culture cannot do so." This is why, Visweswaran explains, "we do not usually turn to anthropology for accounts about what it is to function as racialized subjects."

Abu-Lughod and Dominguez counseled circumspection in relation to uses of culture, but the two offered differing analytical alternatives—"discourse" for Abu-Lughod and an attention to "cultural politics" for Dominguez. Visweswaran, in contrast, promoted rallying around "race" as an analytic perspective, asserting the need to "see race itself as a productive and generative social category" (79). In this regard, she championed approaches such as critical race theory "that radically foreground race and racial identity as modes of sociality and resistance" (77). Her attention to the "productive and generative" work of race stressed "that the experience (and indeed, the category) of race is produced by racism and that different forms of racism produce differing effects of race" (78). This perspective primarily emphasizes the historical legacies of the racial constitution of collectives.

> The middle passage, slavery, and the experience of racial terror produce a race of African Americans out of subjects drawn from different cultures. Genocide, forced removal to reservations, and the experience of racial terror make Native Americans subjects drawn from different linguistic and tribal affiliations: a race. War relocation camps, legal exclusion, and the experience of discrimination make Asian American subjects drawn from different cultural and linguistic backgrounds: a race. The process of forming the southwestern states of the United States through conquest and subjugation and the continued subordination of Puerto Rico constitute Chicanos and Puerto Ricans as races. (78)

These racial identities define the type of subjects that Visweswaran advocates bringing into view via "a conception of race which is socially dynamic but historically meaningful," even though their objectification potentially risks contributing, unintentionally, to the current resurgence in sociobiological notions of race.

Visweswaran's approach brings race to the fore of critical analysis, but the problem is that it also risks reproducing racial thinking in much the way "culture" has been accused of perpetuating race. Herbert Lewis highlights the perils in efforts to articulate this broader sensibility concerning race.[8] Where Visweswaran strives to reanimate the "richly connotative 19th century sense of 'race,'" with its invocations of "blood" as a form of collectivity that encompasses "numerous elements that we would today call cultural," Lewis cautions against a "return to the pre-Boasian conception that combines race, culture, language, nationality and nationality in one neat package" (980). And though the equation of racial identity with the forms of persecution and exploitation highlighted by Visweswaran is insightful, Lewis observes that, pursued further, this logic reactivates a concept that "indissolubly connects groups of people and their appearance with beliefs about their capacity and behavior" (ibid.). Given the criteria she lists, Lewis argues, "it follows presumably that we should recognize as 'races' all those who have suffered one or another form of ill-treatment. Certainly Jews would now return to the status of a 'racial' group (as the Nazis contended), as do Armenians, Gypsies (Rom), 'Untouchables' (Dalits) in India, East Timorese, Muslim and Croats in Bosnia and Serbs in Croatia, educated Cambodians in Pol Pot's Cambodia, both Hutu and Tutsi in Rwanda and Burundi" (ibid.). Every similarly subjected group would be reinscribed and reidentified with the very terms used initially to distinguish them for exploitation and persecution.

Dominguez's concerns about culture's propensity for "perpetuating the very terms—of hierarchies of differential values—that constitute the hegemony" seem equally relevant to this attempt to ensconce race at the forefront of critical social analysis. There follow interminable questions of subdividing and distinguishing such races. Visweswaran's description of the processes that produce "Chicanos and Puerto Ricans as races" leads Lewis to ask, "Are these two different 'races' or one? Can rich, powerful, and self-assured Puerto Ricans belong to this 'race'? Do Dominicans, Ecuadorians, and Cubans each get to be their own race, or can they all be in one race with Chicanos and Puerto Ricans because they all speak (or once spoke) Spanish? Can Spanish-speakers from Spain belong, too?" (980). The problem with formulating research in terms of race is that it becomes very difficult to proceed without reproducing various racialized logics that promote the notion that groups are essentially differentiated—experientially and in terms of innate capacities and dispositions—by race.[9] This is a problem that Gilroy takes as a basis for his critique of "raciology," which I will examine further below.

Faye Harrison takes a somewhat different tack as she engages critically with the history of anthropology in order to arrive at a new analytical sensibility for the discipline. Harrison is more optimistic than Visweswaran about the future of anthropology, which is notable because much of Harrison's considerable scholarship has been directed toward critiquing anthropologists' tendencies to repress or ignore race.[10] Harrison finds that "after an extended hiatus, anthropology has again reached a moment in its history when it cannot evade the pervasive power of racism." Harrison specifies the focus must be on racism—rather than race, as in Visweswaran's approach—and points to "anthropology's unique role in interrogating, theorizing, and potentially disrupting the dynamics of racism."[11] The crux of this distinction between race and racism lies in the way racist discourses have been reformulated to maintain invidious distinctions between social collectives without explicitly invoking race or white supremacist notions.[12]

Harrison explains, "As racism assumes more subtle and elusive forms in the contemporary world, it is being reconfigured without 'race' as a classificatory device for demarcating difference" (610). This assertion, however, raises a perplexing question. What is racism without race? Certainly there are many ways that racialized perceptions and actions operate furtively, studiously avoiding direct attention to their racial basis or outcomes.[13] The enduring impact of racist ideas and beliefs, despite many countervailing legal and political structures, suggests their effectiveness derives from an ability to operate without ostensibly invoking race. But the functioning of "a classificatory device for demarcating difference" without explicit references to race opens onto a larger question of how such classificatory devices operate generally. Is it the case that race, in the past, has represented only one of several or many such devices? If so, in now functioning "without race," has this historical mode of classification undergone such drastic changes that it will no longer be recognizable (a possibility that concerns Harrison), or do these changes instead reveal social dynamics at work in racial discourses that have long been obscured by the unique poignancy and insidious relevance of race? I raise these questions not as abstract philosophical concerns, but because they bring heightened attention to the way Harrison's approach implicitly recoups some basic form of cultural analysis. Indeed, though she too argues against "culture," Harrison's basis for seeing some redeeming perspective in anthropology implies some use for the culture concept in making sense of race.

Harrison basically makes the case for prioritizing racism by underscoring its cultural dimensions. She argues that racism "in all its subtlety and intricate multidimensionality actually works as *a complex social force*" (612, emphasis added). Harrison also refers to racism as an "underlying cultural logic"; in addition, she observes that "racist *beliefs* about blackness are embedded in *a system of material relations* that produces and reproduces *taken-for-granted* power and privileges, such as those associated with whiteness" (ibid., emphasis added). These characteristics of racism each reflect cultural dynamics, which become more evident when Harrison concludes her assessment. "As we devise anthropologically informed strategies for intervening more effectively in the 'culture of racism,' we should be reminded of the need to penetrate beneath the surface of ignorance and knowledge to educate and *enculturate against the very cultural logic of the manner in which ordinary people feel, think, speak, and live their everyday lives in this increasingly multiracial and multicultural society and world*" (emphasis added). Here, culture surfaces as both part of the solution and the crucial terrain of engagement against racism. Both Harrison's solution — "to enculturate against" the culture of racism — and the ground she maps for engaging the reproduction of racism — the realm of "everyday lives" — imply the relevance of culture as a mode of analysis and as a characterization of what it is that really matters in confronting the enduring significance of race. From these anthropological critiques, culture reemerges as simultaneously circumscribed but of irrepressible value to analysis of race.

The significance of this enduring role of culture in relation to race can be fleshed out further by considering Paul Gilroy's arguments, in *Against Race: Imagining Political Culture beyond the Color Line* (2000), that it is time to be done with race and all of its oppressive logics and implications. Gilroy describes how a "crisis of 'raciology'" has emerged out of a host of developments — from new reproductive technologies to the revalorization of blackness in various expressive, public cultures — that undermine the very bases for racial thinking. Gilroy observes, "The meaning of racial difference is itself being changed as the relationship between human beings and nature is reconstructed by the impact of the DNA revolution and of the technological developments that they have energized" (14). Racial thinking is crumbling now "because the idea of 'race' has lost much of its common-sense credibility, because the elaborate cultural and ideological work that goes into producing and reproducing it is more visible than ever before, because it has been stripped of its moral and intellectual integrity, and because there is a chance to prevent its rehabilitation" (29). One basis for preventing its "rehabilitation" lies in cultural critics' finding a means to move "beyond" race in their assessments of contemporary social situations. The stakes in this endeavor are incredibly high. Gilroy acknowledges that such an effort will be particularly difficult "for people who have been subordinated by race thinking," largely because "oppressed groups have built complex traditions of politics, ethics, identity, and culture" on racial edifices (12). But the heady possibilities of our current moment demand such a dramatic gesture.

One might be tempted to assume that Gilroy's stance is largely polemical, but his critique is thoroughgoing, as is his call to reject "this desire to cling on to 'race' and go on stubbornly and unimaginatively seeing the world on the distinctive scales that it has specified." In spite of powerful, novel efforts to fundamentally transform racial analysis — such as the emergence of "whiteness studies" or analyses of the "new racism" — Gilroy is emphatic in "demand[ing] liberation not from white supremacy alone, however urgently that is required, but from all racializing and raciological thought, from racialized seeing, racialized thinking, and racialized thinking about thinking" (40).

In contrast to Visweswaran — and, interestingly, voicing concerns over "cultural politics" that resonate with Dominguez's critique — Gilroy sees a host of problems in "black political cultures" that rely on "essentialist approaches to building solidarity" (38).[14] Nor does he share Harrison's confidence in making racism the centerpiece of critical cultural analysis. Gilroy plainly asserts that "the starting point of this book is that the era of New Racism is emphatically over" (34). A singular focus on racism precludes an attention to "the appearance of sharp intraracial conflicts" and does not effectively address the "several new forms of determinism abroad" (38, 34). We still must be prepared "to give effective answers to the pathological problems represented by genomic racism, the glamour of sameness, and the eugenic projects currently nurtured by their confluence" (41). But the diffuse threats posed by invocations of racially essentialized identities (shimmering in "the glamour of sameness") as the basis for articulating "black political cultures" entails an analytical approach that countervails against positing racism as the singular focus of inquiry and critique.[15] From Gilroy's stance, to articulate a "postracial humanism" we must disable any form of racial vision and ensure that it can never again be reinvested with explanatory power. But what will take its place as a basis for talking about the dynamics of belonging and differentiation that profoundly shape social collectives today?

Gilroy tries to make clear that it will not be "culture," yet this concept infuses his efforts to articulate an alternative conceptual approach. Gilroy conveys many of the same reservations about culture articulated by the anthropologists listed above. Specifically, Gilroy cautions that "the cultur-alist approach still runs the risk of naturalizing and normalizing hatred and brutality by presenting them as inevitable consequences of illegitimate attempts to mix and amalgamate primordially incompatible groups" (27). In contrast, Gilroy expressly prefers the concept of diaspora as a means to ground a new form of attention to collective identities. "As an alternative to the metaphysics of 'race,' nation, and bounded culture coded into the body," Gilroy finds that "diaspora is a concept that problematizes the cultural and historical mechanics of belonging" (123). Furthermore, "by focusing atten-tion equally on the sameness within differentiation and the differentiation within sameness, diaspora disturbs the suggestion that political and cul-tural identity might be understood via the analogy of indistinguishable peas lodged in the protective pods of closed kinship and subspecies" (125). And yet, in a manner similar to Harrison's prioritizing of racism as a central con-cern for social inquiry, when it comes to specifying what diaspora entails and how it works, vestiges of culture reemerge as a basis for the coherence of this new conceptual focus.

When Gilroy delineates the elements and dimensions of diaspora, cul-ture provides the basic conceptual background and terminology. In charac-terizing "the Atlantic diaspora and its successor-cultures," Gilroy sequen-tially invokes "black cultural styles" and "postslave cultures" that have "supplied a platform for youth cultures, popular cultures, and styles of dis-sent far from their place of origin" (178). Gilroy explains how the "cultural expressions" of hip-hop and rap, along with other expressive forms of "black popular culture," are marketed by the "cultural industries" to white con-sumers who "currently support this black culture" (181). Granted, in these uses of "culture" Gilroy remains critical of "absolutist definitions of culture" and the process of commodification that culture in turn supports. But his move away from race importantly hinges upon some notion of culture. We may be able to do away with race, but seemingly not with culture.

Gilroy seems to recognize that some conception of culture remains im-portant to the task of unthinking and undermining beliefs about race. That being the case, Gilroy challenges: "Can we improve upon the idea that cul-ture exists exclusively in localized national and ethnic units—separate but equal in aesthetic value and human worth?" (247–48). Doing so will require an attention to culture that allows for a general vision of social dynamics, rather than the emphasis on the particularities of essentialized cultural styles, identities, and practices critiqued by Abu-Lughod and Dominguez. Gilroy stresses this point: "We do not have to be content with the halfway house provided by the idea of plural cultures. A theory of relational cultures and of culture as relation represents a more worthwhile resting place. That possibility is currently blocked by banal invocations of hybridity in which everything becomes equally and continuously intermixed, blended into an impossibly even consistency" (275). Indeed, Gilroy asks us what might happen if "the idea of culture is usefully and constructively deployed at a different level of abstraction. There, it need no longer be hierarchical, race friendly, or ethnic, and it allows more obviously ethical and aesthetic problems to reemerge in the consolidation of democratic and cosmopolitan formations that are not only humanist but also hybrid, impure, and profane" (282). Versions of how culture might work when differently deployed are fortunately at hand; drawing upon the fundamental plasticity of the notion of culture, they offer useful visions of how we might fashion a more powerful analytic perspective on the social dynamics shaping racial identity.

Robert Brightman, William Sewell Jr., and Cristoph Brumann, each of whom has extensively countered the critiques summarized above, answer Gilroy's question about the deployability of "culture" at different levels of abstraction with an emphatic *yes*.[16] In response to assertions that the concept of culture necessarily entails assumptions about boundedness, homogeneity, coherence, and stability, Brightman and Brumann find, in the past as well as today, rather different qualities being associated with "culture." Reviewing early anthropological works (by Bronislaw Malinowski, Ruth Benedict, Alfred Kroeber, and Franz Boas) and more recent efforts (by Marshall Sahlins, Roy Rappaport, Roy Wagner, and Renato Rosaldo) that each wrestle with the task of defining culture, Brightman concludes that the prevailing characteristics then and now are not invocations of "coherence, timelessness, and discreteness." Rather, he finds stress laid on historicity, on contested social orders, and on flows of exchange between various cultural locales: "Neither in earlier disciplinary history nor as deployed in recent anthropological writings does the culture concept consistently exhibit the attributes of ahistoricism, totalization, holism, legalism, and coherence with which its critics selectively reconstitute it. These are invented images of culture, both arbitrary and partial with respect to a much more diverse and versatile field of definitions and use" (541). However selectively the works by founding figures can be read to promote a critical vision of "culture" as static and homogeneous, Brightman asserts that "history, chaos, contestation, and strategy have been anthropological growth stocks since at least 1980, and disciplinary writing reflects this state of affairs, both in theoretical exposition and in the interpretation of ethnographic materials" (540). On the whole, culture, as with most concepts, bears the features with which we invest it, and it need bear onerous connotations no more than favorable ones.

Brightman argues that the turn "against culture" in anthropology deployed a "straw culture concept," retroactively assembled to privilege and advance recent theoretical positions, such as the turn to "discourse."[17] Brightman asserts "that certain contemporary critiques of culture derive their cogency and persuasiveness from a strategic and selective retrospective construction of the meaning of the concept in earlier conditions in anthropology." Reconstituted precisely as the antithesis of theoretical agendas currently in place, this version of "culture" is presented only to be transcended. Brightman asserts that the move to get "beyond" culture is "the effect of rhetorical strategies that (re)construct an essentialized culture concept in the antipodes of contemporary theoretical argument." Indeed, "recent arguments that the culture construct is evanescent and dispensable foreground conceptual stability at the expense of liability, presupposing that there existed in the past and into the present *a* culture construct with *a* determinate definition, now discredited" (527). Which of the many versions of "culture," Brightman asks, are we to reject? Whatever the basis for such choices, Brightman warns that "anthropologists who self-consciously reject 'culture' in favor of 'discourse,' 'hegemony,' or 'habitus' will traffic partly in old signifieds with new signifiers" (541).

From a somewhat different tack, both Brumann and Sewell argue that a key dimension of deployments of the culture concept is its ability to reference a general aspect of human activity acquired through learning (in contrast to instinct) that systematically imbues material and social relations with meaning. Sewell observes, "This distinction between culture as theoretical category and culture as concrete and bounded body of beliefs is . . . seldom made. Yet it seems to me crucial for thinking clearly about cultural theory."[18] With this distinction in place, one can invoke culture in relation to race without delineating or implying discrete, essentialized forms, such as "white culture" and "black culture." Such an approach has been crucial to my work on whiteness in the United States.[19] There are certainly plenty of reasons for depicting starkly opposed, racial perspectives on topics of contemporary concern—such as whether racism is declining or whether affirmative action should be supported or discontinued—but just as striking to me are the overarching commonalities that white and black Americans share in viewing the world in characteristically American cultural terms. In my ethnographic fieldwork in three distinct neighborhoods in Detroit— an inner-city, "underclass" zone; an adjacent "gentrifying" area; and an outlying working-class neighborhood—I found, in each of these sites, local idioms and discourses that whites and blacks speak with varying degrees of commonality in positioning themselves, neighbors, and strangers in relation to identities marked in terms of both class and race.[20] These commonalities are linked to class structures that cross racial lines and that turn on charged intraracial contests over belonging and difference. Such idioms are cultural but do not parse along the racial lines of whiteness and blackness.

Other ethnographers studying racial dynamics in the United States have also identified discursive forms that whites and people of color share.[21] Steven Gregory's study of black middle-class homeowners is an excellent example.[22] Gregory's attention to the "construction of black class identities through the political culture of grass-roots activism" (17) opens a view onto social forms that operate across racial lines and yet are also distinctly inflected in the process of racial formation. In analyzing the way black middle-class residents of Queens speak a "homeowners' discourse," Gregory reveals—in concerns over local social service agencies and their clients—points of interracial commonalities along the lines of class interests. Furthermore, Gregory's account of how these homeowners "interpret, debate, and publicly perform the present meanings of black class divisions and racial identities" (ibid.) provides a nuanced reading of processes of racial identification and disidentification that would not be possible either by relying solely upon the concept of race or by paying too little attention to cultural dynamics.

Michael Moffatt's study of conflicts in an interracial college dorm provides another example of the usefulness of a cultural approach to racial situations.[23] Moffatt found that these conflicts were assessed similarly by black and white students, who all made reference to the crucial American cultural concept of friendliness. Regardless of race, each of these students traced the origins of conflicts to a perceived lack of friendliness by members of the other racial group. White and black students differed in what they perceived as signs of friendliness, but they were commonly linked in a very American conception that sociality is predicated upon demonstration of this cultural characteristic.[24] The advantage of such a perspective on racial conflicts is that, rather than predicating essentializing differences (i.e., whiteness and blackness), it focuses discussion instead on the very tangible and fundamentally plastic terrain of social cues and perceptions.

The countervailing point to concerns about past misuses of culture in relation to race is that the culture concept holds perhaps the most powerful counterweight to racial thinking, since it depicts, on the one hand, the mutable and artificial aspects of racial identification, and, on the other, all the forms of commonality that undercut racialized inscriptions of essential orders. However, the work of these and other ethnographers neither directly addresses nor specifically counters the charge leveled by Abu-Lughod and Dominguez concerning racial impacts and implications of using culture.[25] Nor should my efforts here to articulate a positive role for culture in response to this critique be regarded as a refutation of their arguments or a rejection of the claims that there are negative racial effects to invoking this concept. Even though I think we need culture to make sense of race, I recognize that Abu-Lughod and Dominguez are right that we need to remain circumspect about the potential for culture to reinscribe racial thinking. The uses I am advocating here will require continued vigilance. To use culture in relation to race will necessarily depend on also engaging with and disrupting popular uses and imaginings of the term that do equate its subjects with static, traditional, and unchanging exotic entities. But it is exactly this type of engagement with embedded assumptions that underscores the central reason for making renewed use of culture in relation to race. From my efforts to teach students about race, I realize that without an overarching attention to culture it is very hard to, first, convey the extent of racial thinking and, second, effectively engage the multiple, overlapping structures of perception and experience that reproduce racial identities and collectives. Many people cannot begin to recognize how thoroughly the significance of race informs social life unless they have the ability to first grasp culture as a field of intelligibility that structures their actions and perception. Fundamentally, one needs a cultural vision in order to denaturalize the view of race as a natural order of difference.

In the United States, in particular, it is critical to engage the processes of socialization that lead whites to see each other as individuals and, in contrast, to see peoples of color as representatives of vaguely comprehended groups. Historian George Lipsitz, in analyzing the economic, political, and social bases for white dominance, labels this process the "possessive invest-ment in whiteness."[26] One of the keys to disabusing white people of this powerful form of racial thinking and perception involves getting whites to recognize the profound group circumstances that contour life chances in racial terms in the United States. That is, we must critically frame and ana-lyze the collective forms that benefit whites as a group, regardless of indi-viduals' personal sentiments about the significance of race. And this work must be done against the grain of white Americans' socialization to see the world strictly in terms of individuals. Such a thoroughgoing socialization can best be disrupted and critically objectified by the concept of culture. A cultural perspective addresses both this inability to grasp the distinctive social conditioning that individualism entails and the attendant ignorance of how collective processes shape our experiences and the very ground of the social order.[27] This approach has the potential to engage whites' racial thinking, at least initially, by shifting discussions away from the charged accusations of racism and onto a ground—the subject of socialization— that may be more conducive to both thinking about race and recognizing its intersection with other critical categories of social identity.

We cannot effectively think through the processes of racial identification and disidentification without a cultural perspective.[28] An inability to grasp culture and its dynamics is central to why many whites are unable to think critically about race or to grasp its various manifestations and operations. Without some understanding that our experience of the world is culturally contoured, it is difficult to regard racism as more than just an individual fail-ing or a vaguely perceived "institutional" by-product. Without a recognition of the interlocking aspects of cultural perceptions and categorical identi-ties, race appears as just another isolated subject of political correctness. But by starting with basic cultural dynamics, it is easy to show how race both inflects and is shaped by judgments Americans make about whether or not certain people appear to be nice, or friendly, or hardworking—each reflecting crucial categorical demarcations that ostensibly make no men-tion of race but that certainly operate at times in racial registers. A cultural perspective allows us to place race simultaneously in the mix of everyday life, shaping perceptions that ostensibly do not appear racial, but without reductively asserting that everything is about race.

Cultural analysis, of course, comes in many forms and encompasses an array of methodological approaches and theoretical assumptions. There are also copious competing and often conflicting definitions of culture, and varying degrees of commitment to its explanatory principles across the disciplines of anthropology, sociology, and history, not to mention the range of interdisciplinary work of cultural studies. Sorting out this confusing assortment of approaches to culture is the subject of my recent book, *Odd Tribes: Toward a Cultural Analysis of White People*, so I will not expound upon this unwieldy subject at length here.[29] But I will close by succinctly stating what I see as fundamentally defining cultural analysis. In broadest terms, culture, as an analytical perspective, treats collective dynamics of belonging and differentiation, the assignation of social meaning to arbitrary biological traits, the naturalization of certain orders of inequality or dominance, the forms of etiquette or decorum that discipline bodies and behaviors, the styles of narrative that organize each of these into tangible forms of meaning that people encounter in a multitude of reinforcing or challenging circumstances, and finally the forms of performance in which categorical identities and more fluid constructions of self are reproduced or revised.[30] Each of these dynamics informs the interpretive work of cultural subjects in making sense of their world and negotiating the uneven social terrains that shape their individual and collective identities. We must grasp these dynamics if we are to make further inroads in understanding and explaining to people how and why race continues to matter.

## Notes

1 Walter Benn Michaels, "Race into Culture: A Critical Genealogy of Cultural Identity," *Critical Inquiry* 18 (1992): 655–85.

2 See Lee Baker, *From Savage to Negro: Anthropology and the Construction of Race, 1896–1954* (Berkeley: University of California Press, 1998), and Regna Darnell, *Invisible Genealogies* (Lincoln: University of Nebraska Press, 2001).

3 Paul Gilroy, *Against Race: Imagining Political Culture beyond the Color Line* (Cambridge, MA: Harvard University Press, 2000), 17.

4 Lila Abu-Lughod, "Writing against Culture," in *Recapturing Anthropology*, ed. Richard Fox (Santa Fe: School of American Research, 1991), 143–44.

5 Virginia Dominguez, "The Messy Side of 'Cultural Politics,'" *South Atlantic Quarterly* 91.1 (1992): 22.

6 Kamala Visweswaran, "Race and the Culture of Anthropology," *American Anthropologist* 100.1 (1998): 76.

7 George Marcus and Michael Fischer, eds., *Anthropology as Cultural Critique: An Experimental Moment in the Human Sciences* (Chicago: University of Chicago Press, 1986), and James Clifford and George Marcus, eds., *Writing Culture: The Poetics and Politics of Ethnography* (Berkeley: University of California Press, 1986).

8 Herbert Lewis, "The Misrepresentation of Anthropology and Its Consequences," *American Anthropologist* 100.3 (1998): 716–33. For additional criticisms of Visweswaran's posi-

tion, see Elizabeth Stassinos, "Response to K. Visweswaran, 'Race and the Culture of Anthropology,'" *American Anthropologist* 100.4 (September 1998); and Janet Bauer, "Genealogies of Race and Culture in Anthropology: The Marginalized Ethnographers," in *Race and Racism in Theory and Practice*, ed. Berel Lang (New York: Rowman and Littlefield, 2000), 123–37.

9  For an example of this problem and a means to formulate an effective research strategy in response to it, see Gary Lee Downey and Juan Lucena, "Engineering Selves: Hiring In to a Contested Field of Education," in *Cyborgs and Citadels: Anthropological Interventions in Engineering Sciences and Technologies*, ed. Gary Lee Downey and Joseph Dumit (Santa Fe: School of American Research Press, 1997).

10  See Faye Harrison, *Decolonizing Anthropology: Moving Further toward an Anthropology for Liberation* (Washington, DC: American Anthropological Association, 1991); Harrison, "The Du Boisian Legacy in Anthropology," *Critique of Anthropology* 12 (1992): 239–60; Harrison, "Introduction: An African Diaspora Perspective for Urban Anthropology," *Urban Anthropology* 17.2–3 (1988): 111–40.

11  Faye Harrison, "Expanding the Discourse on 'Race,'" *American Anthropologist* 100.3 (1998): 610.

12  On current forms of racist ideology being expressed through ostensibly nonracial discourses, see Eduardo Bonilla-Silva, *White Supremacy and Racism* (Boulder, CO: Lynne Rienner, 2001).

13  For a critique of the view that "race is over," see David Roediger, *Colored White: Transcending the Racial Past* (Berkeley: University of California Press, 2002).

14  Such political gestures open onto "the unstable location where white supremacists and black nationalists, Klansmen, Nazis, neo-Nazis and ethnic absolutists, Zionists and anti-semites have been able to encounter each other as potential allies rather than sworn foes" (Gilroy, *Against Race*, 215).

15  See Robert Brightman, "Forget Culture: Replacement, Transcendence, Relexification," *Cultural Anthropology* 10.4 (1995): 509–46; William Sewell Jr., "The Concept(s) of Culture," in *Beyond the Cultural Turn*, ed. Victoria Bonnell and Lynn Hunt, 35–61 (Berkeley: University of California Press, 1999); and Cristoph Brumann, "Writing for Culture: Why a Successful Concept Should Not Be Discarded," *Current Anthropology* 40, supplement (1999): S1–S27.

16  Brightman, "Forget Culture," 510.

17  Sewell, "The Concept(s) of Culture," 39.

18  Gilroy's stance, here, stems from his recognition of "a growing lack of consensus about what the defining cultural or ethnic core of blackness should encompass" (*Against Race*, 179).

19  See John Hartigan Jr., "Whiteness in the Field: Introduction to a Special Issue of *Identities*," *Identities* 7 (2000): 269–79; Hartigan, "The Difference between Whiteness and Whites," *Souls: A Critical Journal of Black Politics, Culture, and Society* 4 (2002): 59–63; Hartigan, "Who Are These White People? 'White Trash,' 'Hillbillies,' and 'Rednecks' as Marked Racial Subjects," in *White Out: The Continuing Significance of Racism*, ed. Eduardo Bonilla-Silva and Ashley Doane, 95–111 (New York: Routledge, 2003).

20  See John Hartigan Jr., *Racial Situations: Class Predicaments of Whiteness in Detroit* (Princeton, NJ: Princeton University Press, 1999).

21   See Pamela Perry, *Shades of White: White Kids and Racial Identities in High School* (Durham, NC: Duke University Press, 2002); Leland Saito, *Race and Politics: Asian Americans, Latinos, and Whites in a Los Angeles Suburb* (Urbana: University of Illinois Press, 1998); Roger Sanjek, *The Future of Us All: Race and Neighborhood Politics in Neighborhood New York* (Ithaca, NY: Cornell University Press, 1998).

22   Steven Gregory, *Black Corona: Race and the Politics of Place in an Urban Community* (Princeton, NJ: Princeton University Press, 1998). See also Jennifer Hochschild, *Facing Up to the American Dream: Race, Class, and the Soul of the Nation* (Princeton, NJ: Princeton University Press, 1995).

23   Michael Moffat, "The Discourse of the Dorm," in *Symbolizing America*, ed. Herve Varenne (Lincoln: University of Nebraska Press, 1986).

24   On this point, see Kyeyoung Park, "Use and Abuse of Race and Culture: Black-Korean Tensions in America," *American Anthropologist* 98 (1996): 492–505.

25   See Livio Sansone, *Blackness without Ethnicity: Constructing Race in Brazil* (New York: Palgrave Macmillan, 2003); Peter Wade, *Race, Nature, and Culture: An Anthropological Perspective* (London: Pluto, 2002); Mary Weismantel, *Cholas and Pishtacos: Stories of Race and Sex in the Andes* (Chicago: University of Chicago Press, 2001); Lorraine Kenney, *Daughters of Suburbia: Growing Up White, Middle-Class, and Female* (New Brunswick, NJ: Rutgers University Press, 2000).

26   George Lipsitz, "The Progressive Investment in Whiteness: Racialized Social Democracy and the 'White' Problem in American Studies," *American Quarterly* (1995): 372.

27   A number of cultural critics focus on liberalism, with its stress on individualism, as a cultural logic that undergirds racial exclusions. See David Theo Goldberg, *Racist Culture: Philosophy and the Politics of Meaning* (Oxford: Blackwell, 1993); Uday Mehta, *Liberalism and Empire: A Study in Nineteenth-Century British Liberal Thought* (Chicago: University of Chicago Press, 1999); Richard Delgado and Jean Stefancic, eds., *Critical Race Theory: The Cutting Edge* (Philadelphia: Temple University Press, 2000).

28   What I mean by a cultural perspective here can be usefully sketched in contrast to the centrality of identity in cultural studies. Stuart Hall explains, "I use 'identity' to refer to the meeting point, the point of suture, between on the one hand the discourses and practices which attempt to 'interpellate,' speak to us or hail us into place as the social subjects of particular discourses, and on the other hand, which produce subjectivities, which construct us as subjects which can be 'spoken'" (in Hall and Paul Du Gay, eds., *Questions of Cultural Identity* [London: Sage, 1996], 5–6). Without dismissing the importance of this perspective on subjects and discourse, culture posits social collectives broadly as objects of description and analysis.

29   John Hartigan Jr., *Odd Tribes: Toward a Cultural Analysis of White People* (Durham, NC: Duke University Press, forthcoming).

30   Anthropologists distinguish two senses of *culture*: one particular (e.g., American culture) and the other generic, referring to a common dimension of human behavior and belief. The lack of a cultural perspective on race today stems from the overemphasis on the former, as is evident in the debates from the 1960s through 1990s over the culture of poverty or the pathology of black culture. Regarding race today, I suggest the latter connotations of culture can provide great insight when paired with an understanding of the institutional and historical dimensions of race.

# Don Robotham

# Cosmopolitanism and Planetary Humanism:
# The Strategic Universalism of Paul Gilroy

One of the most important intellectual trends in the world today is cosmopolitanism and global civil society theory.[1] The basic argument of this viewpoint is that globalization in its economic, political, and cultural dimensions has undermined the saliency of the nation-state and that, therefore, the only intellectually viable position today is one of cosmopolitanism. Leading exponents of cosmopolitanism, theorists such as David Held, do not take a so-called hyperglobalization view—that the nation-state has lost all of its power in the contemporary world. They simply argue that this power has been substantially diminished, conceiving of the world order as one composed of newly "multilayered" allegiances that range from the subnational to the national, from regional to international scales.[2]

Cosmopolitanism has been at pains to contest essentialist notions of identity, notions that give an ahistorical ontological reality to cultural and national identities. It has also opposed itself to hard versions of multiculturalism, versions that are highly critical of the tendency in liberal cosmopolitanism to mask racial and class privilege behind the veil of formal liberal individualism, granting a very limited sociological reality to

The *South Atlantic Quarterly* 104:3, Summer 2005.

nations or identities.[3] In combating these essentialist notions of identity, cosmopolitanism puts forward an equally abstract theory: the constructivist view of such nations, of all social identities.[4] This approach portrays the individual as the only reliable ontological reality and the collective as, in some sense, utterly artificial. Constructivism logically concludes in a formal liberal universalism wherein an abstract humanity—not specific nations or identities—becomes the privileged analytical category. While nations are imagined, humanity is real.[5]

National and cultural boundaries within humanity are, of course, conceded some existence, but this is a transient, historical existence that does not have the same ontological status as the one carried by humanity as a categorical whole. Yet this cosmopolitan position is often inconsistent and unclear. While deploring national identities and nationalisms, it seems to implicitly affirm the durability of Great Power nations, for it is hard to find anyone who seriously envisages the imminent weakening of Britain, France, Germany, Japan, China, Russia, or the United States. Indeed, the backdrop to this color-blind and cosmopolitan critique of African American nationalism is often the counterintuitive and rather self-contradictory claim that such nationalist reasoning is actually much more American than anything else, certainly more than Black Nationalists would ever care to admit.

This constructivist viewpoint can be found not only in liberal cosmopolitanism but in certain versions of Marxism as well. Indeed, there is a very deep opposition to nationalism in some variants of Marxism that regard it wholly negatively as a tool that the bourgeoisie manipulates to distract the proletariat from internationalist solidarities, dragging the working class, by way of jingoism, toward duped complicity with imperialist conquest. In this view, nationalism has provided the basis for class collaboration, most woefully expressed in the collapse of the Second International during the First World War. Typical of this tradition in Marxism, a tradition that views nationalism in a wholly negative light, is the work of Eric Hobsbawm.

With European nationalism in mind, Hobsbawm wrote the following:

> The characteristic nationalist movements of the late twentieth century are essentially negative, or rather divisive. Hence the insistence on "ethnicity" and linguistic differences, each or both sometimes combined with religion. . . . Time and again they seem to be reactions of weakness and fear, attempts to erect barricades to keep at bay the forces of the modern world.[6]

This view concedes a certain reality to nations and nationalism, but only in the negative sense: Nationalism is to be understood as a response brought on by the "anxieties" of modernity, a response with little positive value of its own. The implication is that a proper coming to grips with the real forces shaping the capitalist world, instead of a retreat into the false comforts of nationalism, would lead to the abandonment of national identities and the adoption of an internationalist perspective. This particular tradition regards nationalism much as some Marxists regard religion, as a form of false consciousness, as a fruit of the "invention of tradition" that Marxists are duty-bound to expose.[7] But the tendency to see little or no merit in national identities and nationalism is not only an obstacle to understanding third world nationalism; it also prevents an appreciation of the fundamental basis for nationalism in so-called developed countries. This becomes highly problematic because the liberal tendency to portray nationalism as wholly negative (and the result of "reactions of weakness and fear") ends up handing the nation over to right-wing chauvinists and essentialists. This denial of any merit whatsoever to the nation is most offensive not to wealthy elites, who tend to laud different versions of jet-set cosmopolitanism, but rather to members of popular sectors. Contrary to what negative theories of nationalism conclude, the attachment of working people to the nation is not mainly because of ignorance or chauvinism: it is because the mass of people often associate their most dearly prized rights with the existence and history of the nation and of national struggles. Constructivist theories of national identity, with their negative assessments of the collective, are ill equipped to grasp these realities.

Substantive—as distinct from constructivist—theories of national identity and nationalism are rare in social theory today, being identified (mistakenly, in my view) with simple essentialism. The closest one comes to such a substantive theory is in the work of the late Ernest Gellner.[8] In Gellner's view, nations are the inevitable result (and functional requirement) of modernization as social process. In particular, nationalism and a sense of nationhood arise from an industrialism that, in order to function effectively, requires the creation of a mass education system. Thus, according to Gellner, industrialization and its accompanying systems of public education and intellectual standardization constituted the very citizens who would subsequently be most receptive to nationalist ideas. For Gellner, nations were not simply about the "invention of tradition" by a cultural elite; they had a deeper foundation in objective economic and cultural processes. Gellner, although no nationalist, saw clearly that nationalism, especially in its civic form, could not be accurately regarded in a wholly negative light:[9] as in the historical cases exemplified by Britain, France, and the United States, it had been the bearer of many of the same values that liberals and democrats hold most dear. Despite appearances, Gellner's views should not be confused with a theory of historical materialism. Gellner was a Weberian and a neo-Kantian, someone who very clearly was thinking of industrialism in its *normative* dimension.[10]

Despite Gellner's best attempts, however, anthropology and cultural studies are today dominated by constructivist theories of nations and identities. An outstanding recent example of the problems that cosmopolitanism and constructivism face in addressing nationalism is the book *Against Race: Imagining Political Culture beyond the Color Line.*[11] In this work, Paul Gilroy calls for academics in general and black intellectuals and activists in particular to abandon the concept of race. Instead, Gilroy proposes we should adopt a position in which race and nation no longer figure as central political concepts and in which the particular struggles of black people are dissolved within a general struggle for the rights of all of humanity. Influenced by Frantz Fanon, he calls this position "planetary humanism" (or "strategic universalism") and describes its end state as "postanthropological" (270–71).[12] Interestingly, this view puts Gilroy closer to the position of the "hyperglobalizers," of which, as pointed out above, many cosmopolitans such as Held are highly critical.

The book is not simply an academic exercise. As the presence of the word *political* in its American subtitle indicates, it seeks to have a much broader impact. As in the cases mentioned above, Gilroy puts forward a constructivist concept of identity, which fails to grasp the sociological reality of nationalism and racial consciousness—or how these social, cultural, and political movements are rooted in (and arise from) the actual conditions of life experienced by a given people. In particular, Gilroy has no theory of the *contemporary* social forces that produce nationalism, and, like others in this tradition, he sees nationalism negatively. The result is an abstract juxtaposing of essentialism to universalism in the manner characteristic of liberal cosmopolitanism. The notion that the road to internationalism passes through—does not bypass—nationalism is not appreciated. Moreover, the abstract universalism that Gilroy proposes as an alternative to nationalism is inherently unable to be consistently antiracist and universalistic. This is because these perspectives, as both Held and Gilroy make clear, hold firmly to the view that any attempt to go beyond a social democratic regulation of global capitalism is simply inconceivable and unworkable.[13] But the realization of universalistic goals will always be in conflict with capitalism as a social, economic, and political order. In the end, this humanism must remain purely "planetary" since it will exist solely at the formal-legal and moral levels, masking the substantive power, wealth, and privileges enjoyed in practice by dominant classes, identities, and Great Power nations.

## Against Nation

Gilroy constructs his argument as a critique of black essentialism, but in fact his argument goes much further. It is not simply against nationalist excesses but against the very validity of nationalism in general (and Black Nationalism, in particular) as a deeply rooted political and historical phenomenon. His cosmopolitanism can admit to no deep boundaries—historical, cultural, or national—within a humanity so abstractly conceived. Cosmopolitan theory is usually applied to the issue of the impact of globalization on territorial nation-states. The significance of Gilroy's work, however, is this: it is probably the first attempt to apply cosmopolitanism to Black Nationalism—an identity not constituted as a nation-state. His use of black essentialism as a stick with which to beat Black Nationalism gives us an opportunity to briefly address some broader theoretical issues: what is the basis of national (or racial) identities and what is their reality? Why cannot one simply dissolve these identities into a generally undifferentiated humanity by an act of intellectual will? Why is Gilroy's proposal to address the issues of oppression specific to each nationalism by encompassing them all in a general human rights struggle profoundly misconceived? These are some of the questions this essay seeks to answer.

In order to uphold his viewpoint, Gilroy, like Held, does not argue that national distinctions do not exist. He freely concedes that such distinctions obviously exist but argues that they are superficial. He writes of "the superficialities of history or language, religion or conquest," which are commonly held to distinguish specific peoples (38). If, indeed, cultural distinctions are as superficial as Gilroy holds them to be, then it is conceivable that there would be no point in having separate national struggles. By definition, such a separate movement would be capturing only what was superficial about the history of a people and missing the central fact of their existence—their common humanity.

But is it the case that language, religion, and conquest (or, more to the point, being conquered) represent only the "superficialities of history"? Was the slave trade such a superficiality? Or slavery itself? Or the imperial conquest of Africa? Or apartheid? It is not the case that once one argues for the rootedness of identities in such profound historical experiences one is necessarily an essentialist or a "primordialist," as Gilroy implies. Essentialists argue from the premise of an indefinable, unique ahistorical essence (which may or may not be conceived of as biologically based) characterizing the particular identity, making it what it is and driving its destiny. Primordialists are less explicit but equally mysterious; their arguments tend to take a psychological turn about the need to identify with one's own group, which simply is and has ever been from time immemorial—no further explanation needed! It is clear that neither essentialism nor primordialism explains anything; they largely satisfy themselves with asserting the very thing that needs to be explained. These are hypotheses for which we have no need.

A careful analysis of the operation of economic, social, political, and cultural factors shaping the lives of particular collectivities of people—and in turn being shaped by them over a long period in very specific historical contexts—will adequately explain how some identities are formed and persist with their distinctive characteristics, and how other groups dissolve, disappear, or are absorbed into larger social, political, and cultural units. Contrary to what many think, historical materialist theories seek not only to explain the development of classes, class-divided societies, and the state. Such a view represents a classist reduction of this theoretical approach. On the contrary, such theories have always sought to simultaneously develop a substantive theory of identity, nationality, and nationalism integrated with the theory of classes. A cursory acquaintance with the works of Engels, for example, should make this clear.[14] Whether the theory succeeds in this aim is another matter, but there can be little doubt that the development of an integrated theory of class and identity is the intention.

This notion—that identities are the precipitate of history—is a different idea from that of identities as "imagined communities," as put forward in the work of Benedict Anderson.[15] It is more like what Stuart Hall was referring to when he wrote of the "very profound set of distinctive historically defined black experiences."[16] Anderson's theory is a constructivist one in which identities have a secondary ontological status as "imagined." But the point not to lose sight of is this: the distinctive collective social experience is as real as the individual, if not more so. This common history is first of all collectively experienced—often bitterly experienced—in real life. Literary and other cultural forms do not "create" this experience. On the contrary, they arise out of it and attempt to grasp it at the level of the individual "imagination." They operate at the cultural level to strengthen (or weaken) a community that has already been created by real, common, historical experiences of a most far-reaching kind. Nationalism may be an ideological phenomenon, but national identities are not.

In some cases, but by no means all, these common historical experiences are of great antiquity, going back over hundreds of years.[17] When these hundreds of years of common history include merciless cruelties, degradations, and exploitation by the same oppressor, a particularly fierce nationalism is often the result. This collective sentiment simmers over centuries and then may burst forth with fanatical ferocity. While at the abstract level one can extract the universally human from the particular experience of local groups, all people make history in the concrete. It is this actually concrete common historical experience that generates distinctive national identities and necessarily finds expression in national movements dedicated to that specific cause. Because all history is concrete and because the universal always expresses itself in and through the concrete, never separately and apart as a featureless universal, one cannot confront universal issues and struggles in any manner other than concrete forms. In other words, universalism is not simply a matter of asserting a universal Kantian moral imperative or the priority of international law and human rights over the sovereignty of nation-states. Universalism *has to be made* in substantive political and economic practice over a long period of historical time—and in the face of determined opposition from extremely powerful interests.

One has to understand the more general issues underlying any specific struggle, linking that particular nationalist movement to the political movements of other groups and peoples. But this deeper understanding should not lead one to lose sight of the specifics of a given struggle—or to abandon that specificity in the name of general principles. To do this would mean that the specific oppression and knowledge of particular groups would never be addressed or realized in its distinctiveness. All humans do not experience the particular forms of racial oppression that, say, African Americans experience, no matter how sympathetic these humans may be. An emancipation that is purely human and universal in its very nature will address only the general experiences of oppression common to all oppressed peoples. It will fail to address the very thing that most needs addressing: the specific forms of antiblack racial oppression that are reserved for people of African descent. It will simply leave the conditions of oppression specific to each case untouched. It will also mean that the specific contributions that the Black National movement brings to the human experience will be lost. In other words, planetary humanism will diminish humanity. It is much the same with gender oppression: neither a class nor an abstractly human emancipation of women will get to the heart of the matter. The specific oppressions of gender must be confronted and dealt with *in their specificity.* Likewise, the particularities of national and racial oppression, especially as they affect people of African descent, are not to be evaded from above. This is one reason a nationalist movement of African Americans is a historical necessity. Needless to say, this struggle has to be waged first by African Americans themselves—and not only because of self-interest. In the course of waging this prolonged and difficult struggle, the African American identity is itself forged and ultimately allowed to flourish, making its distinctive contribution to the general development of humanity as a whole.

Nationalism is an extremely varied phenomenon: whether one supports nationalist aims or not must depend on the specific social and political context. One should not imagine that Black Nationalism will solve all the social problems of African Americans, since many of these are not only racial but also articulated with class, gender, and sexuality problems. Equally, one ought never to forget the famously pithy proclamation of Samuel Johnson: patriotism is the last refuge of scoundrels. The forms of national narrow-mindedness that border on and are fed by racism have to be steadfastly opposed. The same applies to essentialism, wherever it is found. But in this given case, the more important point is this: One cannot use the critique of essentialist tendencies in black—indeed, in *all*—nationalism as a means of undermining Black Nationalism as a whole. Nationalism, by definition, is a movement of the entire nation, therefore it is bound to contain within it all the varied political tendencies found within any given nation, from the most conservative to the most radical. There is no such thing as a national movement with a single political tendency, and there could never be. For this reason, one must not give a blank check of approval to nationalism in all its forms and at all times. Everything depends on the concrete set of circumstances, the social and political tendencies found to be dominant in the leadership and the basic aims of the nationalist movement at a given time.

Gilroy's individualism and textualism lead him to conceive of the national distinctions that traditionally have been held to characterize a particular people—art, literature, music, language, history, contiguous territory—as literally constructed by the activist individuals of the particular culture and, thereafter, "propelled" into popular consciousness by the media. He does not approach identities as arising from actual profound collective experiences over long periods of historical time in the manner already discussed. On the contrary, Gilroy, borrowing from Benedict Anderson's theory, argues that the media are used literally to "create" the "forms of solidarity and national consciousness" distinctive to particular people, and that this was how "the idea of belonging" was "propelled" in the nineteenth century (110). Culture, therefore, is really a particularly artful and far-reaching form of propaganda imposed on a vulnerable public but not on the rationalistic cultural critic, someone equipped with the ability to see through its deceptions. Gilroy is striving, he maintains, "to articulate placeless imaginings of identity as well as new bases for solidarity and synchronized action" (111–12). Following this notion of identities as artificial constructs, consider how Gilroy conceives of the process by means of which a black identity gets "created." He writes:

> In the period after emancipation, essentialist approaches to building solidarity and synchronized communal mobilization have often relied upon the effects of racial hierarchy to supply the binding agent that could in turn precipitate national consciousness. Routine experiences of oppression, repression, and abuse—however widespread— could not be transferred into the political arena from which blacks were barred. Instead they became the basis for dissident cultures and an alternative public world. Togetherness produced under these conditions was inherently unreliable. Its instability added to the attractiveness of the authoritarian solutions that offered shortcuts to solidarity, especially where everyday consciousness of racial difference fell short of the models of nationhood that had been borrowed wholesale from the Europe-centered history of the dominant group. (38–39)

The idea here seems to be that African American nationalism (and Black Nationalism as a whole within the West) was, from its inception, "inherently unreliable." This was because of the lack of civil and political rights that would have allowed black grievances to find democratic expression. Being thus bottled up, defensive and often extremist forms of nationalism were developed by various artist-thinkers to compensate for this deficiency and to paper over internal division. Black culture became a "dissident culture" inhabiting "an alternative public world" of social-psychological compensation. This is an astonishing reduction and distortion of the extraordinarily complex and profound economic, social, cultural, and political process by means of which an African American identity was formed in the Americas during and after plantation slavery.

No doubt, as with all cultures in a similar situation, many divisions existed—social, cultural, linguistic, ethnic, geographical, and political—within the populations taken from Africa and enslaved in America. No doubt some tendencies in this culture were purely "dissident"—that is, aggrieved largely by their "exclusion" from white society (to resort to a good New Labour formulation)—and were concerned primarily with how to become incorporated within whiteness.[18] After all, during slavery, the British had a step-by-step process in Jamaica whereby free coloreds—if they were rich enough and light-skinned enough and had prominent whites who would vouch for them—could petition to have themselves statutorily accorded the privileges of "free-born Englishmen." This precocious form of "honorary whiteness" was, in the nature of the case, reserved for a few and served its purpose of drawing some free coloreds away from the fight against slavery.

But anyone who has the slightest acquaintance with slave plantation regimes; the many heroic slave revolts against all odds, especially in countries such as Jamaica, Surinam, and, of course, Haiti; the role played by religion and African political memories; the experience of many defeats and demoralizations (and yet the persistence in struggle over centuries) will know that "dissidence," fostered by exclusion from whiteness, was and is a totally irrelevant issue. It was precisely in the course of overcoming these harsh experiences of slavery that ethnic divisions brought over from Africa were reconfigured and a new African American identity emerged. This unification occurred despite the new ethnic and social divisions (based on color, region, occupation, and politics) that developed within the racial slave plantation society in the Americas.

This is not about "dissidence," or "oppositional identities," or "cultures of insubordination."[19] Gilroy fails to grasp this process in its positivity—the creativity at the core of the history of particular identities in general and of black history in Africa and the Americas in particular. Indeed, without this creativity at the local level, the possibility of a universal human creativity could hardly exist. The point is that the formation of an African American identity was not the result of a "binding agent that could then precipitate national consciousness." As scholars such as Wilson Jeremiah Moses have pointed out, this is an upside-down depiction of the process.[20] The forms of national consciousness that took hold did so because they "reverberated" with the actual social and historical experiences of millions of people. What one needs to focus on, therefore, is the real living experience of these millions and not just the texts of a few cultural activists, texts that more or less adequately or inadequately strived to articulate or clarify their particular version of these experiences. Insofar as these writings evoked a powerful and lasting popular response, it was to the extent that they were able to plumb the depths of this real collective experience, which was at one and the same time a common process and one not experienced homogeneously by all African Americans, let alone by all peoples of African descent in the diaspora.

Likewise, although undoubtedly influenced by European notions of nationhood, it is inaccurate and misleading to characterize this process as "borrowed wholesale from the Europe-centered history of the dominant group." This assertion simply rehashes the questionable diffusionist theses presented in the early postcolonial works of Chatterjee.[21] Such a caricature springs from the depiction of national movements as simply ideational and, as Smith writes, "wholly derivative," not an independent organizational and political process arising from its own circumstances (29–30). As Smith pointed out in his critique of a similar thesis of "imitation" put forward by Elie Kedourie in his book on nationalism, such an idea implies that the minds of the alleged borrowers are "*tabula rasa* ready to be enslaved by newfangled ideologies against which they have no defense" (37).[22] One-sidedly harping on "wholesale borrowing" is, curiously enough, a kind of intellectual nationalism (everything must be pristine and created *ex nihilo*) that fails to perceive what *is* new and innovative amid the anguish about "borrowing." In reality, there is ample evidence that Black Nationalist revolts during slavery, for example, borrowed not from Europe but from Africa. As is commonly known, many early slave revolts in Jamaica were organized along relatively narrow ethnic lines and sought to reestablish (and to some extent did establish) maroon communities modeled on eighteenth-century Akan concepts of statehood.[23]

There is another point worth noting about Gilroy's conception of the process by which African American identity has unfolded and continues to unfold. He does not relate this process to any other historical experience than that of plantation slavery. Gilroy never analyzes the postemancipation period in a detailed and differentiated historical manner—Black Reconstruction and its overthrow, black migration to the North, and the emergence of a black working class in the old (now "sunset") industries of steel, automobiles, and railroads. These tumultuous historical experiences are simply lumped together under a general postemancipation rubric. Although Gilroy often has much to say about the music of Motown, he relates this to the experience with slavery and not to the experience with Henry Ford (194–95).[24] There is nothing in his work about the novel battle with what, in many ways, was a more racist *northern* urban segregation in housing, education, jobs, transportation, entertainment, and other public spheres. Above all, there is nothing about black experiences in the armed forces of the United States, experiences that, in both the nineteenth and twentieth centuries, have been a most profound source of African American identity and nationalism.

There is nothing in Gilroy's book about the struggle against racism in the trade union movement, the entry into two-party politics, and the complicated relationships with the progressive movement. There is nothing about the development of relations not just with the Anglos and Irish of the North but with African Americans from the North, Afro-Caribbean migrants, Poles, Italians, and Jews—the new immigrants arriving in their millions from Eastern Europe at precisely the time when African American migration to the North was getting under way. Nor is there anything on the complicated encounter with Hispanic culture—a vital question today. The actual material history of the racialized black industrial experience in cities such as Detroit, Cleveland, Pittsburgh, Chicago, or Philadelphia (and, in a different way, New York, Los Angeles, and Atlanta) in the twentieth and twenty-first centuries—so absolutely vital for understanding modern black nationalism—does not play a role in his conception of the forces that shaped and still shape black identity. Yet one cannot understand the consequences of racialized deindustrialization for the black community today unless one first understands the racialized industrialization and urbanization that preceded it.

Plantation slavery can, up to a point, explain eighteenth- and nineteenth-century African American identity formation. It cannot explain *contemporary* twentieth- and twenty-first-century developments. The processes that shape contemporary African American identity and provide the foundation for the resurgence of global racism today can be found only by a detailed analysis of the operations of a corporate capitalism that is itself global and racialized. Such an analysis is nowhere to be found in the work of Gilroy. The "empire" of which he wrote in *Empire Strikes Back* (and which he rewrites in *Against Race*) is the colonial empire that was established primarily by Britain and France during the era of mercantile and industrial capitalism and is now safely tucked away in history books. Today, however, the machinations of Britain and France, although not inconsequential, are the least of the problem.

Gilroy, at various points, concedes that there is a vital economic and political context to contemporary African American popular culture. This is the crisis triggered by the entire process of deindustrialization and globalization, a process that has laid waste to critical parts of the American manufacturing sector—automobiles, steel—in which the black working class had traditionally been employed in the North. As pointed out above, this deindustrialization is remarked on without any grasp of the previous period of industrialization. Nonetheless, in discussing various explanations for the rise of an aggressive black popular culture, Gilroy writes:

> Lastly, it is viewed as a structural feature of de-industrialized capitalism that no longer has need for the living labor of terminally broken black communities that are now marginal to the ongoing practice of flexible accumulation and may be contemptuous of the limited economic opportunities offered to them by "neo-slave" employment in a caste of servile, insecure, and underpaid domestic laborers, caregivers, cleaners, deliverers, messengers, attendants, and guards. The segmentation and casualization of employment, health, and dwelling are the foundations on which the destruction of the inner-city's civic order has come to rest. (198)

There are several other points in the book where Gilroy instances a similar sociology of black popular culture, but he does not accept these explanations of "a mechanistic response to racism and material privation" as containing anything but "a tiny rational kernel in a mystical shell," which, ultimately, he says, "do[es] not satisfy" (198–99).

To Gilroy's mind, these materialist explanations smack too much of the nationalist apologetics of black intellectual elites. He writes: "Faced with that struggle and with de-industrialization, the proliferation of intra-communal divisions based upon wealth and money, sexuality and gender, the black elite may find it expedient to fall back on exceptionalist narratives and essential identities. . . . I understand these responses, but I wonder how much they are about a privileged group mystifying its own increasing remoteness from the lives of most black people, whose habits, and tastes can no longer be considered self-legitimating indicators of racial integrity" (270). One of the main aims of *Against Race* is, therefore, to sharply criticize various spokespersons for Black Nationalism in the United States. The targets are, first, certain leading black intellectuals—the work of Tricia Rose, Cornel West, and Ishmael Reed is referenced—who, it is alleged, are in one way or another contributing to a narrow nationalism within the black community (181n5, 98n37).[25] Gilroy's basic charge is that these intellectuals are a petty bourgeoisie alienated from the black community and anxious to impose their class interests and anxieties on the people as a whole. A second target is black popular artists—Ice Cube is repeatedly castigated—who, according to Gilroy, foist an even more damaging popular chauvinism on the black majority through their mainly "visual" art and nationalistic pronouncements. Since, for Gilroy, the essence of fascist aesthetics is "visuality," these movies of Ice Cube are "fascist": end of story. It is true that Gilroy at one point qualifies this extremely broad and basically useless notion of fascist aesthetics. He writes of the "ecstatic, racialized physicality" of the work of Leni Riefenstahl, which is certainly more to the point (178).

Yet, as the following quotation demonstrates, Gilroy in practice deploys an all-inclusive concept of fascism as visuality. He writes: "I have already argued that the camera was directly responsible for the quality of solidarity celebrated by the fascist movements. It did not just attend the festivities arranged to mark and communicate the rebirth of the nation after its period of weakness, decadence and slumber" (170–71). This notion of visuality is so sweeping that it renders itself meaningless. If the camera itself (as distinct from the aesthetics of the director-editor-producer) contains fascist tendencies, then *all* of modern cinema and television, from the most innocuous fantasy to the most highly political docudrama, partakes to some degree in this fascist aesthetic. Such an idea is an absurd argument that black visuality, *eo ipso*, is fascist.[26] But either on the basis of this sweeping notion or on the basis of the narrower concept, this charge is utterly preposterous. The literal physicality of the "hood" has a completely different source and expresses entirely different aesthetic from the spiritualized "strength" found in the films of Riefenstahl, the novels of Ernst Junger or, from another angle, the empty monumentalism of Albert Speer.[27] The aesthetic of black popular culture—oral or visual—does not yearn for the restoration of ancient privileges of aristocracy, class, and race by glorifying a Darwinian brutality shrouded in the ethereal so as to disguise its true substance. There is no mystical "triumph of the will" in black popular culture — visual or oral. It is simply a very bold interpretation of *some critical aspects* of life in deindustrialized northern inner cities, warts and all. In many ways hip-hop is a modern version of what Hitler and Goebbels denounced as *Neger-jazz*, fit to be consumed only by the *Asphaltliteraten* — that is to say, by Jews, Bolsheviks, and the other "rootless cosmopolitans" corrupted by urban life. Yet Gilroy asserts throughout that the black community in the United States is besieged from both above and below. From above a self-seeking petty bourgeoisie strives to discipline and punish them into lining up as a political battalion supporting the narrow aspirations of this black petty bourgeoisie. From below, popular artists, in collusion with the transnational culture industries, dabble in fascism, exploiting and mystifying blackness for the crassest commercial ends (214–15).

## Cosmopolitanism and Planetary Humanism

Gilroy seeks a unilateral political disarmament by the black community. It is not known whether a similar recommendation is being made to Hispanic, Anglo, Jewish, and other identities in the United States — or for all nation-states in the world today. If so, it is a particularly inopportune appeal, given the recent forthright reassertion of "Anglo-Protestant" nativism in the work of Samuel Huntington, strongly reminiscent of the earlier works of Madison Grant and Lothrop Stoddard — *The Passing of the Great Race* and *The Rising Tide of Color against White World Supremacy*, respectively — written at a similar point in the imperial globalization of the late nineteenth century, also a moment of mass international migration.[28]

In return, Gilroy offers to replace nationalism with "planetary humanism," which he thinks will be more effective in eliminating antiblack racism, ending black oppression, and constructing an equalized social world. Gilroy would not be the first to put forward this idea that internationalism dictates the dissolution of nationalist movements. In fact, Gilroy's cosmopolitanism is really a reformulation by a black scholar of the "color-blind" position that has been discredited in the United States at least since affirmative action in the 1960s, even as it still remains enthroned in many liberal, conservative, and Marxist circles throughout Britain and France. It is, therefore, reasonable to ask, What is this "alternative, postanthropological understanding of culture" of which he writes (271)? What is this "planetary" in "planetary humanism"?

One should approach this question by first pointing out what "strategic universalism" is *not*. It has nothing to do with notions of a proletarian internationalism springing out of the socialist tradition. As already noted, Gilroy thinks, like Anthony Giddens, that we are "beyond Left and Right" and that an alternative economic and political system to capitalism is utterly inconceivable today. His concept of humanism reaches back to an earlier era of bourgeois humanism associated traditionally with the Enlightenment. Gilroy is clear in his own mind that he stands in this tradition of Kantian Enlightenment. Referring to Kant and Hegel, he writes of this tradition: "While I value that political pedigree, I want to try to be clear about exactly where this line of thought differs from the noble precursors in those traditions that have contributed so extensively to the ideas and the practices of antiracism" (29). The problem for Gilroy is that the cosmopolitan rationality of Enlightenment rhetoric contained a racist component that has to be cleansed before it can fulfill its universalistic promise. The problem is that Kant suffered from "epidermal thinking in its emergent forms" (46). His point is that the racism of the European rationalistic tradition has to be confronted if one wants, as he does, to see "the development of an emphatically postracial humanism" and a "multicultural democracy" (37, 41).[29] A "wholesale reckoning" is needed in which the issue of Enlightenment racism — what Emmanuel Chukwudi Eze, in a well-known essay, called "the color of reason" — is made into a central issue.[30]

Gilroy's call therefore is for a full and decisive confrontation with this racism, a confrontation that will finally cleanse cosmopolitanism of its compromising racist heritage once and for all. This is clearly not a call for the abandonment of rationalism and universalism. Gilroy, despite his poststructuralist lingo, is not an anti-Enlightenmenter.[31] The call for a consistent rationalism can then become truly universal and embrace a humanity no longer divided into races, cultures, or nations. This is what Gilroy means when he says his goal is "planetary humanism." However, there is a difficulty with this position, a difficulty that needs to be confronted. Can cosmopolitanism be cleansed? The works of nearly every single liberal representative of this tradition, whether Locke, Montesquieu, Raynal, Kant, or Hegel, exhibits a most revealing paradox. Locke, Montesquieu, Raynal, Kant, and Hegel all agree that slavery is wrong. Equally, all of them hasten to insist that slavery, if it is to be abolished at all (this did not arise for Locke, with his investments in the slave trade), must only be abolished slowly.[32] The position of Kant and Hegel did not simply reflect the European views of their time. It reflected a particularly conservative and racist bourgeois outlook, different, for example, from the views of that Scottish jurist of blessed memory—George Wallace![33]

There is also a broader lesson to be learned from this, one that we neglect at our peril. Locke, Montesquieu, Raynal, Kant, and Hegel are luminaries of bourgeois humanism—the "boldest and the best," to use Gilroy's words. There is no tradition of "planetary humanism" or cosmopolitanism without them. The interesting question is why, in spite of their undoubtedly humanist views, they were unable to throw off racist positions. Why were they "not able to withstand" racism (30)? To be more blunt, why were some of them (Kant and Hegel, for example) in the very vanguard of racism? Gilroy asks, but cannot answer, this very crucial question.

Montesquieu, Raynal, Kant, and Hegel wanted slavery abolished and wanted to see a new world brought into existence based only on formally free wage labor. Their outlook is not that of slave masters; on the contrary, it is an antislavery, probourgeois outlook. But they do not want this "humanist" outcome to take place in a manner that could possibly endanger the existing pillars of society. They want an end to feudal and slave privileges and the emergence of a society based solely on reason and humanity. But they want even more that the transition to full capitalism should take place on the basis of the existing hierarchies and privileges. Immediate emancipation must, therefore, be prevented at all costs.

Their support of privilege and property came first, their humanism a distant second. So it has ever been with this tradition, and so it remains. In fact, the forces driving this inconsistency today are far greater than in the eighteenth and nineteenth centuries, since the quantum of property and privilege at stake is incomparably greater. This is why, despite the undoubted sincerity of many cosmopolitans, planetary humanism is properly called bourgeois humanism: because it is a conditional humanism, inherently incapable of being consistently antiracist, of standing up for substantive (not only formal-legal or moral) equality between peoples, even as it argues that slavery and racism are wrong. It is a humanism confined to the planetary sphere because any attempt to bring it down to earth and to make it flesh raises the specter of lost privileges, the very privileges enjoyed by existing elites—including progressive liberal cosmopolitan ones. In fact, one could say that cosmopolitanism, as distinct from internationalism, is the universalism specific to capitalism. The fundamental limitation of cosmopolitanism and planetary humanism lies in their adherence to capitalism—whether this is a critical and dissenting adherence (as is the case with the global social democracy of Held), or a more enthusiastic embrace (by Giddens and his Third Way ideology), or even the more common and unthinking garden variety. As long as global capitalism is regarded as immovable, humanism can only be asserted at the pious level of Kant—or in the form of contemporary international law and human rights. The step to a really existing, substantive internationalism in which states, identities, and individuals are materially equal remains a bridge still hard to cross.

When this cosmopolitanism is confronted with the real exercise of imperial power, it retreats into vague concepts such as "regressive globalization."[34] This term simply registers cosmopolitan shock and impotence in the face of the naked exercise of state power on the global stage, a power that, according to the theory, ought not to have happened. The revelation that, rhetoric and the principles of international law notwithstanding, the global system rests on force, power, and wealth comes as an unpleasant and disorienting surprise. Cosmopolitanism at this point is compelled to develop some version of anti-imperialism, but how can it credibly do so while clinging to purely negative conceptions of nationalism and refusing to reopen the question of moving beyond capitalism? The fact that, as Held insists, we cannot return to the failures of state socialism and of social democracy means that this necessary process of renewal is extremely difficult. But it does not mean that this effort must not be made, which would resign us, by default, to life in the capitalist iron cage.

Held grasps the complexities and contradictions of these issues far better than Gilroy, which is why Held objects so strenuously to the traditional liberal formula, derived from John Stuart Mill and dogmatized by Friedrich Hayek, that equality is the enemy of liberty.[35] But Gilroy does not understand that this is the real secret of his postanthropological humanism. To abandon the struggle for the legitimate national interests of *any* people in return for this poisoned chalice would be catastrophic. It means not just the abandonment of race and the struggles of black people, but also the abandonment of humanity itself.

### Notes

1   David Held, Anthony McGrew, David Goldblatt, and Jonathan Perraton, *Global Transformations: Politics, Economics, and Culture* (Stanford, CA: Stanford University Press, 1999); David Held and Anthony G. McGrew, eds., *The Global Transformations Reader: An Introduction to the Globalization Debate*, 2nd ed. (Cambridge: Polity, 2003); Mary Kaldor, Helmut Anheier, and Marlies Glasius, eds., *Global Civil Society 2003* (Oxford: Oxford University Press, 2004).

2   Montserrat Guibernau, "Globalization, Cosmopolitanism, and Democracy: An Interview," March 11, 2001, www.polity.co.uk/global/held.htm (accessed September 26, 2004).

3   B. Parekh, *Rethinking Multiculturalism: Cultural Diversity and Political Theory* (London: Macmillan, 2000); Nick Stevenson, "Cosmopolitanism, Multiculturalism, and Citizenship," *Sociological Research Online*, 7.1 (2002), www.socresonline.org.uk/7/1/stevenson .html (accessed September 28, 2004).

4   On the importance of constructivism to cosmopolitanism, see David Held and Anthony McGrew, *Globalization/Anti-Globalization* (Cambridge: Polity, 2002), 30.

5   Hoffman suggests ironically that it is globalization which is being imagined! See Stanley Hoffman, "Clash of Globalizations," in *The Global Transformations Reader: An Introduction to the Globalization Debate*, ed. David Held and Anthony McGrew (Cambridge: Polity, 2003), 109–10.

6   E. J. Hobsbawm, *Nations and Nationalism since 1870* (Cambridge: Cambridge University Press, 1997), 164.

7   Eric Hobsbawm and Terence Ranger, eds., *The Invention of Tradition* (Cambridge: Cambridge University Press, 1983).

8   See Ernest Gellner, "Nations and Nationalism," in *New Perspectives on the Past*, ed. R. I. Moore (Ithaca, NY: Cornell University Press, 1983). For a recent review and evaluation of the theory of Gellner, see Brendan O'Leary, "Ernest Gellner's Diagnoses of Nationalism: A Critical Overview; or, What Is Living and What Is Dead in Ernest Gellner's Philosophy of Nationalism?" in *The State of the Nation: Ernest Gellner and the Theory of Nationalism*, ed. John A. Hall, 40–88 (Cambridge: Cambridge University Press, 2000).

9   Ernest Gellner, "Reply to Critics," in *The Social Philosophy of Ernest Gellner*, ed. John A. Hall and Ian C. Jarvie (Amsterdam: Rodopi, 1996).

10  Gellner, "Nations and Nationalism," 19–29.

11  Paul Gilroy, *Against Race: Imagining Political Culture beyond the Color Line* (Cambridge, MA: Harvard University Press, 2000). Subsequent references to this work appear in the text. Interestingly, the book is published in the United Kingdom under the title *Between Camps: Nations, Cultures, and the Allure of Race* (London: Allen Lane, Penguin, 2000). This British title confirms one of the basic points being made here: that Gilroy's argument is as much a case against nation as a case against race. For a critique of Gilroy's earlier work, see Don Robotham, *Culture, Society, Economy: Globalization and Its Alternatives* (London: Sage, 2005).

12  Gilroy's use of the phrase "strategic universalism" is clearly an attempt to contrast it with the "strategic essentialism" once proposed by Gayatri Spivak and referred to approvingly by Stuart Hall. See Stuart Hall, "What Is This 'Black' in Black Popular Culture?" in *Stuart Hall: Critical Dialogues in Cultural Studies*, ed. David Morley and Kuan-Hsing Chen (New York: Routledge, 1997), 472.

13  Gilroy writes of "the outmoded opposition between Left and Right" (*Against Race*, 216). This is very reminiscent of the views of Lord Anthony Giddens set out in Anthony Giddens, *Beyond Left and Right: The Future of Radical Politics* (Cambridge: Polity, 1994). Held, in his interview with Guibernau, is more critical of Giddens. Yet he did nonetheless express the view that "there's no turning back to state-dominated conceptions of socialism, by which I mean both the communist conceptions that emerged out of Soviet Russia

and the orthodox social democratic conceptions of state driven reform." But the issue then becomes: does this necessarily mean that there is no alternative but to turn to some version of Third Way social democracy (Guibernau, "Globalization, Cosmopolitanism, and Democracy")?

14 See F. Engels, *The Origins of the Family, Private Property, and the State,* 4th ed. (Moscow: Foreign Languages Publishing House, n.d.).

15 See Benedict Anderson, *Imagined Communities: Reflections on the Origin and Spread of Nationalism* (London: Verso, 1983). For a fuller discussion of these issues, which is partially drawn to the viewpoint of Benedict Anderson, see Anthony D. Smith, *Nationalism and Modernism: A Critical Survey of Recent Theories of Nations and Nationalism* (New York: Routledge, 1998). The view I put forward here would probably be classified by Smith as a version of "classical modernism." Smith argues that this view has been driven into decline by the rise of postmodern and cosmopolitan critiques.

16 Hall, "What Is This 'Black,'" 473. It should be noted, however, that Hall offered this characterization in a context in which he was trying to deemphasize the distinctiveness of the black experience. In the very next sentence he went on to write that "it is to the diversity, not the homogeneity, of black experience that we must now give our undivided creative attention," further noting that "we are always in negotiation, not with a single set of oppositions that place us always in the same relation to others, but with a series of different positionalities." This observation opens the door through which Gilroy passes, but Hall does not go through this door himself.

17 See Anthony D. Smith, *Theories of Nationalism* (New York: Holmes & Meier, 1983), ix–xxxvi.

18 The formulation of the issue of racial and national oppression as a matter of exclusion versus inclusion suggests that the resolution of this question can be achieved without a profound transformation of the excluding society. On the contrary, the oppressed group can be included without too much drastic social, cultural, economic, and political change.

19 See Gilroy, *Against Race,* 200.

20 Wilson Jeremiah Moses, ed., *Classical Black Nationalism: From the American Revolution to Marcus Garvey* (New York: New York University Press, 1996); Wilson Jeremiah Moses, *Afrotopia: The Roots of African American Popular History,* ed. Eric Sundquist, Cambridge Studies in American Literature and Culture (Cambridge: Cambridge University Press, 1998).

21 Partha Chatterjee, *Nationalist Thought and the Colonial World: A Derivative Discourse* (Minneapolis: University of Minnesota Press, 1993).

22 See Elie Kedourie, *Nationalism* (Oxford: Blackwell, 1996). Gilroy, especially in his emphasis on the role of Kant and the formative role of German nationalism for all nationalisms, provides an account very similar to that in the philosophically conservative work of Kedourie. See in particular *Against Race,* 56–74.

23 See Don Robotham, "The Development of a Black Ethnicity in Jamaica," in *Garvey: His Work and Impact,* ed. Rupert Lewis and Patrick Bryan (Kingston: ISER, University of the West Indies, 1989); and Perry Anderson, *The Overthrow of Colonial Slavery, 1776–1848* (London: Verso, 2000), 55.

24 In fact, Gilroy presents the efforts to go beyond memories of slavery as contributing, how-

ever inadvertently, to black chauvinism. He writes ironically that "it is an old skin that has to be shed before one can hope to attain an authentic life of racialized self-love" (195). He then proceeds to discuss the music of Snoop Doggy Dogg, R. Kelly, and other hip-hop artists whose work ushers in this "newer biopolitics." But the specific social, economic, political, and cultural context that made Motown possible is never discussed. Gilroy also displays an ambiguous attitude to the work of hip-hop artists: insofar as they promote "biopolitics," he disapproves; insofar as they scorn the "visual" art of Ice Cube and the politics of Cornel West, he heartily approves. See *Against Race*, 198 and 214–15.

25 The references are to Tricia Rose, *Black Noise: Rap Music and Black Culture in Contemporary America* (Middletown, CT: Wesleyan University Press, 1994); Cornel West, "Nihilism in Black America," in *Race Matters* (Boston: Beacon, 1993); and Ishmael Reed, *Airing Dirty Laundry* (New York: Perseus, 1995).

26 Here is another example of the sweeping nature of Gilroy's concept of "fascist visuality." He writes: "Pop videos and political advertising alike demonstrate that, although they may not always draw attention to it, fascist techniques and style contribute heavily to the operations of the infotainment telesector. These communicative patterns have been transmitted into black political culture" (158). Apparently, following this notion, much of modern television advertising operates with a fascist aesthetic.

27 See Ernst Junger, *Storm of Steel: From the Diary of a German Stormtroop Officer*, trans. Michael Hoffman (New York: Penguin, 2004); Albert Speer, *Inside the Third Reich: Memoirs* (New York: Simon and Schuster, 1997), esp. chaps. 5, 6, 10, and 11, in which Speer self-servingly discusses the "architectural megalomania" (50) that dominated his career; and Leni Riefenstahl, *The Holy Mountain* (1926) and *The Blue Light* (1932), two classical German "mountain" films in which the Alps are shrouded in an eerie light and presented mystically as metaphors for strength.

28 Samuel P. Huntington, *Who Are We? The Challenges to America's National Identity* (New York: Simon & Schuster, 2004); Madison Grant, *The Passing of the Great Race; or, the Racial Basis of European History* (New York: Arno and the New York Times, 1970); Lothrop Stoddard, *The Rising Tide of Color against White World Supremacy* (Honolulu: University of Hawai'i Press, 2003). Grant published originally in 1918 and Stoddard in 1922. The neo-nativist tendency is by no means confined to Huntington: the use of the odd-sounding term *homeland* or *Heimat* also resonates powerfully with another, far more menacing, nativist European tradition. *Heimat* is probably better rendered into English as "hearth." But there is no question that in a country with strong civil society traditions, any such Germanic-sounding nomenclature as the "Department for the Security of the Hearth" would have created both a linguistic and a political uproar.

29 Gilroy calls this "multicultural democracy," "the testing route I favor" (41).

30 Emmanuel Chukwudi Eze, "The Color of Reason: The Idea of 'Race' in Kant's Anthropology," in *Anthropology and the German Enlightenment*, ed. Katherine M. Faull, 200–241 (London and Toronto: Associated University Press, 1995).

31 Despite many remarks about the "cultural syncretism" of Phillis Wheatley and Olaudah Equiano (117) and the importance of "creolization" for Afro-Caribbean culture and "diaspora identities," which are said to be "creolized, syncretized, hybridized, and chronically impure cultural forms" (129), Gilroy is not an uncritical supporter of "hybridity." For example, he dissents from "invocations of hybridity in which everything becomes equally

and continuously intermixed, blended into an impossibly even consistency" (275). It is not clear to me how this remark is to be squared with his earlier views in the book.

32  Anderson, *Overthrow*, 30–62, 131–211.

33  See ibid., 50.

34  See Mary Kaldor, Helmut Anheier, and Marlies Glasius, "Global Civil Society in an Era of Regressive Globalization," in Kaldor, Anheier, and Glasius, *Global Civil Society 2003*, 3–33.

35  See Guibernau, "Globalization, Cosmopolitanism, and Democracy."

**Vijay Prashad**

How the Hindus Became Jews:
American Racism after 9/11

In November 2001, I traveled to Washington, DC, for the second Annual South Asian Literary Festival. At a panel discussion, someone asked me a pointed question: "Last year you had come here to promote your book, *Karma of Brown Folk*, and spent quite a long time being critical of the concept of the model minority. Now, with all these *desis* being harassed after 9/11, what do you think of our being a model minority?"

Certainly, Human Rights Watch and Amnesty International, not to speak of the Indian American press and the social network of rumor, had alerted us to the large number of *desis* (those who claim South Asian origin) who have been hassled by airlines, by the police, and by strangers—all wary of those of us who look like terrorists. In a comprehensive review of over a thousand hate attacks on Arabs and *desis*, Human Rights Watch noted, "This violence was directed at people solely because they shared or were perceived as sharing the national background or religion of the hijackers and al-Qaeda members deemed responsible for attacking the World Trade Center and the Pentagon."[1] A report from the South Asian American Leaders for Tomorrow found that in the week after 9/11, the U.S. media

The *South Atlantic Quarterly* 104:3, Summer 2005.
Copyright © 2005 by Duke University Press.

"reported 645 bias incidents directed towards Americans perceived to be of Middle Eastern descent."[2]

Before the government reported on the details of the 9/11 attacks, ordinary people took it on themselves to punish anyone with a turban—that is, anyone with headgear that resembled the turban worn by Osama bin Laden. On 9/11, within *minutes* of the attacks, four men chased after a Sikh man who had escaped from the towers and now had to escape once more for his life. In Richmond, Queens, three white youth severely beat up a Sikh man, other men shot at two Sikh boys, and a white man began to yell at a Sikh man on the Northern State Parkway, "You fucking Arab raghead, you're all going to die, we're going to kill every one of you," as all four of those in his car gave the Sikh man the finger. Men got the brunt of these attacks, because turbans are worn mainly by men. Those turbans served to distinguish the "evildoers."

Women faced hostility in different spaces, generally not as routine assaults by those emboldened to be vigilantes for 9/11. But there are also women who faced the crowd: Meera Kumar, on September 12, 2001, was removed from an Amtrak train in Boston; in Huntington, New York, an elderly drunk driver tried to run down a Pakistani woman, followed her into a store, and threatened to kill her because she's "destroying my country"; in Los Angeles, on September 13, 2001, an Iranian woman was punched in the eye by another woman who wanted to register her displeasure at those who look like terrorists; on September 15, 2001, in Tulsa, Oklahoma, when Kimberly Lowe, a Creek Native American, stopped her car to confront a group of white males who had yelled, "Go back to your own country," they pinned her down and drove over her till she died.

She was mistaken for the wrong kind of Indian.

So when the man at the panel discussion asked me if I had been mistaken about the term *model minority* after what had been called the "racial profiling" of *desis*, I took a few minutes to react. Well, a year ago, I had suggested that *desis* are whites on probation and that if we ever misbehaved, the power structure would revoke our privileges. So it was easy enough to say that our probation is over, and we are now to be served with a sentence of disapprobation.

But this is false. After all, within days, the attacks on *desis* began to diminish and the U.S. state resumed its general assault on the contingent class. Racism is not simply prejudice, although this is an important form of subordination. In advanced industrial societies where there is a "natural rate of unemployment," the contingent class that is either permanently unemployed or underemployed finds itself stigmatized as incompetent or worse. To keep this class in a subordinate position, the state intensifies its repression through systematic police brutality, incarceration, or harsh forced-work policies (workfare), and also by the disavowal of public education. That a disproportionate part of the contingent class is of color, and because of the culture of racism in U.S. history that has forged what it means to be both a danger (all but white) and a success (white), the form of subordination is almost identical to the architecture of U.S. racism.[3] What *desis* experienced in the months after 9/11 was not state racism, which is reserved for the contingent class, but the enraged prejudice of society fostered by the corporate media and enflamed by the rash words of politicians.

The state's response to 9/11 had little in common with the routine racial profiling against the contingent class; it had much more to do with the McCarthyism against Communists half a century ago. The government began to play the game of six degrees of separation, picking up anyone who knew anyone who knew one of the hijackers or worshiped at a mosque that they attended, or whose names appeared in their address books, or whose name came up in interrogation of anyone picked up for these reasons, or again, anyone who had been under the government's dragnet as radical Islamists in one form or another. And then there were those Muslims who became accidental radical Islamists—pilots, students with expired visas, and youth with criminal records.[4] The repression post-9/11 is akin to McCarthyism, but here the target is not communism, but Islam— and, ancillary to it, all political ideologies that challenge the hegemony of imperialist globalization. If guilt by association became acceptable due to McCarthyism, it has returned once again after 9/11 to make those who are Muslim culpable for 9/11. We are in the condition of the Green Scare.[5]

Those of us who look like terrorists but are not Muslims seem to want to carry a sign that says, "I am not a Muslim," as if to say, "I am not a terrorist."

Rumors flew about that the Indian Embassy in Washington asked its nationals to wear a *bindi*, to help distinguish "Indians" from Arabs and Afghans.[6] A gay friend called to say that this was the first time that he knew of the Indian government asking its male citizens to adopt drag. Another friend bitterly mentioned that the *bindi* had once served as the accumulation of resentment against *desis*, at least in the 1980s, when the Dotbusters of New Jersey began a hate campaign against Indian immigrants. Now that Madonna had made the *bindi* fashionable, the rumor mills had begun to offer it as protection against the revanchism that followed 9/11. Talk of the *bindi* went about as a way for some to suggest it as an adequate sign of being a Hindu, or at least not a Muslim.

What we miss is that as Islam becomes imperialist globalization's Green Menace, *Muslim* has come to stand in for those who look or sound like immigrants.

So if *Muslim* stands in for *immigrant*, we should follow philosopher Etienne Balibar's insistence that immigration "becomes the main name given to race within the crisis-torn nations of the post-colonial era."[7] *Muslim* begins to be seen in the logic of race, with all those who *look like* Muslims being treated in a certain way, and all those who *are* Muslims being harassed by the state, but—and this returns to my point about the contingent class— whereas in France (Balibar's home terrain), Algerians *do* form part of the contingent class in sizable numbers, this is not the case in the United States. Black Muslims certainly figure among the U.S. contingent, but the harassment they face is mostly for being black in the contingent world.[8]

All Muslims are suspects by association, but those who had come into even fleeting contact with the organs of Islamic radicalism are fair game for arrest and interrogation.[9]

Many who are not Muslims try to tell the country that they are not the bad ones, that being Sikh or Hindu or even atheists they should not be harassed. But the gaze of imperial whiteness does not discriminate between the dusky bodies. In *its* eyes, we are all Muslims.

Because of the power of the state and the corporate media, we are not immune to this logic. We have begun to see ourselves through their eyes. As we walk down the street, whatever our religion or provenance, we wonder whether those around us see us as a problem. "Mom, look at the terrorist! I'm frightened!"

Cringe, cower, paste that sickly smile on your face, exaggerate your American accent, and disappear into the fantasy life in your mind: a renewed nostalgia for the homeland.[10]

Some Indian Americans sought shelter from this storm not so much in the category of "whiteness," but in an attempt to manufacture an alliance with Jewish American organizations. The game for this set of influential Indian Americans was to see in Jewish Americans a model for their own attempt not simply to gain respectability in mainstream America, but to gain power in Washington. These are the "Hindus" who want to repudiate the hundreds of millions of Muslims in South Asia, to create an image of the Indian as a victim of Muslim terrorism in South Asia, and therefore the Indian American's dilemma as akin to the Jewish American's distress over Muslim terrorism in Israel. That those who operate with terrorist means are not simply Muslims is the exact idea that had to be demolished, because what allowed "Hindus" and "Jews" to become kin relied principally on the reduction of Palestinians and Kashmiris to "Muslim."

The text above slips between Indian and Hindu, and speaks of Muslim and Jew with confidence, although sometimes in quotes. The hesitancy comes partly because there is far too much heterogeneity within these categories: *Hindu* is not a coherent entity, rent as it is not only by theological disputes but also by the many political disagreements, as well as the everyday divides of gender and caste. But there is a far more particular reason for the tentativeness with these terms. If we run three of the terms in sequence (*Jewish-Hindu-Muslim*), one point is revealed: they are no longer terms that define only religions or religious experience. *Muslim* has come to refer to a global community of Muslims who adhere to a singular theocratic ideology (Islam) reinforced by a clergy that interprets a single book (the Koran). The varieties of religious experience within *Muslim* are rarely acknowledged, or else very rarely explored by the uninitiated. The term *Jewish* has come to refer less to religion and more to culture. We assume that regardless of their political or theological commitments, all those who are born in a Jewish family are Jews because of the culture of Judaism. The association of something called "Jewish culture" enables conservative activists of the Hindu Right to claim that regardless of one's religion or politics, any Indian is culturally a Hindu. Hindu culture, in this logic, is like Jewish culture, and the modular form of a religious culture being the culture of a people circumvents any suggestion of diversity within the category: all those who are Indian are part of Hindu culture, even if they are not Hindus, and Jews are always Jews because, despite their religious and political differences, they exist within Jewish culture. If "Muslims" form part of the global community of Islam, then Indian Muslims are more Muslim than Indian; if all those of India are Hindus, then Indian Muslims are Hindus when they deny their place in the global community of Islam. This conservative chain of command is of central concern for this essay, and even though I won't refer to this problem explicitly again, it forms an important consideration for us.

Events and processes that appear to be fundamentally outside the story of the United States, at least after 9/11, are a fundamental component of domestic race and racism. It is my contention that race in the United States after 9/11 has to be seen on a global scale, because planetary events lean upon the social construction and reconfiguration of identity within the United States. Jewish American identity has, at least since 1967, been in direct contact with the place of Israel in world affairs, and since 9/11, the importance of the links between India and Israel have fashioned one section of the *desi* community. Those of us who study racism and racial formation in the United States need to pay more and more attention not to the comparative study of racism, but to the way race in the United States is constructed with an eye to global events. In my own earlier work I argued that the fear factor of "blacks" created the conditions for the construction of the Indian American (and the Asian American in general) as the model minority, whereas now I will argue that this is insufficient. It is the terror of the "Muslim" alongside antiblack racism that provides the political space for Jewish Americans and Indian (or sometimes *Hindu*) Americans to mitigate their cultural difference from the mainstream, but crucially to put themselves forward as those who, because of their experience with terrorism, become the vanguard of the new, antiterrorist battleship America.

### An Axis of Good?

On September 8, 2003, Israeli Prime Minister Ariel Sharon arrived in New Delhi to spend the second anniversary of 9/11 with his Indian counterpart. This was the first visit by an Israeli prime minister in its five-decade history, and it came at a propitious time. Right-wing governments ruled in Tel Aviv, New Delhi, and Washington, and all three wanted to fashion an alliance against what they understood to be their principal adversary: what they called Islamic terrorism.[11]

While the alliance emerged between the governments, others plotted an alliance between two minority communities within the United States: Jewish Americans and Indian Americans. If Israel and India (as well as the United States) formulated a new approach to each other, then Jewish Americans and Indian Americans might do so with each other. The idea that Jewish Americans are a valuable model for Indian Americans is not novel. In 1994, when Gopal Raju, the publisher of *India Abroad* (the leading Indian American weekly newspaper), founded the Indian American Center for Political Awareness (IACPA), he had much the same thing in mind. Raju's worthy goal had been to draw Indian Americans into U.S. politics and to educate U.S. representatives on things Indian.[12] When Raju started IACPA, he hired onto its staff Ralph Nurnberger. Nurnberger, who is now the governmental affairs counsel at the prestigious and controversial Washington lobbying firm Preston Gates,[13] brought to IACPA his experience as the legislative liaison for the American Israel Public Affairs Committee (AIPAC). A former staff member of IACPA told me that Raju hired Nurnberger because he believed that Indian Americans needed to follow the example of Jewish Americans.[14] Another small minority within the United States, Jewish Americans, Raju is reported to have said, had made decisive inroads into the U.S. Congress on behalf of Israel. Indian Americans, he held, needed to adopt this strategy on behalf of India.

After 9/11 the links between Jewish American and Indian American groups, as well as members of Congress, increased astronomically. In the summer of 2002, two high-profile Indian American groups began talks with the two premier lobbying outfits that claim to represent both the Jewish American community and Israel, the American Jewish Committee (AJCommittee) and AIPAC. The Indian American groups wanted to learn how best to influence policy in Washington. Talks by AIPAC leaders and workshops by AJCommittee staff members introduced the Indian American organizations to lobbying in the corridors of American power. A year later, AJCommittee honored India's national security adviser at its annual dinner, while it held a special dinner for India's home minister. In addition, a host of U.S. congressional leaders gave talks at Indian American gatherings, favorably compared Indian Americans to Jewish Americans, and applauded the increased links between India and Israel. Leaders of the India Caucus in the U.S. House of Representatives, elected officials from both the Democratic and Republican Parties, took turns praising Indian Americans, whose access to votes and cash appeals to politicians from heavily Indian American districts, including parts of New Jersey, Illinois, New York, and Texas. In such districts, Indian Americans have the highest per capita income.

For a community that numbers about 1.5 million, only about 0.5 percent of the U.S. population, such attention is unprecedented and incredible. For a community that is generally invisible in the halls of power, it came as a surprise to suddenly experience such attention.

## The Myth of the "Same Extremist Enemy"

Shortly after 9/11, a group of Indian Americans formed the Indian American Political Action Committee (INAPAC) in New Jersey. Not long after its creation, INAPAC substantially dissolved, and another lobbying group emerged in Washington: the United States India Political Action Committee (USINPAC). It took over the space opened up by INAPAC and allowed itself to be adopted by AJCommittee and AIPAC. USINPAC held two related briefs: to ensure that Indian Americans enjoy the same amount of political power it feels is held by the Jewish American community, and to deploy that power in the service of India, preferably in an Indo-U.S. alliance in the image of the U.S.-Israeli entente. The ideological unity between Israel, India, and the United States preached by USINPAC is this: to fight terrorism, namely "Islamic militancy," "Islamic fundamentalism," "Islamic extremism," or, in the words of Congressman Tom Lantos (Democrat from California), "mindless, vicious, fanatic Islamic terrorism."[15] If we all agree that the enemy is Islamic terrorism, then the United States, Israel, and India have an urgent need for an axis.

INAPAC, and then USINPAC, has worked closely with members of the AJCommittee and AIPAC. Ann Schaffer, director of the AJCommittee's Belfer Center for American Pluralism, said of the AJCommittee's assistance toward INAPAC, "We shared with them the Jewish approach to political activism. We want to give them the tools to further their political agenda." When asked about the common "political agenda" between Jewish Americans and Indian Americans, the AJCommittee's Washington, DC, regional director, Charles Brooks, said, "We're fighting the same extremist enemy. We want to help them become more effective in communicating their political will."[16] Who is that global enemy? The proffered answer is Islamic extremism, but in some incarnations, the enemy seems to be global Islam in general, or else anyone who dares to challenge the supremacy of the current geopolitical dispensation (which goes by many names: free-market theorists call it globalization, whereas its critics call it imperialist globalization; the U.S. State Department describes it as the export of democracy, whereas its critics call it U.S. imperialism). What is crucial to my analysis is that U.S. power does not target global Islam as its enemy, even as al-Qaeda is the current assailant. The animus of U.S. imperialism is directed at all those forces that resist its hegemony, from the guerrillas in the Americas (FARC in Colombia, for example) to the North Korean regime. It is convenient for al-Qaeda, Sharonism, and Hindutva (Hinduness) to reduce U.S. policy to an enmity against Islam itself for their own reasons (for al-Qaeda, to appeal to its radical Islamist base; for Sharonism and Hindutva, to purport that their state policy is identical to U.S. state policy).

The chairman of the board of trustees for INAPAC, Jesal Amin, argued that the "terrorists" who target Israel are "interconnected with the Muslim terror groups operating elsewhere in the Middle East and South Asia." Amin, who is active in the Republican Party in a very prosperous and overwhelmingly white area of New Jersey, adopts the view that is commonplace among Israeli conservatives that any Muslim who acts against the interests of Israel, or here India, is a terrorist, whether it is the Palestinian Liberation Organization or Hamas, the Jammu and Kashmir Liberation Front or the Lashkar-e-Toiba. But he is not alone in this strategic reduction. Sue Ghosh Sticklett, a member of USINPAC's Defense and Strategic Affairs Committee, told a conservative publication, "Our no. 1 legislative priority in 2004 is terrorism. . . . the terrorism directed against India is the same as that directed against the United States and Israel. We would like to see closer ties between the United States and India. Right now, India feels that Israel is a closer friend than the United States, and we would like to change that."[17] In other words, it is valuable to reduce all forms of violence to "terrorism" in order to facilitate a geopolitical, economic alliance between India and the United States—regardless of the costs that others must bear for the prosperity that it will generate for a few.

Since the 1980s, one strand of the Indian American community has made it very clear that it lives within a worldview known as Hindutva (Hinduness). A political ideology within India that draws from European racist ideas of nationhood, Hindutva has taken the view, since its emergence in the 1920s, that Muslims do for it what Jews do for Nazism. In the United States such a view makes no sense, and it is translated into what I have called "Yankee Hindutva," where the Hindutva adherent relies upon liberal multiculturalism to give it space to develop its generally illiberal political identity that opposes not only Muslims, whether conservative or liberal, but also anything that it deems to be progressive and therefore a challenge to Hindutva. If there is any movement that cannot be held at bay, such as feminism, Hindutva attempts to accommodate it by attempting to glorify women who are independent and "traditional."[18] Amin and Ghosh Sticklett's theory is so common now among upwardly mobile Indian Americans that one of its children, twenty-one-year-old Nishkam Gupta, enlisted to fight in the 2003 U.S. war in Iraq as part of his desire to "fight the larger war against terrorism, a war that would directly benefit Hinduism and its cause."[19] Kapil Sharma, a consultant for the generally liberal IACPA, says, "We should be educated about each other's issues, so we can talk about Kashmir and Palestine"—the two areas of the world that, in the Indo-Israeli convergence, are now considered as parallels.[20] The Hindutva-Sharonist framework has leaked into the lives of those generally not predisposed to cruel and macho nationalism.

There are several problems with the formulation offered by people such as Amin, Sticklett, and the AJCommittee. They assume that the Jihad International grows out of whole cloth from Islam, from a few *suras* in the Koran, or else from the medieval history of Arabia.[21] There is a complete disregard for the history of the Jihad International—how it came to be, its social forces, how the United States and the Saudis, for instance, encouraged and financed it as an alternative to the growth of republicanism and communism.[22] The Jihad International draws from the frustrations of a generation of mainly men who had been betrayed by the states that claimed the mantle of anticolonial republicanism. Drawing from the detritus of social thought in their home regions, these groups remained largely anachronistic and without strength until the United States gave them legitimacy and the Saudis began to fund them, principally for the Afghan campaign against the Soviets, but also in the war over Marxist South Yemen.[23]

Groups like Hamas and the various factions in Kashmir certainly share ideological resources with the broader Jihad International, but they are also rooted in nationalist struggles.[24] There is little doubt that Hamas and the various *jihadi* factions in Kashmir are a serious problem for the social development of their respective regions. Although Hamas does provide basic social services alongside its general policy of violence, this welfare is hardly to be considered valuable given the context within which it is offered. But to cast the Palestinians and the Kashmiris and others as the "extremist enemy" without a sense of how such factions attained prominence in their various struggles is to miss the hand of imperialism. Such a view also omits the many other Palestinian and Kashmiri organizations that revile the tactic of terror and the general social vision of Hamas and the Kashmiri groups, as well as the views of those who want as much to make a living as to change the world. To leave all this out erases the visions of social justice in such places, renders Islam itself into a one-dimensional tragedy, and casts out any hope for the progressive elements that strive against immense odds to turn the direction of the struggle around.

Furthermore, to render "terrorism" and "terrorists" as the enemy fails to distinguish between the *tactics* that a people use and the *social and political conditions* that generate their hostility: to defeat those who use terrorism, one has to understand and deal with the conditions that produce those who take to terror.[25] All this is irrelevant to AIPAC-USINPAC.

## The Myth of the Pro-Israel Lobby

On July 16, 2003, the AJCommittee, the AIPAC, and the USINPAC held their first joint briefing. Congressman Frank Pallone, a New Jersey Democrat and former cochair of the India Caucus of the U.S. Congress, said, "One of the first things I would hear whenever I went around to the Indian American communities was how we can emulate the Jewish community, particularly how can we emulate AIPAC—in terms of their lobbying abilities, their grass-roots abilities, their ability to organize the community politically."[26] Kumar Barve, the highest elected Indian American and majority leader in the Maryland House of Delegates, told the *Washington Post*, "I think Indian Americans see the American Jewish community as a yardstick against which to compare themselves. It's seen as the gold standard in terms of political activism."[27] "A lot of folks in the Indian American community," reported Ajay Kuntamukkala, the president of the South Asian Bar Association of Washington, DC, "look at what Jews have done and try to model themselves after it."[28]

There are fewer than 6 million Jews in the United States, just about 2 percent of the population. If *they* can determine U.S. foreign policy, then they should certainly be a model for all communities that have the same agenda.

AIPAC, without a doubt, is a very strong lobbying organization. With an annual budget in excess of \$15 million, a group of registered lobbyists, and a staff in the hundreds, AIPAC can send out the troops to patrol the halls of Congress if any bill inimical to Sharonist interest appears on the floor. The genius of AIPAC is that it sits at the center of almost a hundred pro-Israel groups and coordinates their donations. These myriad political action groups—"which draw money from Jewish donors and operate under obscure-sounding names—are operated by AIPAC officials or people who hold seats on AIPAC's two major policymaking bodies."[29] Money lubricates the U.S. political system, and AIPAC has been able to strategically use its funds to gain the support of a slew of elected representatives.

Political scientist Stephen Zunes points out, "The Aerospace Industry Association which promotes these massive arms shipments to Israel is even more influential" than the pro-Israel lobby. The "general thrust of US policy would be pretty much the same even if AIPAC didn't exist. We didn't need a pro-Indonesia lobby to support Indonesia in its savage repression of East Timor all these years."[30] In other words, AIPAC is powerful not because of its use of money alone, but decisively because of the strategic convergence of interests between Israel, AIPAC, and the U.S. Congress.[31]

The U.S. Congress stands united behind Israel. Any dissension is met with the reproach of anti-Semitism. If this is the work of the pro-Israel lobby, then it has achieved a remarkable feat: a totally bipartisan Congress with little opposition to its general goals. However, as most electoral and campaign finance data show, most American Jews tend to lean toward the Democratic Party, so why should the Republicans come out so strongly for Israel?[32]

Two public policy organizations give us a sense of an answer: the Washington Institute for Near East Policy (WINEP) and the Jewish Institute for National Security Affairs (JINSA). Martin Indyk, who worked as research director at AIPAC, founded WINEP in 1985 to produce policy papers on Israel in order to strengthen U.S.-Israeli relations. In 1988, WINEP published *Building for Peace: An American Strategy for the Middle East,* which focused on what the Bush administration must do about the Israeli-Palestinian process. WINEP concluded that the U.S. government should "resist pressures for a procedural breakthrough until conditions have ripened," that is, until the Palestinian resistance had been broken. Six members of the WINEP study group that wrote this report entered the administration of George H. W. Bush, which, as it happened, adopted the Sharonist line to alienate the PLO despite its recognition of Israel at the Palestinian National Council of November 1988.[33]

While WINEP tends to hew the line of whatever Israeli party comes to power, JINSA is the U.S. offshoot of the Likud Party. Set up in 1997, both JINSA and the Project for a New American Century (PNAC) drew from the most conservative hawks in the U.S. establishment for its board of directors: Richard Cheney (now vice president), John Bolton (now undersecretary of state), Douglas Feith (now undersecretary of defense), Paul Wolfowitz (now deputy of defense), Lewis Libby (now the vice president's chief of staff), Zalmay Khalilzad (now U.S. ambassador to Afghanistan), Richard Armitage (now deputy secretary of state), Elliott Abrams (now National Security Council adviser), and Richard Perle (formerly on the Defense Policy Board). Perle and Feith, among others, drafted a paper titled "A Clean Break: A New Strategy for Securing the Realm," published by the Institute for Advanced Strategic Political Studies (Washington and Jerusalem), that urged the Israeli government to repudiate Oslo, to permanently annex the occupied territories, to overthrow the regime of Saddam Hussein (and restore the Hashemite monarchy)—this last, "an important Israeli strategic objective in its own right." Netanyahu, as prime minister of Israel at the time, rejected the report, particularly the adventurism against Iraq. When George W. Bush came to power in 2001, he adopted it, not because he was pushed by the pro-Israel lobby but because of the U.S. neoconservative vision for U.S. power in the world.[34]

The idea of the power of the pro-Israel lobby is attractive because it draws upon at least a few hundred years of anti-Semitic worry about an international conspiracy operated by Jewish financiers to defraud the European and American working poor of their livelihoods. The "Jew," without a country, but with a bank, had no loyalty to the nation, no solidarity with fellow citizens. The anti-Semitic document *Protocols of the Elders of Zion* is a good illustration of this idea.[35] The Nazis stigmatized the "Jew" as the problem of poverty and exploitation and obscured the role played by capitalism in the reproduction of grief. The 6 million Jews in the United States do not determine U.S. foreign policy, nor are they united as one. Jews in America, like other communities, are rent with division, not united behind one agenda. When Charles Brooks of the AJCommittee says, "We're fighting the same extremist enemy," the question to ask is, Who is included in "we"?

AJCommittee and AIPAC do not speak for all Jews in the United States, for the mythical "American Jewish community." The community is fractured on its support for the various political parties and agendas in Israel, as well as the importance of being behind Israel at all. Those who dissent from Sharonism are, however, part of a weakened tradition that has been unable to combat the overwhelming but incorrect notion that any criticism of Israel is anti-Semitic.[36] In my two decades in the United States, in almost all the struggles with which I have been involved (from the antiapartheid movement to the El Salvador solidarity work to labor struggles to antiwar work, to work against the destruction of the U.S. welfare net, and so on), there have always been those of Jewish ancestry. The river of radicalism runs deeply through the world of American Jewry. This tradition is well analyzed by the philosopher Judith Butler:

> The ethical framework within which most progressive Jews operate takes the form of the following question: will we be silent (and thereby collaborate with illegitimately violent power), or will we make our voices heard (and be counted among those who did what they could to stop that violence), even if speaking poses a risk? The current Jewish critique of Israel is often portrayed as insensitive to Jewish suffering, past as well as present, yet its ethic is based on the experience of suffering, in order that suffering might stop.[37]

The strand of anti-Sharonist politics among American Jews draws strength from the litany of anti-Sharonist organizations within Israel itself.[38] Again, this is a weak tradition with limited traction over a society that has produced an overwhelming consensus.

AIPAC and its confreres are powerful, but they do not determine U.S. foreign policy. They are powerful not just because of their money, but because their views converge with those of the neoconservative elements that dominate the Middle East policy formation team of the ruling coalition in Washington. Until the 1967 war, few American Jews wanted to identify themselves with Israel. In his 1957 survey of Jewish American attitudes, the sociologist Nathan Glazer found that Israel "had remarkably slight effects on the inner life of American Jewry."[39] Only one in twenty American Jews traveled to Israel before June 1967, and intellectuals at an AJCommittee symposium on Jewish identity held a few months before the war barely considered Israel in their comments. After the war, when Israel became a crucial player in U.S. strategy, Israel became, according to Norman Podhoretz, editor of the neoconservative *Commentary*, "the religion of the American Jews," at least of the mainstream Zionist organizations.[40] When AIPAC and the AJCommittee go to Washington now, they meet receptive, even eager ears. The lobbyists did not create the conditions for Israel's elevation. U.S. foreign policy did the work for them.

### The Myth of the Model Minority

If AIPAC does not have a major, or decisive, impact on U.S. foreign policy, it has certainly come to play a crucial role in the Jewish American community. As Esther Kaplan of Jews for Ethnic and Racial Justice said on her radio show, *Beyond the Pale*, in 2002, groups like AIPAC and AJCommittee leverage their closeness to U.S. power to claim the mantle of the Jewish American mainstream for themselves. Even if AIPAC does not represent the majority or the plurality of American Jews, it claims to be representative and attempts to fulfill its claim. AIPAC's proximity to Sharonism and its claim to be the representative of Jewish America mean that the community appears to be far more conservative than it perhaps is. Do all Jewish Americans align with the views of AIPAC and the AJCommittee, or indeed with Sharon? No. What is more important is the way immigrant or ethnic organizations pose as representative to the power structure regardless of their actual depth in their community.

Immigrants in the United States have an idiosyncratic relationship to the world of politics. Take the case of *desis*. Despite the racist divisions in our civil society, there is no referendum or election process for the leader of each of the social communities. So how does "ethnic leadership" emerge? There are some organic processes—for example, the efforts of community organizations that not only represent the community but also constitute and reproduce it. The regional and linguistic groups (Gujarat Samaj, Tamil Sangam) are one example, and so are the national professional groups (Asian American Hotel Owners Association, American Association of Physicians of Indian Origin). Then there are those groups that work within the community to transform practices undesirable to some or to fashion a new *desi* social culture (women's rights groups, gay and lesbian groups, workers' rights groups). The people who could be leaders are those who put their energy into these organizations and into the reproduction of the *desi* community through the festivals and protests, the gatherings for joy and justice. But, as with most post-1965 immigrant groups, the leaders of these organizations are not the most visible representatives of the community in the realm of electoral politics.

It takes little to set up a political shop: the name of an organization, a patron among one or the other party or lobby group, some letterhead, a fairly dynamic leader, and preferably a photograph or two of this leader with an important white politician from one of the two major parties and/or an important politician from the homeland. The picture with the white politician is almost sufficient to indicate that our fearless leader has cachet in the world of Washington, and his or her backdoor to power allows him or her to play a disproportionate role as the "representative" of the immigrant community before the established power structure. These figures become brokers for the major parties as they try to reach out to the immigrant communities for votes, and they become symbolic figureheads for the community itself. USINPAC is one such immigrant entity.

AIPAC and the Indian American high-profile groups not only use their closeness to U.S. power; they also wield the myth of the model minority to capture the hearts and minds of their constituency and to make a broader appeal in a country wedded to antiblack racism. The Indian American community is rent with divisions, and within U.S. domestic politics the tendency has been for Indian Americans to lean toward liberalism (in its organized form, the Democratic Party).[41] While there is no good survey data on Indian American social and political attitudes, my own reading of the ethnographic literature and my own political involvement in the community suggest that the bulk of *desis* are against immigration controls and the death penalty, for the right of a woman to control her own body (or at least against the ban on abortion), for better wages for working people, for better care for the elderly, for health insurance coverage. Among second-generation *desis* the trend of liberalism runs deeper.[42] With the fear of terror, manipulations by groups like USINPAC, and the consolidation of professional success for a sizable section of the community, there has been a perceptible turn to conservatism.[43]

Jesal Amin, of INAPAC, praises Indian culture for its emphasis on higher education: "We have made the American dream come true. Many Indians are professional. One of the reasons for working together with the Jewish community is that we are so similar in terms of education, and from an economic point of view."[44] Tom Lantos, a Jewish Democrat from California and an immigrant from Hungary, goes over the top: "There is a natural symbiotic relationship between the Indian community and the Jewish community," he said. "It begins with respect for life. There is no community for whom the sacredness of life is as prominent in its philosophy than the Indian community and we Jews—when we drink, we say 'Rafiat' which means life." On a more practical level, he says, "there is a profound relationship in our passionate commitment to education. We have a passionate commitment to respect for others, for the rule of law and for democracy, and lately, we've been brought together by our joint fight against mindless, vicious, fanatic Islamic terrorism."[45]

How does one even begin to analyze these banal generalities? Do all Jews and Indians have a passionate respect for others? Even those Indians (perhaps he means Hindus) who killed innocent people in Gujarat in 2002, or those Jews (as Israeli citizens) who killed the Palestinians of Jenin in 2002? Is the assumption that a people have a culture that is singular not itself a species of racialist thinking that we must abhor? These are some basic questions that are worth posing.[46] When Congressman Lantos says that Jews and Indians are passionate about education, when Amin says that Jews and Indians are similar in terms of education, do they mean that there are people in the world who are *not* interested or invested in education, who would *prefer* illiteracy? What does it mean to say that some people are favored, are chosen, if not to also say that there are others who are misbegotten?

In 1965, after a century of struggle and sacrifice, the movement for civil rights won an impressive victory. The U.S. state adopted a bill that gave every citizen formal equality before the law, thereby annulling the premise of Jim Crow segregation. The victory was immense, but partial. It demolished formal equality, but it did not say anything about the everyday inequality that had been structured into every aspect of social life. As one of the architects of the classical civil rights movement, Bayard Rustin, put it, "The very decade which has witnessed the decline of legal Jim Crow has also seen the rise of *de facto* segregation in our most fundamental socioeconomic institutions."[47] The movement against racism was interested in much greater freedoms than simply the right to vote, one of which was the demand for reparations or a transfer of capital stolen from labor that had not been paid for centuries. The famous 1963 march on Washington was called, for instance, the March on Washington for Civil Rights *and Jobs*. The reforms of the U.S. state did not address this crucial demand. When the generally peaceful and hopeful civil rights movement transmuted into the more violent and embittered Black Power movement, the U.S. state and its intellectuals revised their older racist notions and practices for what has been called the New Racism of our epoch. That is, the state must now treat everyone equal before the law, economic demands are left outside the purview of the question of race, and certain previously oppressed people (such as Jews and Asians) can obtain some privileges, while those who are the descendants of enslaved people are left penniless, hopeless, and therefore one step from criminality.

When the mainly black community of Watts, Los Angeles, rose in rebellion in 1965, the U.S. state appeared incensed and shocked. In a mainstream periodical in 1966, one of the first positive articles about Asians appeared. Once reviled as the Yellow Peril, Chinese Americans, the article said, believe in "the old idea that people should depend on their own efforts—not a welfare check—in order to reach America's 'promised land.'" This autonomous effort, the magazine noted, came at "a time when it is being proposed that hundreds of billions of dollars be spent to uplift Negroes and other minorities."[48] That same year, Irving Kristol asked in the *New York Times Magazine*, "Can the Negro be expected to follow the path of previous immigrant groups [Jews and Italians] or is his a special, 'pathological' case?" What is being said is this: the Asians work hard without complaint, and so should the blacks; the Jews work hard, and so should the blacks. This erases the hard work and low pay endured by African Americans, most of whom, because of the incomplete dismantling of the Jim Crow structure, did not have access to any other kind of work. Kristol wrote, "The real tragedy of the American Negro today is not that he is poor, or black, but that he is a latecomer—he confronts a settled and highly organized society whose assimilatory powers have markedly declined over the past decades."[49] But Africans had been brought to the Americas long before Jews and Italians, so that when Kristol says "latecomers," he must mean to the feast of capital, since most blacks worked to produce the bounty that was divided among some whites in an earlier time. By this logic, blacks are blamed for the failures of American history.[50]

Jews, long reviled by the U.S. power structure, like Asians, became acceptable only in the late 1960s, as beneficiaries of the New Racism and of the victory of Israel in 1967.[51] The Indians that came to the United States because of the 1965 immigration reforms also benefited from this New Racism: before these laws we were regarded as blacks, but after them we could aspire to whiteness. Arriving in the United States in droves between the mid-1960s and the early 1980s, Indian Americans rose in the ranks of their professions and made very high salaries. But their attainments are *not* caused by natural or cultural selection. If this were the case, the 1 billion Indians in India would all be doctors and nurses, engineers and scientists. Rather, it was the result of *state* selection, whereby the U.S. state, through the special skills provision in the 1965 Immigration Act, fundamentally configured the demography of Indian America. Between 1965 and 1977, 83 percent of the migrants came with advanced degrees.

State selection, not the natural selection of millennia, brought highly qualified *desis* to the United States. Those who hold power in the United States use the anomalous demographic of professional *desis* to show that we succeed while other minorities fail, that we succeed because we work hard, while they fail because they are either incapable or lazy. The history of why we succeed is lost in this simple story. And thanks to its loss of history, the stereotype tends to confirm antiblack racism.

Why should Jewish Americans and Indian Americans get together? Because they are human beings, because some may share ideological positions, because a few may share personal tastes—these are less offensive ways to create solidarity than to bear heavily upon us with the burden of stereotyped traditions (peaceful people, etc.) or else to leverage our friendship on the backs of blacks. The latter, as the novelist Toni Morrison wrote, is a typical, homespun strategy for advancement in the United States: the immigrant, she noted, must participate "freely in this most enduring and efficient rite of passage into American culture: negative appraisals of the native-born black population. Only when the lesson of racial estrangement is learned is assimilation complete. Whatever the lived experience of immigrants with African Americans—pleasant, beneficial, or bruising—the rhetorical experience renders blacks as non-citizens, already discredited outlaws."[52] Jews and Indians, both of whom live in a racist polity, take shelter in the false praises of their greatness. Far better to be seen as good than evil, but at what social cost do a people want acclaim? Who pays for *desis* to be the "model minority"?

The high-profile organizations leverage their proximity to power and their ideology of the model minority to attract large numbers of *desis* into their ranks, or else into the tug of their beliefs. The cost of this, however, is to leave *desis* outside the major struggles for social justice that is the best thing about America.

### Strange Bedfellows

Politics does make strange bedfellows. Two decades ago, the alliance between Indian American and Jewish American groups would have seemed impossible.[53] For one, the Indian government was not openly in favor of the Israeli state—a mark against it, from AIPAC's point of view. When it declined to issue visas to Israeli delegations, particularly to sports teams, the Indian government earned the ire of U.S.-based Jewish organizations. In 1987, the Anti-Defamation League, for instance, wrote, "It is time for the international community to let India know that unless it ceases to inject its anti-Israel policies into events aimed at furthering the spirit of international cooperation, it will be forced to forfeit its frequent role as host nation."[54]

The alliance between Indian American and Jewish American mainstream organizations plainly has little to do with "cultural values," but a lot to do with the geopolitical alliance between India and Israel. When it comes to Israel, the AJCommittee and the AIPAC will make alliances with anyone who, for whatever reason, is willing to defend the right of the Sharonists to make mayhem in West Asia. Jason F. Isaacson, director of government and international affairs of the AJCommittee, told the press, "All three countries [India, Israel, and the United States] really need to stick together not only because of the common threats of terrorism but because of commonalities and values, and that is the message we are going to convey."[55] These common values are not shared by all Indians, Israelis, and Americans in the same way: they may want to do different things when faced with specific forms of terror that come from very particular social forces.

What does this have to say about race in post-9/11 America? As the "Muslim" increasingly bears the mark of Cain, it opens up immense opportunities for middle-class people of color to demonstrate their patriotism in anti-Islamic terms. For the contingent working class, such an opportunity is not afforded, as I suggested in the opening section. Those who are of color in this class fragment bear the brunt of systemic racism, and their patriotism is easily eclipsed by their imputed immorality and criminality. Those who are not prone to functional unemployment or contingent status and are of color as a block are mainly immigrants like those from South Asia. Race, since 9/11, has not included *desis* as victims of racial profiling and thereby expanded the targets for state racism. It has instead fashioned a complex racial landscape where groups jockey to get out from under the racist gaze of society and the racist policies of the state. For such immigrants, the post-9/11 scenario offers few decent options: either claim solidarity with a people who have become the image of international terrorism, or else pledge your patriotism through abjuration of any cultural links with Islam or Muslims, indeed to make the "Muslim" your enemy. If the "Muslim" becomes your enemy, and if you have the cultural capital to fly above the quicksand of the contingent class, then you have the opportunity to be "American."

### Notes

This essay draws from the last chapter of my book *Namaste Sharon: Hindutva and Sharonism under US Hegemony* (New Delhi: LeftWord, 2003). Thanks to Prakash Karat and Sudhanva Deshpande for their commentary on it. I began to write on these themes because of a provocation from Toufic Haddad and Tikva Honig-Parnass of the magazine *Between the Lines* (Jerusalem). The essay developed thanks to extended discussions from a host of colleagues, notably Elisabeth Armstrong, Ania Loomba, Sunaina Maira, and Magid Shihade. Ania Loomba read the essay very carefully and gave me several important suggestions, notably to expand upon the categories of Hindu, Muslim, Jewish, and Indian and to bring back the excised point on the *bindi*. I gave this essay as a talk at Cornell University (thanks to Shelly Wong and Viranjani Munasinghe), the University of Pennsylvania (thanks to Dharma Naik, and to Howard Winant for his question afterward), the University of California, Davis (thanks to Sunaina Maira and Wendy Ho), and in the Lowell Lecture series at the Gustavus Myers Center for the Study of Bigotry and Human Rights (thanks to Loretta Williams). I am grateful to John Jackson for asking me to contribute to this issue, and for his patient solidarity.

1   Amardeep Singh (for Human Rights Watch), *"We Are Not the Enemy": Hate Crimes against Arabs, Muslims, and Those Perceived to Be Arab or Muslim after September 11* (New York: HRW, 2002), 3.

2   South Asian American Leaders of Tomorrow, *American Backlash: Terrorists Bring War Home in More Ways Than One* (Washington, DC: SAALT, 2001), 3. The project leader

for this report was Debasish Mishra, with Deepa Iyer, Kiran Chaudhri, Kulmeet Dang, Poonam Desai, Ankur Doshi, Parvinder Kang, Sunny Rehman, and Vivek Sankaran.

3   I make this argument in *Keeping Up with the Dow Joneses: Debt, Prison, Workfare* (Boston: South End, 2003).

4   For an excellent study of the state's pressure on Muslim youth, see Sunaina Maira, "Citizenship in a Time of War: South Asian Muslim Youth in Cambridge after 9/11," *Subcontinental* 1.1 (2003): 41–52. It has been suggested to me on a number of occasions that the hatred is directed not at "Muslims" but at "Arabs," or at least at "Muslims and Arabs." This might be so. It would require far more specific analysis than I can do in this space. Few would be able to distinguish between Arabs and Persians, Arabs and South Asians, or indeed between the various and distinguishable Arabs who live across the Arab lands from the Mashreq to the Maghreb. On this point my analysis is vulnerable from lack of more ethnographic work. I am looking forward to the completion of Sunaina Maira's extensive research on South Asian Muslims after 9/11 in the Boston region, of Louise Cainkar's research project on the impact of 9/11 on Arab and Muslim communities in the United States (an early example of Cainkar's work is in her "No Longer Invisible: Arab and Muslim Exclusion after September 11," *MERIP* 224 [2002], available at www.merip.org/mer/mer224/224_cainkar.html), and of Salah D. Hassan's work on Arabs after 9/11, notably in "Arabs, Race, and the Post–September 11 National Security State," *MERIP* 224 (2002) (available at www.merip.org/mer/mer224/224_hassan.html), as well as Columbia University's large-scale project titled "Muslims in New York City" (including Amaney Jamal's work on mosques in the life of Muslim Americans, with an eye to 9/11, and Hisham Aidi's work on Islam and inner-city youth).

5   Vijay Prashad, "The Green Menace: McCarthyism after 9/11," *Subcontinental* 1.1 (2003): 65–75. The color green is generically used by Muslims as Islam's standard.

6   An Indian magazine article reported just after 9/11, "In this atmosphere thick with fear, talk that the Indian embassy had asked Indian women to use the bindi—to identify themselves as not Arab or Afghan—got around fast. The embassy, of course, denies it ever issued any such directive" (Kamla Bhatt, "Alone in the Crowd," *Outlook*, October 1, 2001).

7   Etienne Balibar, "Racism and Nationalism," in *Race, Nation, Class: Ambiguous Identities*, ed. Etienne Balibar and Immanuel Wallerstein (London: Verso, 1991), 51.

8   For an early note on the status of migrants from North Africa in France, see Mahfoud Bennoune, "Maghribin Workers in France," *MERIP Reports* 34 (1975): 1–12. For a general statement, see Janet Bauer and Vijay Prashad, "Dilemmas at the Border: An Introduction," *Cultural Dynamics* 12 (2000): 275–81, an introduction to a set of essays including Leora Auslander, "Bavarian Crucifixes and French Headscarves: Religious Signs and the Postmodern European State," *Cultural Dynamics* 12 (2000): 283–309.

9   For an excellent analysis of the new racial category "Middle Eastern, Arab, or Muslim," see Leti Volpp, "The Citizen and the Terrorist," *UCLA Law Review* 49 (2002): 1575–1600.

10  All this is a poor imitation of Frantz Fanon's "The Fact of Blackness," in *Black Skin, White Mask* (London: MacGibbon & Kee, 1968).

11  The details are in my *Namaste Sharon*, but for a liberal view of it, see Robert Hathaway's "Washington's New Strategic Partnership," *Seminar* 538 (June 2004).

12  The IACPA's greatest contribution to Indian American visibility in Washington has been

its internship program. After opening its office in 1996, IACPA hosted young Indian Americans for a summer and placed them in the offices of congressional figures who are, in one way or another, crucial in Indian American– and Indian-related matters. The interns got an education in the mendacity of the political process, and the lawmakers had a crash course in Indian American lives and issues. By all accounts the internship program has worked very well, and many former interns remain active in the policy field.

13 Preston Gates has represented the Choctaw Indians for a gaming concession, and it represented the antilabor elements that continue to block labor laws and regulations in the Mariana Islands, a U.S. territory in the South Pacific. Jim Vandehei, "Mississippi's Choctaw Indians Find an Unlikely Ally in a GOP Stalwart," *Wall Street Journal,* July 3, 2000, and Jim Vandehei, "Saipan Looks to Powerful Lobbyist," *Wall Street Journal,* July 19, 2000.

14 Debasish Mishra, former executive director of IACPA, told me this on May 23, 1998. While Raju was more interested in creating power for Indian Americans in Washington, it seems that Nurnberger might have had an ideological ax to grind. "The three democracies [India, Israel and the United States] are now poised to cooperate in counter-terrorism efforts. It must be stressed this is not a Christian-Jewish-Hindu coalition gearing up against Islam. Rather it is an effort by civilized, democratic nations to combat terrorism by extremists." Bhaskar Dasgupta, "Brajesh Mishra Proposes India-Israel-America Axis to Combat Terror," *Hindustan Times,* June 27, 2003. As we will see below, this verbal posture is not tenable.

15 Alan Cooperman, "India, Israel Interests Team Up," *Washington Post,* July 19, 2003.

16 Larry Ramer, "Pro-Israel Activists Seeking Allies among Immigrants from India," *Forward,* October 11, 2002.

17 Joseph D'Agostino, "Conservative Spotlight: USINPAC," *Human Events,* December 11, 2003.

18 Vijay Prashad, *Karma of Brown Folk* (Minneapolis: University of Minnesota Press, 2000), 133–56.

19 Mira Kamdar, "A Move to the Right? The Shifting Sands of South Asian American Politics," *Subcontinental* 1.2 (2003): 65.

20 Ramer, "Pro-Israel Activists."

21 For an excellent refutation of this view, see Natana J. Delong-Bas, *Wahhabi Islam: From Revival and Reform to Global Jihad* (New York: Oxford University Press, 2004).

22 For more on this, see Vijay Prashad, *Darker Nations: The Rise and Fall of the Third World* (New York: New Press, forthcoming 2005).

23 For Yemen's story, see Fred Halliday, *Arabia without Sultans* (Harmondsworth, U.K.: Penguin, 1974), and "*Arabia without Sultans* Revisited," *Middle East Report* 27.3 (1997).

24 On Hamas, see Beverly Milton-Edwards, *Islamic Politics in Palestine* (London: I. B. Tauris, 1999), and on the Kashmiri struggle, see Manoj Joshi, *The Lost Rebellion: Kashmir in the Nineties* (New Delhi: Penguin, 1999).

25 "Terrorism is a tactic, not an enemy," wrote former senator Bob Kerrey ("Fighting the Wrong War," *New York Times,* April 11, 2004).

26 Aziz Haniffa, "The Sacredness of Life Is Most Prominent in Indian and Jewish Philosophy," *India Abroad,* July 25, 2003.

27 Alan Cooperman, "India, Israel Interests Team Up."

28  Eric Fingerhut, "A Growing Partnership: Jewish, Indian American Communities Working Together," *Washington Jewish Week*, October 24, 2002. Then comes the fawning: Professor Ram Roy, a political scientist who spoke at a 2003 conference on Jews and Indians in Washington, DC, said, "It is heartening to note this powerful, well-organized experienced group [AJCommittee] is trying to establish an alliance with Indian groups." Aziz Haniffa, "How to Make Uncle Sam Listen: Tips from Jewish Americans," *India Abroad*, July 25, 2003.

29  John J. Fialka, "Linked Donations? Political Contributions from Pro-Israel PACs Suggest Coordination," *Wall Street Journal*, June 24, 1987.

30  "US Aid to Israel: Interpreting the Strategic Relationship: Report from a Palestine Center Briefing by Stephen Zunes," *For the Record*, February 1, 2001, 50–52. My analysis is entirely the other side of Jeffrey Blankfort's otherwise very thoughtful "The Israel Lobby and the Left," in *The Politics of Anti-Semitism*, ed. Alexander Cockburn and Jeffrey St. Clair (Oakland: AK, 2003).

31  The spy scandal of 2004 had no traction in Washington, even though it involved AIPAC. The FBI alleges that the lobbying group had a direct pipeline to both the Pentagon and the Israeli government and that it funneled classified information. There is no yellow tape around the AIPAC office, and the scandal has all but disappeared.

32  In recent years, the American Jewish vote for the Democratic Party has begun to split. Murray Friedman, "Are American Jews Moving to the Right?" *Commentary*, April 2000.

33  Joel Beinin, "Pro-Israel Hawks and the Second Gulf War," *MERIP*, April 6, 2003.

34  There is an account of the convergence between the neoconservative agenda and Sharonism in Michael Lind, *Made in Texas: George W. Bush and the Southern Takeover of American Politics* (New York: Basic Books, 2003), chap. 6, "Armageddon."

35  The classic text that covers this history is Norman Cohn, *Warrant for Genocide: The Myth of the Jewish World Conspiracy and the* Protocols of the Elders of Zion (London: Serif, 1996).

36  Indeed, there is even no agreement on the role of "anti-Semitism" in U.S. progressivism, for on one side is Ellen Willis, whose essay "Is There Still a Jewish Question? Why I'm an Anti-Anti-Zionist" argues that the Left's anti-Zionism is pretty much anti-Semitism, whereas Philip Green's "'Anti-Semitism,' Israel, and the Left" argues that the charge of anti-Semitism is leveled against anyone who disagrees with the pro-Israel orthodoxy. Both essays are in *Wrestling with Zion: Progressive Jewish-American Responses to the Israeli-Palestinian Conflict*, ed. Tony Kushner and Alisa Solomon (New York: Grove, 2003). A forceful dissent from the Willis view, and a more philosophical analysis than Green's, is available in Judith Butler's "The Charge of Anti-Semitism: Jews, Israel, and the Risks of Public Critique," also in the Kushner and Solomon volume. Esther Kaplan's "Globalize the Intifada" points out that although "the road to victory will be littered with email postings that are a bit strident and flyers that are insensitive to Jewish history, . . . this new wave of activism has healthy roots, ones that tap deep into despair at the worsening occupation and anger at US complicity—not into ancient wells of Jew hating" (Kushner and Solomon, *Wrestling with Zion*, 87–88).

37  Judith Butler, "No, It's Not Anti-Semitic," *London Review of Books*, August 21, 2003. A revised version of this essay appears as "The Charge of Anti-Semitism" in Kushner and Solomon, *Wrestling with Zion*.

38 For a full rendition of this strand, see Tom Segev, Roane Carey, and Jonathan Shainin, eds., *The Other Israel: Voice of Refusal and Dissent* (New York: New Press, 2002).

39 Nathan Glazer, *American Judaism* (Chicago: University of Chicago Press, 1957), 114.

40 Norman Podhoretz, *Breaking Ranks: A Political Memoir* (New York: HarperCollins, 1980), 335. See also Norman G. Finklestein, *The Holocaust Industry: Reflections on the Exploitation of Jewish Suffering* (London: Verso, 2000), 19–21.

41 There is almost no literature on the political attitudes of South Asian Americans. One poll shortly before the 2004 presidential election found that Indian Americans favored the candidacy of John Kerry by a wide margin (53 percent to 14 percent, but with 30 percent undecided). Richard Springer, "Indian Americans Favor Kerry in New Poll," *India West*, October 1, 2004; Jim Lobe, "Asian Americans Lean toward Kerry," *Asia Times*, September 16, 2004; and George Joseph, "Poll Finds 20 Percent of Asian Americans Are Undecided Voters," *India Abroad*, September 24, 2004.

42 The ethnographic literature is well represented by Madhulika Khandelwal, *Becoming American, Being Indian: An Immigrant Community in New York City* (Ithaca, NY: Cornell University Press, 2002); Padma Rangaswamy, *Namaste America: Indian Immigrants in an American City* (University Park: Pennsylvania State University Press, 2000); Sandhya Shukla, *India Abroad: Diasporic Cultures of Postwar America and England* (Princeton, NJ: Princeton University Press, 2003); Sunaina Maira, *Desis in the House: Indian American Youth Culture in New York City* (Philadelphia: Temple University Press, 2002).

43 As Kamdar points out in "A Move to the Right?"

44 Ramer, "Pro-Israel Activists."

45 Aziz Haniffa, "The Sacredness of Life."

46 And I have done so in *Everybody Was Kung Fu Fighting: Afro-Asian Connections and the Myth of Cultural Purity* (Boston: Beacon, 2001).

47 Bayard Rustin, "From Protest to Politics: The Future of the Civil Rights Movement," in *Down the Line: The Collected Writings of Bayard Rustin* (Chicago: Quadrangle Books, 1971), 112.

48 "Success Story of One Minority Group in U.S.," *U.S. News and World Report*, December 26, 1966.

49 Irving Kristol, "The Negro Today Is Like the Immigrant Yesterday," *New York Times Magazine*, September 11, 1966, 138.

50 See Prashad, *Karma of Brown Folk*, 167–68.

51 See Karen Brodkin, *How Jews Became White Folks and What That Says about Race in America* (New Brunswick, NJ: Rutgers University Press, 1998).

52 Toni Morrison, "On the Backs of Blacks," *Time*, Fall 1993 special issue, 57.

53 But not nearly as strange as that between Christian dispensationalists and Zionists.

54 Anti-Defamation League, *India's Campaign against Israel* (New York: ADL, 1987), 7.

55 Suman Guha Mozumder, "Indo-Israeli Groups to Co-Host Reception on Capitol Hill," *India Abroad*, July 11, 2003.

# Notes on Contributors

ELIZABETH ALEXANDER is the author of three books of poems and a collection of essays, *The Black Interior*. Graywolf Press will bring out her fourth book of poems, *American Sublime*, in fall 2005. She teaches at Yale University.

AMIRI BARAKA is a world-famous poet, novelist, cultural critic, and political activist. His books include *Blues People* (1963), *Black Fire* (1968), and *The Autobiography of LeRoi Jones* (1984).

TESS CHAKKALAKAL is an assistant professor in the English department at Williams College. She is currently completing a manuscript on the relationship between Harriet Beecher Stowe's *Uncle Tom's Cabin* and conventions of the early African American novel.

THEODORE A. HARRIS is a collagist, mural painter, and poet who has been commissioned to create visual art for drama, dance theater, and documentary films. His art and poetry have appeared in many magazines and journals, such as *boundary 2, Theatre Journal, African American Review, Souls, XCP: Cross Cultural Poetics, Drumvoices Revue, Radical Society, Black Renaissance Noire, Left Curve*, and *Callaloo*, and in the anthologies *In Defense of Mumia* (1996), *ROLE CALL: A Generational Anthology of Social and Political Black Literature and Art* (2002), *Bum Rush the Page: A Def Poetry Jam* (2002), and *All the Days After: Critical Voices in Poetry and Artwork* (2003). The excerpt published here is from the manuscript *Our Flesh of Flames: Text by Amiri Baraka and Collages by Theodore A. Harris*, forthcoming in 2005 from Africa World Press. An online exhibition of his art from 1989 to 2005 may be viewed online at the Haverford College Center for Humanities HHC Web Gallery, www.haverford.edu/hhc/gallerywelcome.html.

JOHN HARTIGAN JR. is an anthropologist in the Americo Paredes Center for Cultural Studies at the University of Texas, Austin. He is the author of *Racial Situations: Class Predicaments in Detroit* (1999) and *Odd Tribes: Toward a Cultural Analysis of White People* (2005).

SHARON P. HOLLAND is an associate professor of African American studies and English at the University of Illinois at Chicago. Her first book is *Raising the Dead: Readings of Death and (Black) Subjectivity* (2000), and her second project is *The Erotic Life of Racism* (forthcoming).

JOHN L. JACKSON JR. is assistant professor of cultural anthropology and African and African American studies at Duke University. He is author of *Har-*

*lemworld: Doing Race and Class in Contemporary Black America* (2001) and *Real Black: Adventures in Racial Sincerity* (2005).

MARCYLIENA MORGAN is associate professor of communications at Stanford University. In 2002, she founded the Hiphop Archive at the W. E. B. Du Bois Institute at Harvard University. Her research has focused on youth, gender, language, culture and identity, sociolinguistics, discourse, and interaction. She is the author of *Language, Discourse, and Power in African American Culture* (2002) and editor of *Language and the Social Construction of Identity in Creole Situations* (1994). She is currently completing a book on hip-hop culture, *The Real Hiphop: Battling for Knowledge, Power, and Respect in the Underground.*

VIJAY PRASHAD is the author of eight books, most recently *Keeping Up with the Dow Joneses: Debt, Prison, Workfare* (2003). He teaches at Trinity College in Hartford, CT.

DON ROBOTHAM is professor of anthropology at the Graduate Center of the City University of New York. He is the author of *Culture, Society, Economy: Globalization and Its Alternatives* (2005).

NICHOLE T. RUSTIN is completing a book entitled *Jazz Men: Masculine Difference, Race, and the Emotions in 1950s America* and is coediting a collection of essays on jazz and gender. Rustin is a research assistant professor at the University of Illinois at Urbana-Champaign, where she teaches African American cultural history and gender studies.

BRACKETTE F. WILLIAMS earned a PhD in anthropology from Johns Hopkins University (1983). She has conducted fieldwork in Guyana and the United States. Since 1997, when she received a John D. and Catherine T. MacArthur Fellowship, she has been conducting research and writing on classification and capital punishment in the United States. The piece here is an excerpt from her novel in progress, *Pretty Black's Hole.*

# Harlan Davidson

## THE PROGRESSIVE ERA AND RACE: REACTION AND REFORM, 1900–1917

DAVID W. SOUTHERN
WESTMINSTER COLLEGE

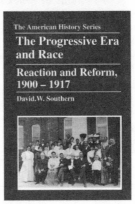

The American History Series

**The Progressive Era and Race**

Reaction and Reform, 1900 – 1917

David.W. Southern

This comprehensive, unflinching volume vividly portrays the ruthless exploitation, brutality, and violence inflicted on African Americans in the early twentieth century. In the South, where most blacks resided, white progressives followed racist demagogues, consolidating the Jim Crow system. In addition, southern whites liberally employed fraud, intimidation, and violence to repress blacks. Most northern progressives, meanwhile, were either indifferent to the fate of southern blacks or actively supported the social system in the South, while reformers became ensnared in a web of "scientific racism" that convinced them that blacks were inferior. Despite the adversity, African Americans courageously fought racism. The last chapter of the book reveals how the modern civil rights movement emerged— including the Niagra Movement and the rise of the NAACP—during the hostile feud between Booker T. Washington and W.E.B. Du Bois. And unlike many of the other short books on this subject, space is given to many other important African American leaders as well. **256 pages. Includes Photographs, Bibliographical Essay, and Index. Paperback, $15.95 ISBN: 0-88295-234-X © 2005**

*"The strengths of this book are manifest: graceful and engaging prose; an organization that builds momentum as the narrative progresses; broad-ranging analyses of how race permeated virtually every aspect of American life; and many fascinating discussions of the changing definitions of race. . . . A moving volume that will fit well into Harlan Davidson's American History Series."*

Loren Schweninger,
University of North Carolina at Greensboro

**Harlan Davidson, Inc.** • 773 Glenn Avenue, Wheeling, Illinois • Phone 847-541-9720 • Fax 847-541-9830 • E-mail: harlandavidson@harlandavidson.com

## One Hundred Years of
## *The Souls of Black Folk*: A Celebration

© University of Massachusetts Amherst

Originally published in 1903, *The Souls of Black Folk* is W. E. B. DuBois's biting critique of the racist and nationalist ideologies that animated the political culture of post-Reconstruction, Jim Crow America. This special issue celebrates and considers the influence of *Souls* during the last one hundred years. Featuring the work of a new generation of DuBois scholars, it suggests that a full appreciation of *Souls* requires reading it both as literary art and as political theory.

PUBLIC CULTURE
Society for Transnational Cultural Studies

*Contributors*:
Anne E. Carroll
Vilashini Cooppan
Robert Gooding-Williams
Sheila Lloyd
Charles Nero
Cheryl A. Wall
Alexander Weheliye

Robert Gooding-Williams and
Dwight A. McBride,
special issue editors
Volume 17, number 2  Spring 2005

DUKE
UNIVERSITY PRESS

# DU BOIS REVIEW

## SOCIAL SCIENCE RESEARCH ON RACE

This new peer-reviewed journal is devoted to research and criticism on race in the social sciences. It provides a forum for discussion and increased understanding of race and society from a range of disciplines, including but not limited to economics, political science, sociology, anthropology, law, communications, public policy, psychology, and history. Each issue contains an editorial overview, invited lead essays, original research papers, and review essays covering current books, controversies, and research threads.

The first volume will include such noted authors as Claude Steele on "The Psychology of Race", William Darity on "Blacks in the Global Economy", Mary Waters on "Immigrants and the Civil Rights Revolution", Cathy Cohen on "Gender, Sexuality, and Politics", Claire Kim on "Race and Politics", and review essays by Eduardo Bonilla-Silva, Glenn Loury, Alice O'Connor, Adolph Reed, Jr., Rogers Smith, and Barbara Ransby.

**EDITORS**

**LAWRENCE BOBO**
*Harvard University, USA*

**MICHAEL DAWSON**
*Harvard University, USA*

Published on behalf of the
W.E.B. Du Bois Institute for
African and African American
Research, Harvard University

**VOLUME 1, 2004**

Subscriptions:
**$135.00/£85 institutions print plus online**
**$125.00/£75 institutions print only**
**$115.00/£72 institutions online only**
**$65.00/£40 individuals print only**

To subscribe in the U.S.A., Canada, or Mexico,
please contact **Cambridge University Press**
by phone at **800-872-7423**, via fax at **845-353-4141**, or by email to
**journals_subscriptions@cup.org**

To subscribe from elsewhere,
please contact **Cambridge University Press**
by phone at +44 (0) 1223 326070, via fax at +44 (0) 1223 325150,
or by email to **journals@cambridge.org**